"He will be the sure foundation for your times,
a rich store of salvation and wisdom and knowledge;
the fear of the Lord is the key to this treasure."

-Isaiah 33:6, NIV

Jr. Devotional   Charles Mills

SECRETS
FROM THE
TREASURE
CHEST

REVIEW AND HERALD® PUBLISHING ASSOCIATION
HAGERSTOWN, MD 21740

Texts credited to NIV are from the *Holy Bible, New International Version.* Copyright © 1973, 1978, 1984, International Bible Society. Used by permission of Zondervan Bible Publishers.

Texts credited to NKJV are from The New King James Version. Copyright © 1979, 1980, 1982, Thomas Nelson, Inc., Publishers.

Bible texts credited to NRSV are from the New Revised Standard Version of the Bible, copyright © 1989 by the Division of Christian Education of the National Council of the Churches of Christ in the U.S.A. Used by permission.

This book was
Edited by Raymond H. Woolsey
Designed by Willie S. Duke
Photos by Joel D. Springer
Typeset: 11/12 New Century Schoolbook

00 99 98 97 96   6 5 4 3 2 1

Printed in U.S.A.

R&H Cataloging Service
Mills, Charles Henning, 1950-
        Secrets from the treasure chest.

        1. Teenagers—Prayer—books and devotions—English. 2. Devotional calendars—Juvenile literature. I. Title.

                242.6

ISBN 0-8280-1055-2

DEDICATION

To my parents,
Robert and El Rita
Mills, who always
answered my ques-
tions whenever I hon-
ored them by asking, and
to my wife, Dorinda, who
continues the tradition.

DEAR ADULTS:

The seeds for this book took root several years ago when the editors of *Guide* magazine invited me to ask kids what they'd ask God if they had the chance. Their questions stunned me. Many were deep, heart-searching, and often troubling.

When the Review and Herald® Publishing Association requested that I write a devotional, I immediately replied, "Only if kids can be involved." *Secrets From the Treasure Chest* is my response to what I consider an urgent need in our church today. Junior boys and girls are facing a confusing, turbulent future. If we parents, teachers, and spiritual leaders don't address the pressing questions tumbling about in their active minds, we haven't done our Christ-ordained duty. They'll find answers one way or another. This sinful world contains a ready library of misinformation and dangerous philosophies.

Please consider this volume a launching pad for further discussion and guidance. As you know, answers can sometimes create more questions. I'm depending on you to take over the controls and move our precious boys and girls closer and closer to Jesus.

Much prayer and soul-searching went into every word you'll read. Now my prayers are with you.

May God bless our efforts.

'Til He comes,
Charles

🔑 DEAR JUNIORS: 🗝️

Here's what happened. I sent a letter to a bunch of church schools in North America and Canada, inviting kids ages 10-15 to ask anything they wanted about God, homelife, school, relationships, the Bible, even themselves.

A *ton* of questions poured into my mailbox like a paper storm. Kids want to know about everything! So I got out my faithful Bible, gathered a pile of resource material, fired up the ol' computer, pleaded for God's help, took in a deep breath, and wrote what you're about to read.

You'll notice that on some of the more personal questions, the juniors who asked them chose not to mention their names. That's OK because some stuff is kinda sensitive, and we certainly don't want to embarrass anyone.

Many of the areas we talk about are very mature and adult. So I answered them in a very mature and adult fashion. You may have to do some pretty serious thinking, but hey, deep thinkers deserve deep answers, right?

To those who asked the questions, I say *"Thank you!* This is your book. You made it possible."

To those who read the answers, I say "Listen for God to speak to your heart. I only wrote the words. He'll give them meaning for your life."

It's my prayer that juniors everywhere will catch a glimpse of Jesus in this book. He's the only One with *all* the answers.

See you in heaven!

Mr. Mills

"He will be the sure foundation
for your times,
A rich store of salvation and wisdom
and knowledge;
The fear of the Lord is the key
to this treasure."
—Isaiah 33:6, NIV

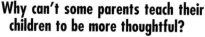

Why can't some parents teach their children to be more thoughtful?

—Cassandra, 13, Alaska

Sounds like you've met some kids who are having trouble being nice. Sad, isn't it?

While it's true that parents have a God-given responsibility to raise their sons and daughters to be Christlike, some don't, simply because they don't know how to be Christlike themselves. No one ever taught them.

Or maybe some parents work very hard to show their children how to live as Jesus lived—helpful, forgiving, always thinking of others first— but the kids refuse to listen. They like being the way they are. Gets them lots of attention.

Try this. Be as thoughtful and loving as you can. Let your life be a shining example of goodwill and respect for others. By your actions you can help teach those kids what they haven't learned at home, or demonstrate that a thoughtful attitude brings much more joy and longer-lasting attention.

Never underestimate the power of prayer. Each morning, before you head for school, ask your Friend Jesus to give you the strength to be kind, even when others aren't. And plant this Bible text firmly in your thoughts: *"Be merciful, just as your Father is merciful"* (Luke 6:36, NIV).

You might be surprised by the result!

I would like to know if Baptists, Catholics, etc., don't know they're in the wrong religion. How do we know we're in the right religion? I understand by the Bible, but they have Bibles too, so how can we prove it?
—*Samantha, 13, Alabama*

Your question contains part of the answer. The Bible is the true test. So how can two people read the same verses and come up with such different conclusions?

Truth is, they can't. The Bible insists that the seventh day is the Sabbath. That's a fact. It says that when you die, you sleep until Jesus comes to wake you up. Fact again. Scripture clearly states that there's going to be a new earth someday, after sin has been *completely* destroyed. Another fact.

Problem is, some people don't think it's important to believe what the Bible says. "It doesn't matter what day you keep as Sabbath," they'll state, "as long as you love God. I'd rather believe that my dead grandmother is happy in heaven than sleeping in the cold ground. Sinners are such terrible people, God is going to burn them forever."

In other words, they try to fit the Bible to what they want to believe instead of the other way around.

But a true Christian knows better. He or she says, *"Your word is a lamp to my feet and a light for my path"* (Psalm 119:105, NIV). God dearly loves members of all religions. Those who study their Bibles prayerfully quickly learn how to love God in return.

(From time to time, as in this case, the answers to a question may extend over two or more days.)

I would like to know if Baptists, Catholics, etc., don't know they're in the wrong religion. How do we know we're in the right religion? I understand by the Bible, but they have Bibles too, so how can we prove it?
—*Samantha, 13, Alabama*

Maybe this has happened to you too. You're driving to the store on Sunday morning and you see the parking lot of a local church jammed with cars. Perhaps you even hear the beautiful singing coming through the open front door.

"Look," you say. "They're keeping the wrong day."

Wait a minute! Don't you think God loves to be praised on Sunday? Or Tuesday? Or Friday? Sure He does. Wouldn't you?

Those wonderful people aren't keeping the *wrong* day. They just aren't keeping the *right* one.

The Bible makes it clear that the seventh-day Sabbath is a special day filled with very specific promises. God asks us to keep it as a sign that we believe in His creative power.

Monday is not a sign of His creative power. Neither is Wednesday. Same with Sunday. They're just days of the week.

But Saturday, the seventh day, is a holy day set aside by God for worship and remembrance. So the next time you see the parking lot of a church filled on a day other than the true Sabbath, understand that while God is enjoying the praise, He knows those precious people are missing out on the power and promise of His true Sabbath.

"I love them that love me," God says in Proverbs 8:17. By honoring His holy Sabbath, we show *Him* just how much *we* care.

I would like to know if Baptists, Catholics, etc., don't know they're in the wrong religion. How do we know we're in the right religion? I understand by the Bible, but they have Bibles too, so how can we prove it?
—*Samantha, 13, Alabama*

Have you ever tried to prove something to someone? You state your case, show evidence supporting your point of view, try to reason, convince, charm. If that doesn't work, you yell!

But if a person is perfectly satisfied with believing the way he or she does, that person usually listens politely, then goes off with his or her mind unchanged.

Proving something is difficult if the other person sees no reason to change his or her way of thinking.

Most churchgoing folk who don't believe as we do usually are perfectly satisfied with their religion. It's comforting and friendly. But we know they're missing out on something. God offers great blessings to those who dig into His Word, looking for the truths we love.

How do we prove they're not on target when it comes to what the Bible teaches? By arguing? No. By showing them where they're wrong? I don't think so. By yelling? Hardly.

The best way to prove something is to show its benefits in our own lives. *"Now that you have purified yourselves by obeying the truth . . . , love one another deeply, from the heart"* (1 Peter 1:22, NIV). When we live the truth, those without it will notice, and long for the happiness we've found.

How can you live a perfect life?
—Frank, 11, Florida

You can't. But Jesus can live perfectly in you. Let me explain.

Sinful people like us, who also happen to love Jesus, have a problem. We want to always be kind, patient, and forgiving, and reflect God's character to everyone we meet. But the more we try, the more we mess up. Know what I mean?

So we throw our hands up in frustration and say, "Forget this! I'm a sinner and that's how I'll always stay."

Then we read a verse in the Bible such as *"Be ye therefore perfect, even as your Father which is in heaven is perfect"* (Matthew 5:48).

"What?" we gasp. "I can't be as perfect as God!"

Yes, you can. Here's how. When you ask Jesus to come into your heart, He quickly makes Himself at home and directs the Holy Spirit to get busy and point out those bad habits and personality flaws that need attention. From that moment on, when God the Father looks at you, He doesn't see a sinner. He's sees His precious Son Jesus living in you, guiding you, helping you get through the troubles and overcome the temptations that come your way.

So, in God's eyes you're perfect because you've accepted Christ's perfect forgiveness and perfect peace.

Listen to these beautiful words: *"But if Christ is in you, your body is dead because of sin, yet your spirit is alive because of righteousness"* (Romans 8:10, NIV). You may be dead in sin. But Christ's righteousness makes you alive . . . and perfect.

Recently I made a new friend. When my old friend returned to school, she got upset and said I had to choose between her and my new friend. I told her I wanted both. Now she hardly speaks to me and hangs out with other girls. What should I do?

—Girl, 13, Montana

Nothing hurts more than when a friend turns his or her back on you, especially when you don't know why.

It sounds like both you and your old friend are feeling kind of rejected. She thinks you forgot all about her when you started a new relationship. So she's withholding her attention, trying to hurt the person she thinks hurt her.

Making new friends is important. You can't stop doing that. But some people, especially old friends, need lots of reassurance whenever someone new is added to the circle. Make sure you spend some extra time with that person, saying how happy you are to know her. Love has the power to make *many* people believe that they're needed and special.

Listen to these words from the Bible. *"A friend loves at all times"* (Proverbs 17:17, NIV). Notice it doesn't say "whenever she feels like it" or "if everything is going his way." Someone who stops loving you, for whatever reason, either doesn't know how to love or wasn't a true friend to begin with.

Tell your old buddy that you miss her. If she chooses to return to your circle, great. If she doesn't, say you'll be happy to wait, just in case she changes her mind. That's being a friend . . . at all times.

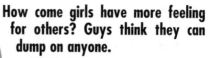

How come girls have more feeling for others? Guys think they can dump on anyone.

—*Girl, 12, Maine*

Some guys certainly do have a problem in the "feeling for others" area. Of course, some girls show a distinct shortage of warm fuzzies too. But generally, you're right. Girls do tend to be a little more sensitive by nature.

When God created man and woman, they were both supposed to be tender and loving, sharing equally in the work of caring for this earth. But something happened.

Our friend Ellen White puts it this way: "The transgression and fall of Adam and Eve brought sin and wretchedness upon the human race, and man followed his own carnal desires, and changed God's order" (*Conflict and Courage*, p. 36).

One of the changes that quickly developed, at least in some cultures, is that the male is supposed to be the leader, the aggressor—the one who takes charge and bosses women around. Dumb idea. But the concept continued to take hold, until in Christ's day women were considered nothing more than property—useful only for making babies and fixing supper.

Today there are guys—old and young—who still think they were created to be "king of the world." So they dump on everyone, especially women. Females in some cultures who haven't had the same opportunities as men seem to be more passive and sensitive. This is changing.

"Let the peace of God rule in your hearts," urges Paul in Colossians 3:15. Good advice for both men and women.

About how many people get heart attacks? What's the average age? What does the Bible say on what to eat?

—*Jorge, 11, California*

I think my friend Jorge has learned something. Notice how he's making the connection between heart attacks and what we eat. Good for you, Jorge!

As of this writing, 1.3 million people a year have heart attacks. Four out of five victims are 65 or older. Women have twice as many as men, and are twice as likely to die from them (statistics from the American Heart Association).

Modern-day scientists and medical experts are finding more and more evidence that diet affects health. "Eat lots of fruits and vegetables," they cry. "Keep roughage running through your system. Drink plenty of water. Cut down on sugars and fats. Skip meats for more nourishing natural proteins."

Sound familiar?

"I give you every seed-bearing plant on the face of the whole earth and every tree that has fruit with seed in it. They will be yours for food" (Genesis 1:29, NIV).

The proper diet was prepared in Eden. In the simple foods formed by the Creator's hand, we find all the nourishment and strength needed to live a healthy life. God's menu—along with proper exercise, rest, and growing faith—will help keep our hearts ticking for years and years to come.

How long has the world been around?

The museum guide smiles and says, "And over here you see the skeletal remains of a compsognathus, one of the smallest of the predatory dinosaurs. These fascinating creatures lived somewhere between 65 and 210 million years ago."

"When?" you gasp to yourself.

The guide continues. "Man and woman finally stood upright and began forming structured families about 6 million B.C."

"How long ago?" you question.

"You see, there was this big bang in the universe," you're told. "Swirling energy and matter joined to form stars and planets, setting in motion the sparkling heavens we know today. This happened 4.5 billion years before we were born."

"Billion years?" you think, shaking your head.

A verse pops into your mind. *"In the beginning God created the heavens and the earth. Now the earth was formless and empty, darkness was over the surface of the deep. . . . And God said, 'Let there be light,' and there was light"* (Genesis 1:1, 2, NIV).

What's going on here? Karlos, modern science offers one answer to your question; the Bible another. Before we can come to a conclusion as to how old the world is, we have to decide whom we want to believe: science or the Bible.

Science insists this world happened by chance. The Bible reports that God said, *"Let us make man in our image"* (verse 26, NIV). Evolution or creation? Happenstance or design? Choose.

How long has the world been around?
—*Karlos, 14, New Mexico*

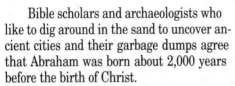

Bible scholars and archaeologists who like to dig around in the sand to uncover ancient cities and their garbage dumps agree that Abraham was born about 2,000 years before the birth of Christ.

Then if you figure in the generations from Abraham back to Adam, as listed in Genesis 5 and 11, you can safely establish that our world, including New Mexico, is somewhere between 6,000 and 10,000 years old.

"But," you say, "a program I saw on television the other night said our world was, like, billions and billions of years old. Why such a difference?"

Some people don't want to believe that God spoke and stuff appeared as if it had been there for a long time. But the Bible reports that the Creator said a few words and full-grown trees materialized out of nowhere. A couple more words, and adult birds fluttered in the sky. Soon afterward, a man who'd never been a child opened his eyes and saw God's smiling face.

To believe in Creation is to believe in a God who loves you, who died for you, and who's coming again to take you to heaven.

Evolution offers no Saviour, no reason to live, no glorious future. *"You are all sons of God through faith in Christ Jesus" (Galatians 3:26, NIV).* I choose to believe the Bible, Karlos. How about you?

Why is it so hard to talk and tell my friends about Jesus? How do I get them to listen? I told one friend, and she just laughed at me, called me crazy, and told me to get a life.
—*Girl, 11, Maine*

Someone laughed at you, huh? You're in good company. Listen to this: *"All who see me mock me; they hurl insults, shaking their heads [saying]: 'He trusts in the Lord'"* (Psalm 22:7, 8, NIV). Looks like one of the Bible writers understands what you're going through.

Jesus Himself heard people laughing at Him too. It even happened when He was trying to help a hurting family. *"When they came to the home of the synagogue ruler, Jesus saw a commotion, with people crying and wailing loudly. He went in and said to them, 'Why all this commotion and wailing? The child is not dead but asleep.' But they laughed at him"* (Mark 5:38, 39, NIV).

He healed the sick girl. The laughing changed to astonished praise.

People laugh for a lot of reasons. Maybe they're embarrassed, feeling guilty, confused, even angry. But that never stopped Jesus from doing good. And it must not stop you.

The next time someone giggles at your witness, just smile and change the subject. They heard what you said. Now it's time for the Holy Spirit to continue the work you've started in their hearts.

Why is it so hard to talk and tell my friends about Jesus? How do I get them to listen? I told one friend, and she just laughed at me, called me crazy, and told me to "get a life."
—*Girl, 11, Maine*

No one likes to be told they're wrong, even if you can prove they are. Often when Christians try to tell friends about Jesus, they begin by pointing out errors in the life, focusing on habits or beliefs that need changing.

What did Christ do? How did He approach sinners?

It's a lovely afternoon by the Sea of Galilee. A large crowd of people has gathered to hear Jesus speak. Among the assembly are rough, crude fishermen, heartless business people, bored housewives with wandering eyes, tricky traders, violent soldiers, and maybe even a few outright criminals running from the law.

Christ stands and faces the crowd, opens His mouth, and speaks. *"Blessed are the poor in spirit, for theirs is the kingdom of heaven. Blessed are those who mourn, for they will be comforted. Blessed are the meek, for they will inherit the earth" (Matthew 5:3-5, NIV).*

No judgments. No finger-pointing. No proclamations of wrongdoing. Jesus offers hope, encouragement; His words overflow with love and concern. What a wonderful witness!

Why is it so hard to talk and tell my friends about Jesus? How do I get them to listen? I told one friend, and she just laughed at me, called me crazy, and told me to get a life.
—Girl, 11, Maine

Let me ask *you* a question. Can you save someone's soul?

"Of course not," you say. "That's God's job."

Can you forgive sins?

"Don't be silly! Only God can do that."

Maybe when we share Jesus with our friends, we're going about it all wrong. "That's a sin," we say. "You shouldn't do that," we plead. "You're breaking God's law," we announce.

One day a woman was pushed down at Jesus' feet. "We caught her sleeping with a man who wasn't her husband," the angry crowd shouted self-righteously. Why they didn't drag the man in too we'll never know. Maybe he could run faster than they could.

Jesus looked at the tear-stained, embarrassed, frightened face of the young woman. Then He glanced at the fuming countenances of her accusers and said, *"If any one of you is without sin, let him be the first to throw a stone at her" (John 8:7, NIV).*

Everyone left, for all were sinners. Then Jesus knelt and gazed into the eyes of the woman. *"'Neither do I condemn you,' Jesus declared. 'Go now and leave your life of sin'" (verse 11).*

When we witness, let's not condemn, but encourage. Talking about Jesus will suddenly seem a lot easier.

Why is it so hard to talk and tell my friends about Jesus? How do I get them to listen? I told one friend, and she just laughed at me, called me crazy, and told me to get a life.

—*Girl, 11, Maine*

Getting someone to listen to you when you want to talk about Jesus can be difficult. Ask any evangelist. He or she might send out brochures, place advertisements on the radio and television, even go from door to door, personally inviting people to come to the meetings. Then on opening night maybe just a handful of folks show up. Why? Because the devil works very hard to make sure no one has the time or desire to learn about Jesus.

So what do we do? How do we get them to listen?

Here's the answer. *Make Jesus desirable!* Show your friends how Christ can help them live healthier, improve their relationships, even increase their IQ! People will always find time to better themselves.

And how do you do this? By showing them a real-life example of what Jesus can do. Show them *you*. Tell them that you used to be afraid but that now you trust in God. Tell them that you once worried about the future until you learned that Jesus will be there. Tell them that you felt guilt for your past sins until you discovered how willing Christ is to forgive.

Don't just witness with words. Become living proof of God's power. People will see and want to learn more. *"Delight yourself in the Lord and he will give you the desires of your heart"* (Psalm 37:4, NIV). Show others how delightful Jesus can be.

24

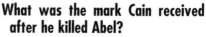

What was the mark Cain received after he killed Abel?
—*Rachel, 11, Indiana*

After Cain killed his brother Abel in a jealous rage, God told him he was under a curse. No crops would grow out of the ground for him anymore. He'd have to become a restless wanderer on the earth.

"That's too hard a punishment," Cain moaned. "And whoever finds me will kill me because of what I've done."

Here's what the Bible says next. *"But the Lord said to him, 'Not so; if anyone kills Cain, he will suffer vengeance seven times over.' Then the Lord put a mark on Cain so that no one who found him would kill him"* *(Genesis 4:15, NIV).*

First of all, we need to remember that at the time of the incident this world wasn't exactly overpopulated. Then as Adam and Eve's family grew, details of the infamous murder were passed down from father to child to granddaughter to great-grandson. Everyone knew the story.

I believe Cain's mark wasn't so much a blotch on his skin or some words printed on his forehead. It was his reputation as a murderer that stayed with him until the day he died, setting him apart from everyone else, making him an outcast.

Could Cain have removed the "mark"? Perhaps, if he'd asked forgiveness for his sin. But he didn't. He kept saying in his heart, "Am I my brother's keeper?"

If only he'd chosen to turn to God instead of running from Him. Let's make sure we keep our reputations unmarked.

What can you do to be a good friend to your poorer brother?

—*Benjie, 11, Ontario*

You see them on the streets, huddled in unheated apartment buildings, looking longingly into store windows, or sitting across from you in church.

Perhaps there's a poor boy or girl in your school. I'm so glad Benjie wants to be friends with everyone, even those who suffer in poverty.

First, look in the mirror and imagine that your family has suddenly lost everything. Everything! *That's* what a poor person looks like—same as you, only penniless. They aren't diseased or dangerous or frightening. They're just people, like you.

Now, how would you want the kids at school to treat you while you and your family were in this condition? Should they think of you as different? Special?

No. You want to be treated the same as everyone else. You want to laugh, tell secrets, score a perfect mark on your math test, have the teacher compliment you on finishing your assignment on time. You want to be included in the baseball game or the special club that meets every Tuesday after school.

Why is it so important for the Christian to learn how to be friends with those struggling in poverty? *"The poor you will always have with you,"* says Jesus in Matthew 26:11 (NIV). And as long as there are men and women, boys and girls, down on their luck, they'll need friends to make their days brighter and their future more hopeful.

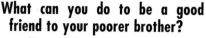

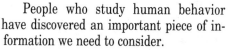

What can you do to be a good friend to your poorer brother?
—*Benjie, 11, Ontario*

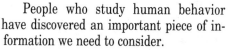

People who study human behavior have discovered an important piece of information we need to consider.

Seems everyone, *everyone*, has certain basic needs. These include security, respect, hope, acceptance, and love. Financial struggles tend to increase these needs in the lives of families.

Security: make sure your friend's home is safe. Ask a knowledgeable adult to help you check things out. Purchase secure locks for the doors and a couple of inexpensive fire alarms. Call each afternoon after school to make sure your buddy got home safely.

Respect: never, *never*, make fun of those who are struggling with poverty. Treat them as you want to be treated—fairly and equal.

Hope: speak encouragingly about the future. Offer to help your friend with his or her homework. If they're getting better grades than you, ask them to give you some pointers.

Acceptance: invite poor classmates into your circle of friends. Make them feel welcome and important.

Love: introduce your brother or sister to the creator of love—Jesus Christ. Offer to take them to Sabbath school and church. Share your church papers.

And remember Jesus' words: *"Whatever you did for one of the least of these brothers of mine, you did for me"* (Matthew 25:40, NIV).

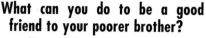

Why are parents so overly protective?
—*Derick, 12, Alaska*

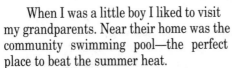

When I was a little boy I liked to visit my grandparents. Near their home was the community swimming pool—the perfect place to beat the summer heat.

"Now, Charlie," my grandfather would say each afternoon as he drove me to the pool, "have fun. But remember, I don't want you jumping off the high dive."

This place had an awesome diving platform. It was, like, 3,000 feet high. Airplanes had to change course to keep from running into it.

So guess what I did one afternoon. With arms and legs fanning the air, in total disregard for my overly protective grandfather, I launched myself off the high dive. *Wow!* For about two seconds I felt like an astronaut. Then I landed, right on top of a swimmer who was dog-paddling across the deep end. Didn't even see him until the last microsecond before impact.

He didn't die, and neither did I. But he sure was mad, and my back hurt for a week. When I confessed my sin to my grandfather, he nodded thoughtfully.

"How did you know I was gonna land on that guy?" I asked.

Grandfather looked at me. "I didn't know you were going to," he said softly. "But I knew it was a possibility."

Loving parents even try to protect their children from what *might* happen. So does God. *"The Lord will keep you from all harm—he will watch over your life"* (Psalm 121:7, NIV).

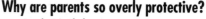

Why are parents so overly protective?
—Derick, 12, Alaska

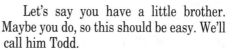

Let's say you have a little brother. Maybe you do, so this should be easy. We'll call him Todd.

Now Todd, being a typical, active 2-year-old, likes to explore. He's everywhere—under the sink, on top of the desk, crawling along the back of the couch, clopping along behind you as you go about the important stuff you do each day.

In your room you've set up your latest science project, with spinning wheels, colorful posters, and a bottle of chemicals necessary for your experiment. You're 12, and you know all about chemicals. Todd's 2, and he thinks anything that's colorful, small, and sits in a bottle is candy.

"Don't go into my room!" you tell Todd firmly. He nods and heads straight down the hall to your door. But when he tries to open it, it won't budge. You've locked your room up tight.

Why? Aren't you being a little overly protective? Doesn't Todd have the right to wander around the house on his own? Doesn't he have a right to be 2 years old?

Your love for Todd has caused you to lock away an entire room because of one bottle of chemicals. Derick, maybe there's something at the mall, or on your street, or at your friend's house, that your parents see as dangerous to your physical or spiritual life. Ask them what it is. Then ask them to show you how to avoid it. *"Discipline your son,"* God instructs parents, *"and he will give you peace" (Proverbs 29:17, NIV).*

JANUARY

20

How old are you? What color is your hair? Do you have missionary books, and are you a missionary?
—*Katie, 10, Alabama*

Well, here's a curious young lady. I guess she figured she should know a little more about the man who's attempting to answer all these important questions.

I was born February 14, 1950, in Seoul, Korea. My parents were missionaries, and I spent many years in strange, faraway places such as Singapore, the Philippines, Japan, Lebanon, and California.

In my travels I've met thousands of young people who love the Lord just as you do. And I discovered how smart they are and how they want to do what's right and help other people live better lives.

Maybe, because I associate with so many boys and girls, my hair is trying to stay young too. It's dark brown, with just a few strands of gray peeking out.

Although I haven't written any "missionary" books, I do enjoy writing adventure books for juniors.

May I share with you my favorite Bible text? It's in Philippians 2:5. If every boy and girl, man and woman, would do what the verse says, our world would be a much better place. Listen. *"Let this mind be in you, which was also in Christ Jesus."*

Why don't you decide to put this text into action today. Think like Jesus. Act like Jesus. And love like Jesus.

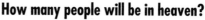

How many people will be in heaven?
—Quentin, 13, Oklahoma

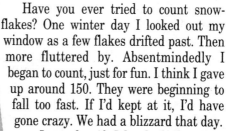

Have you ever tried to count snow-flakes? One winter day I looked out my window as a few flakes drifted past. Then more fluttered by. Absentmindedly I began to count, just for fun. I think I gave up around 150. They were beginning to fall too fast. If I'd kept at it, I'd have gone crazy. We had a blizzard that day.

I wonder if John had the same problem when he was writing chapter 7 of Revelation. God was showing him what would happen at the end of time. Here's how he described one of the scenes he saw: *"After this I looked and there before me was a great multitude that no one could count, from every nation, tribe, people and language, standing before the throne and in front of the Lamb"* (Revelation 7:9, NIV).

That's a lot of people, Quentin.

But even with such a multitude singing praises, God will know if you're not there. Or if I'm not there. He'll be searching the throng for your face and for mine. And when He sees us, He'll smile.

John also wrote: *"And I heard a loud voice from the throne saying, 'Now the dwelling of God is with men, and he will live with them. They will be his people, and God himself will be with them and be their God. He will wipe every tear from their eyes. There will be no more death or mourning or crying or pain'"* (Revelation 21:3, 4, NIV). Let's look forward to heaven together.

How did Mary and Joseph, the parents of Jesus, die?
—*Jessica, 11, California*

The Bible doesn't say. Like so many of the details of Jesus' life, we can only speculate on what happened to them.

Mary was at the Crucifixion, but Joseph wasn't. We can only surmise that Jesus' earthly father must have been dead by that time. Listen to what happened. *"Near the cross of Jesus stood his mother, his mother's sister, Mary the wife of Clopas, and Mary Magdalena. When Jesus saw his mother there, and the disciple whom he loved standing nearby, he said to his mother, 'Dear woman, here is your son,' and to the disciple, 'Here is your mother.' From that time on, this disciple took her into his home"* (John 19:25-27, NIV).

Even during this awful time, as His life was fading away in agony, Jesus made provision for His mother. Joseph had taught Him how to build with His hands, to labor honestly, to be an effective workman. Mary, sweet Mary, had taught her Son how to live for others and put their needs first. She had also taught Him how to die.

In this earth we may never know what happened to Mary and Joseph. But they left their mark on the Son they raised. I praise God every day for parents who dedicate themselves to training their boys and girls for heaven.

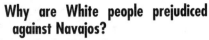

Why are White people prejudiced against Navajos?

—*Rhonda, 14, New Mexico*

According to my dictionary, one of the meanings of the word "prejudice" is: "to take a stand, as in a conflict, usually without just grounds or sufficient information."

In other words, you form an opinion without knowing all the facts.

If I say the word "Africa," what pops into your mind? Lions? Elephants? Natives living in grass huts? Some people think that's all Africa is—until they get on an airplane and pay Africa a visit. After seeing the modern cities, enjoying the rich culture, meeting the proud, caring people who populate that beautiful continent, their opinions change rather rapidly. Africa is many things, *including* lions, elephants, and grass huts.

So to begin to answer your question, those White people who are prejudiced against Navajos haven't taken the time to understand the beauty of that Native American nation. They haven't studied their mysterious culture, faced their problems, listened to their dreams. They don't want to get involved with the challenges facing their Indian neighbors, so they build thorny walls of misinformation and hate in order to keep themselves from feeling guilty about their indifference.

"Whoever loves his brother lives in the light. . . . But whoever hates his brother is in the darkness and walks around in the darkness; he does not know where he is going, because the darkness has blinded him" (1 John 2:10, 11, NIV).

JANUARY
24

Why are White people prejudiced against Navajos?
—*Rhonda, 14, New Mexico*

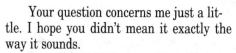

Your question concerns me just a little. I hope you didn't mean it exactly the way it sounds.

You asked, "Why are White people prejudiced . . ." as if all White people have this terrible problem. Wouldn't it be more realistic to ask, "Why are *some* White people prejudiced . . . ?"

You made what's called a generalization. Without even knowing it, you lumped all White people together, as if every one of them thought the same way about Navajos.

Generalization is one of the nastiest ingredients of prejudice. It lumps a group or family or nation of people together as if they were all alike, acting the same, believing the same. That's not possible. Everyone's different.

What would you think if I visited your school and saw a seventh grader standing in the hallway, with no one else in sight? And then I went out and told everyone, "The kids at that school are lazy. They just stand around when they should be in class." I generalized based on what I thought I saw one person doing. My mind became prejudiced without ever knowing that the student in the hallway was sent there by his teacher to practice a speech he was to give in class.

"Dear friends, since God so loved us, we also ought to love one another" (1 John 4:11, NIV). That includes training ourselves to guard our every word and action, keeping even the hint of prejudice out of our lives.

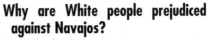
Why are White people prejudiced against Navajos?
—*Rhonda, 14, New Mexico*

Those who put people or groups of people down are giving themselves an excuse not to love them. And most selfish of all, it's a way for some to feel better about themselves. How terribly mean!

How do you do battle with prejudice? First, you make sure you use God's eyes when you look at people whose skin color, culture, or history isn't the same as yours. *"The Lord does not look at the things man looks at. Man looks at the outward appearance, but the Lord looks at the heart"* (1 Samuel 16:7, NIV). You'll be surprised how alike we all are when you learn to ignore the differences.

Next, keep far away from prejudiced people. They like to poison others with their hate. This makes them feel less guilty when they can get others to think as they do.

Be Christlike in your associations with all people. God loves everyone equally, and so should we. Take the time to learn the history and culture of those who aren't like you. Your life will be enriched by what you discover.

And finally, be proud of who *you* are, of *your* history, *your* culture. Ask the elders in your family to share stories from the past. Anchor yourself in who you are so that if someone demonstrates prejudice against you, you can say, *"I will heal their waywardness and love them freely, for my anger has turned away from them"* (Hosea 14:4, NIV).

What does "going out" mean? How old should you be? Most of the boys I know don't know Jesus, and it's hard.
—Girl, 11, Maine

To "go out" with someone is to spend much more time with that person than with anyone else. If a classmate says, "Heather and Jason are going out with each other," he or she's really saying, "Heather and Jason like to do stuff together such as go to the mall, study, or watch videos."

Going out with someone is a very natural way for two people to learn each other's habits and personalities.

How old should you be? That depends. Have you consistently shown your parents that they can trust you? Are you honest with them? Do you keep your word? And more important, has the guy you want to go out with done the same?

Juniors face a dilemma when it comes to special friendships. You regard the boys in your life as friends and, possibly, potential boyfriends. You know them quite well from school or church. Your parents, on the other hand, may view those very same young men as potential threats to your happiness and peace of mind. And in a world filled with drug abuse and violence, moms and dads shudder at the dangers waiting so close at hand.

So if you want to "go out" with some lucky guy, design the date to maximize the fun while minimizing your parents' fears. If the guy doesn't like the plan, tough. He's got to learn to be man enough to meet *your* conditions and date by *your* rules. *"The man [and woman] of integrity walks securely"* (Proverbs 10:9, NIV).

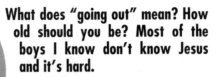

What does "going out" mean? How old should you be? Most of the boys I know don't know Jesus and it's hard.
—*Girl, 11, Maine*

It's very hard, isn't it? Dealing with someone who doesn't have Jesus in his or her heart makes *everything* more difficult than it has to be.

Many guys, and a few girls, I suppose, think of Jesus as the great "You can't do that" God who likes to take away fun. So they ignore Him and do whatever they feel like doing. This always results in broken promises, broken relationships, and broken hearts.

You, on the other hand, know Jesus. You understand He has your best interest at heart and He's trying to look out for you, to keep you from making terrible mistakes. That's why He created rules and pleads with you to follow them. Anytime you feel a little hindered by God's laws of love, take a look at the relationships around you. Review the marriage success rate across the nation. *That's* what happens when Jesus is left out of relationships. *That's* the result of choosing not to know Him.

Listen to what God says to you. *"Don't copy the behavior and customs of this world, but be a new and different person with a fresh newness in all you do and think. Then you will learn from your own experience how his ways will really satisfy you"* (Romans 12:2, TLB).

Don't allow someone who doesn't know Jesus to take control of your heart. Guys like that come and go, but Jesus is forever!

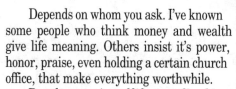

What is the meaning of life?

—*Ryan, 14, Indiana*

Depends on whom you ask. I've known some people who think money and wealth give life meaning. Others insist it's power, honor, praise, even holding a certain church office, that make everything worthwhile.

But the meaning of life as outlined in God's holy book has nothing to do with any of the above. Listen. *"Then God said, 'Let us make man in our image, in our likeness, and let them rule over the fish of the sea and the birds of the air, over the livestock, over all the earth, and over all the creatures that move along the ground'"* (Genesis 1:26, NIV).

Only as we work in partnership with God to care for this world, including all the people and creatures in it, can we discover the real meaning of life.

Notice what sin has done since Eden. Satan has turned men's and women's hearts against nature. We eat animals instead of nurturing them. We destroy forests instead of protecting them. We rob the earth of its natural resources instead of using them wisely. Evil has turned our minds away from the meaning of life, leaving us with trivial goals and selfish desires.

Ryan, it's your job, and mine, to counter what other people do, and dedicate ourselves to caring for this earth as God intended. Only then will we know the meaning of life and enjoy living it.

When is Jesus coming?
—*Erik, 13, Ontario*

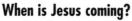

We've all heard the Bible texts describing what the world will be like when Jesus comes: Wars and rumors of wars, earthquakes, pestilence, men's hearts failing them for fear, people running to and fro on the earth, natural affections turning cold, anger, hate, lust.

Sound familiar?

Even the people alive right after Jesus lived on this earth believed the world was ripe for His quick return. When He didn't show up, Peter wrote, *"First of all, you must understand that in the last days scoffers will come. . . . They will say, 'Where is this "coming" he promised? Ever since our fathers died, everything goes on as it has since the beginning of creation'"* (2 Peter 3:3, 4, NIV).

Ever feel that way? Where is He? Why hasn't He come back?

Erik, no one knows the day or hour when Jesus will return the second time. God says so in the Bible. But we can be ready today, and tomorrow, and the next day. We can begin to prepare for our future life in heaven with Jesus so when He does come back, we can say, *"Lo, this is our God; we have waited for him, and he will save us"* (Isaiah 25:9).

When it will happen is not important. If it were, God would have told us. *That* it will happen should fill our hearts with gladness and set our lips to singing. He's coming, Erik. He's coming. You can count on it!

How do we know there are planets farther away in the galaxies?
—Christopher, 12, Alaska

Something tells me Christopher has been looking up into the clear, unpolluted Alaskan night sky. Awesome, isn't it? Like jewels on black velvet.

Makes you wonder. What's up there? Is some other boy standing on a distant speck of light looking back at us?

We know there are planets in far-off galaxies because science and the Bible say so.

But as Christians our final word is the Bible. *"God made two great lights—the greater light to govern the day and the lesser light to govern the night. He also made the stars"* (Genesis 1:16, NIV).

"God . . . hath in these last days spoken unto us by his Son, whom he hath appointed heir of all things, by whom also he made the worlds" (Hebrews 1:2).

"By faith we understand that the universe was formed at God's command" (Hebrews 11:3, NIV).

Our planet contains an element missing in all the other "worlds" scattered about God's universe—evil. Someday that will change. We'll spend eternity getting to know the sinless beings who live on some of those tiny sparkles we see in the night sky. I can hardly wait. How about you, Christopher?

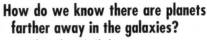

How do we know there are planets farther away in the galaxies?

—*Christopher, 12, Alaska*

Our friend Ellen White had quite an adventure one day. God gave her a vision. Listen to this spine-tingling report recorded in *A Sketch of the Christian Experience and Views of Ellen G. White*, pages 32, 33.

"The Lord has given me a view of other worlds. Wings were given me, and an angel attended me from the city to a place that was bright and glorious. The grass of the place was living green, and the birds there warbled a sweet song. The inhabitants of the place were of all sizes, they were noble, majestic, and lovely. They bore the express image of Jesus, and their countenances beamed with holy joy, expressive of the freedom and happiness of the place. I asked one of them why they were so much more lovely than those on the earth. The reply was, 'We have lived in strict obedience to the commandments of God, and have not fallen by disobedience, like those on the earth.' . . .

"I begged of my attending angel to let me remain in that place. I could not bear the thought of coming back to this dark world again. Then the angel said, 'You must go back, and if you are faithful, you . . . shall have the privilege of visiting all the worlds and viewing the handiworks of God.'"

What a glorious preview of things to come! Christopher, next time you gaze into the clear Alaskan night sky, you can look forward to the day when you'll travel to worlds far beyond the Milky Way, and share stories of God's forgiving love.

Why does God let some people live and some other people die?
—Brian, 12, West Virginia

Not long ago I watched an interview with a young woman who'd survived a terrible airplane crash. Many passengers had lost their lives. She, and a few others, had miraculously walked away with nary a scratch.

"God must have something important planned for my life," she said with tears in her eyes. "That's why He let me live."

My immediate reaction to her statement was "Does that mean God had nothing important planned for the people who didn't survive? He just let them die because He was through with them?"

Brian, how we answer your question reveals the basis for our entire belief in God. It has to do with His *will*—that means His set of wants for our lives. Jesus said, *"For the Father's will is that everyone who looks to the Son and believes in him shall have eternal life"* (John 6:40, NIV). The apostle John, who learned to love at Jesus' feet, wrote, *"I wish above all things that thou mayest prosper and be in health, even as thy soul prospereth"* (3 John 2).

God's will centers on life, not death. He wants us to enjoy a healthy, prosperous existence, spiritually and *physically*. Don't ever think that your heavenly Father is sitting around waiting to pull the plug on your existence when He thinks you've lived long enough. That young woman survived because she was sitting in the right place at the right time. The others died because they weren't. In most cases, it's that simple. God can always overrule, of course, as He sees best in His great plan.

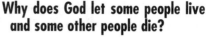

Why does God let some people live and some other people die?
—Brian, 12, West Virginia

The car's trunk bulges with suitcases, motel reservations have been made, there's film in the camera, and the dog is safely at the boarding kennel. IT'S VACATION TIME!

Before Dad turns the key in the ignition, everyone bows and asks God to protect them on their journey.

Sound familiar? It should. Every Christian I know prays before leaving on a long trip. So do I.

Then you hear the terrible news that one of the families at your church was killed in a multicar accident on a foggy road miles from home. "Why?" you ask. "They prayed!"

People die for a lot of reasons. If you jump out of an airplane without a parachute, you can pray all the way to the ground, but it won't help. Someone who has smoked three packs of cigarettes a day for 40 years shouldn't be surprised when the doctor says, "You've got lung cancer," even if that person recently became a Christian and asked God for a long, healthy life.

Evil affects both praying people and nonpraying people. But those who love God and obey His laws have a definite advantage. They're constantly preparing their minds and bodies to meet the challenges and dangers of life. *"The name of the Lord is a strong tower; the righteous run to it and are safe" (Proverbs 18:10, NIV).* Studying God's Word increases wisdom, and wisdom helps you live a safer, and usually longer, life.

Why does God let some people live and some other people die?

—*Brian, 12, West Virginia*

God wants us to live—forever. Satan does everything he can to keep that from happening. The wisdom we gain from studying God's Word helps us battle sin and its effects. That's what life is for the Christian—constant combat with evil.

But God's battle plan is powerful. It prepares us in three ways. First, our bodies are strengthened. Drugs and alcohol have no place in God's army. By faithfully following heaven's health laws, we increase our defenses against the attacks of disease.

Next, our minds are barricaded with pure thoughts, repelling the unceasing onslaught of filth hurled at us by the world.

Then, our souls find hope and rest in the knowledge of God's persistent presence in our lives.

All this makes us safer drivers, more careful workers, friendlier neighbors; we handle relationships better, learn how to avoid potential dangers while traveling, and live longer.

One Bible writer put it this way: *"The Lord is my rock, my fortress and my deliverer; my God is my rock, in whom I take refuge. He is my shield and the horn of my salvation, my stronghold. I call to the Lord, who is worthy of praise, and I am saved from my enemies"* (Psalm 18:2, 3, NIV).

Brian, God doesn't *let* people live or die. He teaches us how to live in safety, and how to die with hope for a new life to come. Why don't you become one of God's soldiers this very minute?

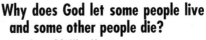

Why does God let some people live and some other people die?
—Brian, 12, West Virginia

I had a cousin who died. His name was Jonny. Although he passed away many years ago, his mother always cried at the mention of his name. Not long ago she died too.

I hate death. So does God. It wasn't supposed to happen in His perfect universe. But Adam and Eve chose to live apart from the Creator, separating themselves, and their future generations, from heaven's sustaining power. Death became a natural result of that terrible choice and separation from God.

All people die because of sin, and not necessarily their own. Even Jesus lost His life on a cruel cross. It was His way of saying, "Watch and learn, Brian . . . and Cassandra . . . and Karlos. Even though evil can kill Me, My Father can restore Me to life again. And He can do the same for you."

"But I, when I am lifted up from the earth, will draw all men to myself" (John 12:32, NIV). At the foot of the cross we see death at its most terrible—and its most hopeful.

Someday, because of what Jesus did, I'll see my cousin Jonny again. I'll see Aunt Helen, too. We'll live in a universe forever cleansed of sin and death.

When loved ones die, our hearts break with sadness for what sin has done. But at the same time we know that if they loved Jesus they'll live again, forever. And we, along with the apostle Paul, can say, "Where, O death, is your victory? Where, O death, is your sting?" (1 Corinthians 15:55, NIV).

Why didn't Jesus have a wife? They say He went through everything other people go through. Most people get married. Why didn't He?

—Jini, 14, Alabama

At first glance it does seem strange that the One who created marriage didn't choose a wife for Himself. What a comfort and encouragement a loving companion would have been to Him as He worked for the salvation of souls.

But Jesus knew who He was, even at an early age. He knew the life He'd be forced to live—one filled with rejection, pain, suspicion, uncertainty, all of it ending in a horrible death. Perhaps He didn't want to put a wife through such suffering.

His chosen lifestyle wasn't exactly appealing, either. Jesus once said, *"Foxes have holes and birds of the air have nests, but the Son of Man has no place to lay his head"* (Matthew 8:20, NIV).

I believe Christ understood the requirements of a successful marriage. He knew it takes time, energy, and sacrifice. But all those things He'd already committed to you and me and to anyone needing salvation. That's why He lived and died alone, so we could benefit from His complete, unbroken attention.

There's a lesson here for all. We must make sure we're willing to meet every requirement of marriage *before* we say "I do." Listen to what Paul said: *"Husbands, love your wives, just as Christ loved the church and gave himself up for her"* (Ephesians 5:25, NIV).

Jesus didn't get married because He'd already chosen the love of His life—you and me.

How many universes are there until you reach heaven?
—*Karen, 12, Oklahoma*

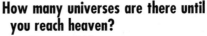

Every time a new telescope is designed and pointed toward the night sky, astronomers gasp.

Each time science figures out a new way to look at far-off galaxies and stars, astronomers shake their heads in amazement.

Every time some updated, more powerful, computer-operated instrument scans the sky, searching for signs of life beyond our solar system, stargazers have to rewrite their textbooks.

Why? They're always finding whole new worlds, entirely uncharted galaxies, and completely unknown star systems whizzing about the dark void of space.

So a scientist may rattle off a number in answer to your question, but don't put too much stock in it. Even they don't. The count keeps increasing. So I'm not even going to guess. You want facts, not guesses.

Here's a fact you can keep in mind. While describing our future heavenly home, our friend Ellen White wrote: "With undimmed vision, they [God's people] gaze upon the glory of creation—suns and stars and systems, all in their appointed order circling the throne of Deity. Upon all things, from the least to the greatest, the Creator's name is written, and in all are the riches of His power displayed" (*The Great Controversy*, pp. 677, 678). Now you know something most astronomers don't. Cool!

When we go to heaven, will there be peace and happiness?

—*Antoinee, 11, California*

Anytime this old world gets you down, close your eyes and think about these features of the new earth:

A river of life, clear as crystal, flowing from the throne of God (Revelation 22:1). A tree bearing *12* fruits (verse 2). No sin or curse (verse 3). We see God face-to-face (verse 4). No night (verse 5). People live in peaceful dwelling places and secure homes (Isaiah 32:18). No violence (Isaiah 60:18). Families plant vineyards and eat the fruit (Isaiah 65:21).

Instead of thorns, fir trees (Isaiah 55:13). Wolves and lambs, leopards and baby goats live together in harmony (Isaiah 11:6, 9).

And here are my two favorite texts for describing our lives in heaven. *"He [God] will wipe every tear from their eyes. There will be no more death or mourning or crying or pain, for the old order of things has passed away"* (Revelation 21:4, NIV).

"They will neither harm nor destroy on all my holy mountain: for the earth will be full of the knowledge of the Lord" (Isaiah 11:9, NIV).

Yes, Antoinee. When we get to heaven, we'll all enjoy eternal, blessed, long-prayed-for, long-hoped-for, mind-expanding, body-healing, soul-cleansing, song-raising, smile-making, foot-jumping, love-building, and God-praising peace and happiness. I can *hardly* wait! How about you?

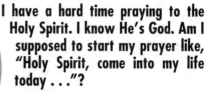

I have a hard time praying to the Holy Spirit. I know He's God. Am I supposed to start my prayer like, "Holy Spirit, come into my life today . . ."?
—*Natalie, 14, Montana*

Here's something to try. Instead of speaking to one particular member of the Godhead, why don't you just pray to "God." You can be sure that all three—the Father, the Son, and the Holy Spirit—are listening intently to your prayer. They'll know which one is supposed to respond.

The idea of three Gods being one God is kind of confusing until you learn more about Them. The Father, Son, and Holy Spirit are one in thought (They are in complete agreement with Each Other), but They do different things. The Son, Jesus, is the Creator God. He made everything. And because He died for us, He's the God who can forgive us when we sin.

The Holy Spirit works in us by nudging our conscience when we've done something bad. He makes us want to be good, to act kind, to love others. He gives us the power to forgive those who mistreat us, and kindles hope when all seems lost.

God the Father serves as our judge. Don't think He's out to condemn us. Hardly. He works constantly to make sure that Satan doesn't accuse us wrongly. Instead of the title "Judge," perhaps a better label for the Father would be "Protector."

When God says, *"Call to me and I will answer you and tell you great and unsearchable things you do not know" (Jeremiah 33:3, NIV),* He means it. When you whisper your prayer, the greatest Power in the universe is listening. That's power times three!

Why did God make earth if He had other planets to love and care for?

—Heather, 11, Oklahoma

Some time ago there was trouble in my family. My sister couldn't find a job. My brothers were concerned about their children. There were financial worries, marriages under stress, and even some serious spiritual doubts to be overcome.

In the middle of all this mess, I asked my mom and dad a pointed question. "Don't you wish you hadn't had us kids?" I queried. "Wouldn't it have been better for you if you'd just lived your life without us?"

Their response was immediate. "You children have brought us so much joy and happiness through the years. We couldn't think of a world without you in it."

Heather, even though God had an entire universe of beautiful beings willing to worship Him, something was missing. We were missing. His love was so great, He not only brought us into existence, He also allowed His only Son to suffer and die a terrible death to keep us free from Satan's snare, to assure our place in His everlasting kingdom.

My parents repeatedly demonstrate to us children the verse found in Zephaniah 3:17: *"The Lord your God is with you, he is mighty to save. He will take great delight in you, he will quiet you with his love, he will rejoice over you with singing"* (NIV).

Why did God make earth? Because He couldn't think of a universe without us in it.

How do you say no when you're not ready to date?
—*Girl, 11, Maine*

No one wants to be left out. But sometimes girls and guys don't feel comfortable in a dating situation. Perhaps they're not sure how to act or what to say. Maybe they're simply shy or would rather have fun with lots of friends instead of being the date of just one person in particular.

As with everything else in life, honesty is the best policy. If some guy asks you for a date and you're not ready, tell him, "Thanks for the invitation, but I'd rather not be tied down to just one person yet. Check back with me in a month, or a year, or when you get your first BMW. But it was nice of you to ask."

This way the guy doesn't think there's something wrong with him, and he can start saving for the car. And you've expressed yourself in an open, honest way.

How do you know when you're ready to go on that first date? When you feel confident in yourself. When the guy who's asking you out has proved himself a good Christian by showing respect for others, especially those in authority.

Have your first date at a place where you feel comfortable and safe, so you can enjoy the special attention of another person for an hour or so. Dating is like trial relationships. Some are great, some are pitiful. But you learn, and grow.

"Even a child is known by his actions, by whether his conduct is pure and right" (Proverbs 20:11, NIV). Ask Jesus to tag along on your date. He enjoys watching you learn and grow, too.

Is God Black or White?

—*Kyle, 12, Indiana*

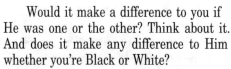

Would it make a difference to you if He was one or the other? Think about it. And does it make any difference to Him whether you're Black or White?

Facts are, we don't know what color God is, because we haven't seen Him.

Jesus was born into a Jewish family. Jews usually have lighter skin tones, but some are darker than others depending on the ancestral line.

So, to the question "Is God Black or White?" I'd have to answer "Yes." He's also Brown, and Pink, and Yellow, and Golden. He's the color of all nations, all people, all boys and girls.

Consider this text. *"And I will put my Spirit in you and move you to follow my decrees and be careful to keep my laws" (Ezekiel 36:27, NIV).* It reminds me of the words to a song I've sung many times: "Into my heart, Into my heart, Come into my heart, Lord Jesus. Come in today, come in to stay. Come into my heart, Lord Jesus."

When you allow God to live in your heart, He becomes exactly the same color as you.

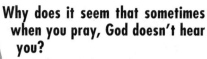

Why does it seem that sometimes when you pray, God doesn't hear you?

—*Stephanie, 13, Ontario*

Because that's what the devil wants you to think. "You're not important enough for God," he'll whisper in your thoughts. "He's not interested in your stupid problems. You're too sinful, or selfish, or mean. God listens only to nice people who say the right words and smile all the time."

Listen to what David—that's right, Mr. Giant-killer himself—once prayed. *"How long, O Lord? Will you forget me forever? How long will you hide your face from me? How long must I wrestle with my thoughts?" (Psalm 13:1, 2, NIV).* Sounds like he was having a slight communication problem as well.

But David finally overcame his doubt. He wrote, *"Come and listen, all you who fear God; let me tell you what he has done for me. I cried out to him with my mouth; his praise was on my tongue. If I had cherished sin in my heart, the Lord would not have listened; but God has surely listened and heard my voice in prayer. Praise be to God, who has not rejected my prayer or withheld his love from me!" (Psalm 66:16-20, NIV).*

It doesn't matter what the devil says. God hears every prayer from every mouth. And that includes yours and mine. As a matter of fact, God's even one up on you. *"For your Father knows what you need before you ask him" (Matthew 6:8, NIV).* How's that for hearing what you have to say?

So, Stephanie, when you pray, ignore those feelings that the devil tries to plant, and continue talking to your friend Jesus.

Why do people steal even though they're rich or they could afford to buy it?
—*John, 13, Alaska*

For a number of reasons. First, some think it's exciting to take something that doesn't belong to them. They like the thrill of seeing if they can outsmart the law, or their neighbor, or the store security guards.

Some steal because they think the world owes them something. If they can't get what they want through the usual, lawful means, they simply rip it off.

Third, some rich people steal because that's how they obtained their wealth, and they don't want (or know how) to stop. Stealing has become a habit.

Fourth, some do it because it makes them feel good about themselves. They like to think they're smart or clever.

And fifth, some might be angry at someone, or some company. So they take out their revenge by pilfering items owned by that person or business.

Thieves are looking for something that's missing in their lives. Whether they're rich or poor, ripping off people will never fill the void in their heart, even if they have to build warehouses in which to store their loot.

But you know better. You know where true happiness is. *"I delight greatly in the Lord. . . . For he has clothed me with garments of salvation and arrayed me in a robe of righteousness, as a bridegroom adorns his head like a priest, and as a bride adorns herself with her jewels" (Isaiah 61:10, NIV).* And it's all legal!

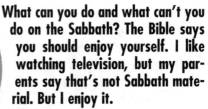

What can you do and what can't you do on the Sabbath? The Bible says you should enjoy yourself. I like watching television, but my parents say that's not Sabbath material. But I enjoy it.
—*Tim, 14, West Virginia*

Sabbath *is* supposed to be a day filled with joy, Tim. As a matter of fact, it was designed to be the one day of the week we enjoy the most! But many kids (and even a few adults) haven't figured out how to make it such a joyful time.

First, the Sabbath isn't all that different from a Tuesday or a Thursday. For most of society, it's simply a day like any other, except many people don't have to work. They mow their lawns, watch TV, attend a ball game, or go shopping. No big deal.

But Bible-believing Christians know better. They've discovered something unusual about the day, something fascinating. It began in Eden. *"By the seventh day God had finished the work he had been doing; so on the seventh day he rested from all his work. And God blessed the seventh day and made it holy" (Genesis 2:2, NIV).*

Tim, if you believe in God, which I'm sure you do, then you'll believe what God says. He announced in the Bible that the seventh day, Saturday, was blessed and holy. So don't ever consider Sabbath like any other day. It's special because it was made holy by the God you love.

What can you do and what can't you do on the Sabbath? The Bible says you should enjoy yourself. I like watching television, but my parents say that's not Sabbath material. But I enjoy it.
—*Tim, 14, West Virginia*

We've discovered that the seventh day of the week is special, blessed of God. So how do we make the day different? We begin by doing what Christ did. *"On the Sabbath day he went into the synagogue, as was his custom" (Luke 4:16, NIV).*

"But going to church is boring," some juniors whine. Then, do what Christ did. *"And he stood up to read" (verse 16).* In other words, He got involved in the service. He didn't just sit around waiting to be entertained.

Keeping the Sabbath holy requires action! If the day passes and you've just moped about, wishing for sundown, you've missed the whole point. You didn't make the day special at all.

"So what can I do?" you ask. March up to your pastor and ask to be a part of the church service. It may take a moment for his heart to start beating again, but then he'll probably lift his hands and sing the doxology. Pastors love it when juniors want to get involved.

No, you don't have to preach or anything. But you could greet people at the door, offer to care for noisy children, help take up the offering, shovel snow, read the Scripture text, turn pages for the organist, collect the hymnbooks, lead the singing, and so on. *"The Sabbath was made for man, not man for the Sabbath" (Mark 2:27, NIV).* It's your day. Don't waste it.

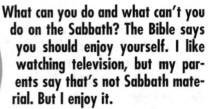

What can you do and what can't you do on the Sabbath? The Bible says you should enjoy yourself. I like watching television, but my parents say that's not Sabbath material. But I enjoy it.
—*Tim, 14, West Virginia*

Sabbath is holy, and should be filled with action! Church involvement gets things off to a good start. But what about the rest of the day?

"Remember the Sabbath day by keeping it holy. Six days you shall labor and do all your work, but the seventh day is a Sabbath to the Lord your God. On it you shall not do any work" *(Exodus 20:8, 9, NIV).* True Sabbath-keepers make a change in their lives at sundown on Friday. They switch from being workers to being servers. They stop making a living and start living for others. For 24 hours, they become *blessing* seekers, not *pleasure* seekers. They have one goal in mind—to draw closer to God.

That's the test. *That's* how you should judge what you want to do during God's holy hours. Ask yourself, "Will this activity teach me something new about my Saviour? Will this behavior serve to help another human being understand God's power better? By doing this, am I seeking a blessing, or simply entertainment?"

"If you keep your feet from breaking the Sabbath and from doing as you please on my holy day, if you call the Sabbath a delight and the Lord's holy day honorable, and if you honor it by not going your own way and not doing as you please or speaking idle words, then you will find your joy in the Lord" (Isaiah 58:13, 14, NIV). There's no Sabbath delight waiting for you on TV.

What can you do and what can't you do on the Sabbath? The Bible says you should enjoy yourself. I like watching television, but my parents say that's not Sabbath material. But I enjoy it.
—*Tim, 14, West Virginia*

God blessed the seventh-day Sabbath. He calls us to dedicated action during His holy hours. Every activity should bring someone closer to God, especially if that someone is *you*.

Tim, your heavenly Father realizes you live a busy life. School, friends, playtime, activities, studies, work, hobbies, relationships, and, yes, even watching TV, take up huge chunks of your week. Factor in sleep, and there's nothing left!

But God has important stuff to tell you. He's got answers to your many spiritual questions, solutions to the problems crowding your life, hope to combat your concerns, strength to prop up your weaknesses.

You know how you like it when your mom, dad, or the adult you live with takes the time to listen to you, to pay attention to your needs? Well, God wants you to pay attention to Him during His Sabbath. He wants to communicate with you through the experiences you enjoy during those holy hours.

So I'm not going to give you a list of do's and don'ts for Sabbathkeeping. Juniors are smart enough to figure things out for themselves once they know the facts as you now know them. Just remember: *"The Lord is with you when you are with him. If you seek him, he will be found by you"* (2 Chronicles 15:2, NIV). Make next Sabbath, and every Sabbath, a time to be with God.

Will our animals go to heaven?

—*Kendra, 13, Alabama*

People and animals were never supposed to be separated. In Eden God told Adam, *"Rule over the fish of the sea and the birds of the air and over every living creature that moves on the ground"* (Genesis 1:28, NIV). *"[God] brought [the animals] to the man to see what he would name them; and whatever the man called each living creature, that was its name"* (Genesis 2:19, NIV).

Not only did the Creator ask Adam to care for the animals; He even let him name each and every one of them! This was not just a passing relationship God was forming between people and nature. It was designed to be an everlasting bond.

Sin really messed things up. It created enemies where there used to be friends, distrust where there used to be harmony, and introduced to both human beings and animals the most heartbreaking result of evil—separation from God through death.

I still miss a dog I had when I was a kid. His name was Toodles, a fox terrier-beagle mix. He was my best friend in all the world. Now he lives only in memory and fading photographs.

Kendra, I believe that someday, when sin has been wiped from the universe, and Eden has been restored as the Bible promises, the everlasting people-animal bond will be reestablished, and my little Toodles will run by my side through the meadows and mountains of the new earth. No, there's no Bible text to prove it one way or the other. But since God says He's preparing a home for me, He's got to know what I long to have waiting at the front door of my heavenly mansion. And God can do anything.

How many years has the Bible been around, and how many churches have used it?
—*Karen, 12, Oklahoma*

The Bible is as old as human thought. As a matter of fact, that's where it remained for generations. Stories were told and retold around countless campfires and from ancient pulpits—stories of Creation, of sin, and of a great flood.

Over time, these remembrances, reinforced by the Holy Spirit through prophets, found their way onto stiff sheets of parchment, each word painstakingly penned by people who wanted future generations to hear the stories unaltered. Soon the pages of these "books of history" were joined, forming such collections as the Law, the Prophets, and the Writings. Later these groups came together in specific languages to form such books as the Hebrew Canon and the Greek Septuagint, thus forming the Old Covenant or, as we know it, the Old Testament.

Contemporaries of Jesus penned the different books of the New Covenant as letters to churches and detailed reports to friends. Listen to how Luke begins his writings: *"Many have undertaken to draw up an account of the things that have been fulfilled among us, just as they were handed down to us by those who from the first were eyewitnesses and servants of the word. Therefore, since I myself have carefully investigated everything from the beginning, it seemed good also to me to write an orderly account for you, most excellent Theophilus, so that you may know the certainty of the things you have been taught"* (Luke 1:1-4, NIV).

How many years has the Bible been around, and how many churches have used it?

—Karen, 12, Oklahoma

John Wycliffe translated the Bible into English in 1382. Another English Reformer, Miles Coverdale, began *printing* the first copies of the complete Scriptures in English in 1535.

Every church congregation who worships the God of heaven has used the Bible in some form or another. But some groups focus on just a small collection of verses to build their entire religion. This leaves gaping holes in their beliefs, holes through which Satan can pour doubt and uncertainty.

In order to claim the Bible as the foundation of a religion, every word, every doctrine, every book must be included. Among other things, Bible-believing churches must: obey God's commandments (Revelation 12:17); keep holy the seventh day (Saturday) Sabbath (Exodus 20:8-11); practice tithe paying and observe the Lord's Supper (Leviticus 27:30; John 13:12-15); live healthfully (1 Corinthians 10:31); refrain from adorning themselves (1 Timothy 2:9).

A congregation should keep this important text at the very center of their beliefs: *"But when the kindness and love of God our Savior appeared, he saved us, not because of righteous things we had done, but because of his mercy. He saved us through the washing of rebirth and renewal by the Holy Spirit, whom he poured out on us generously through Jesus Christ our Savior, so that, having been justified by his grace, we might become heirs having the hope of eternal life" (Titus 3:4-7, NIV).* We obey because we love Jesus. Jesus saves because He loves us.

Why did God send a flood on the earth?

—*Victoria, 11, California*

At face value, the Flood seems kind of mean. After all, women and children were killed by it. Animals, puppies, birds—every living thing except the occupants of the ark—vanished in the raging waters. Why?

The world of Noah wasn't anything like the world of his ancestor Adam. Listen to this chilling description: *"The Lord saw how great man's wickedness on the earth had become, and that every inclination of the thoughts of his heart was only evil all the time"* (Genesis 6:5, NIV). Every thought was evil all the time! How would you like to live in that world?

So was God angry, furious, beside Himself with rage? Be careful how you interpret these next words: *"The Lord was grieved that he had made man on the earth, and his heart was filled with pain. So the Lord said, 'I will wipe mankind, whom I have created, from the face of the earth . . . for I am grieved that I have made them'"* (verses 6, 7, NIV).

Action born from grief is different from action springing from anger. We grieve for others. We're angry for ourselves. God wanted to "wipe mankind . . . from the face of the earth" in order to stop the pain and suffering they were continually bringing upon themselves because of their sinful lives. With heartbreaking anguish, the Creator realized that, at this time in history, death was more humane than life.

But something changed His mind. He saw Noah.

Why did God send a flood on the earth?
—*Victoria, 11, California*

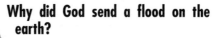

The world was so corrupted, lives were so filled with pain and suffering, that God decided its inhabitants would be better off dead. Then He noticed someone unusual. *"Noah was a righteous man, blameless among the people of his time, and he walked with God"* (Genesis 6:9, NIV).

It seems that not everyone had chosen to live by Satan's rules. Noah was busy bucking tradition, fighting evil, being and doing good, even though it wasn't popular. In Noah, God saw a way of escape for humanity.

"Make yourself an ark of cypress wood," He commanded (verse 14). *"I am going to bring floodwaters on the earth to destroy all life. . . . Everything on earth will perish"* (verse 17).

Noah got right to work. But he didn't just hammer and saw; he also preached—for 120 *years* he preached about what was going to happen to the earth. And his construction project wasn't hidden away someplace where no one could see it. It was right out in plain view where, if someone else believed God's terrible warning, he or she could plan to come on board—or build a similar ark for his or her family, neighbors, and friends.

But no one chose to trust God's word. And when the waters came, just Noah and his family survived. If only more people had believed and built instead of laughing and continuing in their sins . . . God never puts out a warning without an avenue of salvation. For every flood, He provides plans for an ark.

If your friend becomes your enemy, how can you become friends again?
—*Joel, 12, Florida*

I'm glad you asked that question, because it shows you want your friend back. Good for you!

The best way to accomplish this is to find out what made your buddy become your enemy in the first place. Perhaps there was a misunderstanding. Maybe you did something foolish and hurt his or her feelings. Could it be that one of you let selfishness or greed get in the way of your relationship?

After you've identified what caused the problem, get busy and try to figure out a way of overcoming it. Does someone need to swallow a mouthful of pride and say "I'm sorry"? Is forgiveness in order? Sometimes just sitting down and talking about stuff can clear the air.

I'll let you in on a little strategy I use when someone chooses to stop being friends with me. I go straight to that person and say, "Look, our friendship is more important than anything. I won't give up until we've straightened this mess out. Please help me find a way to make us friends again."

This works most of the time. But if a person truly doesn't want to be your pal anymore, you can't force that person to change his or her mind.

And if the experience of losing a friend hurts you, remember these words: *"[God] heals the brokenhearted and binds up their wounds"* *(Psalm 147:3, NIV)*. In this evil world, Jesus may sometimes be the *only* friend we have.

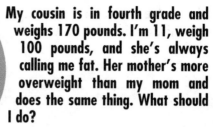

My cousin is in fourth grade and weighs 170 pounds. I'm 11, weigh 100 pounds, and she's always calling me fat. Her mother's more overweight than my mom and does the same thing. What should I do?

—*Girl, 11*

Many people who battle overweight get so frustrated that they do strange things. Sometimes they desperately try to shift attention away from their shortcomings by pointing out (or in this case imagining) shortcomings in others.

Your cousin and her mother probably feel bad about themselves. They wish they were more slender. And they're tired of hearing (or they imagine that they hear) other people make unkind remarks about *their* weight. So they fight back with their own hurtful remarks.

Try this. The next time your cousin calls you fat, say something like "Yeah, it's hard to keep the pounds off when food looks so inviting. I really should try to stay in better shape." Both of these statements are true for everyone, including you and me—and your cousin. By using such nonthreatening words, you're placing yourself on her side in a supporting role. No longer is your lack of fat intimidating. She feels she's found someone who understands the battles she has to fight.

And to give you strength as you deal with this situation, here's a terrific text to plant firmly in your mind: *"Commit your way to the Lord; trust in him and he will do this: He will make your righteousness shine like the dawn, the justice of your cause like the noonday sun"* (Psalm 37:5, 6, NIV).

Allow God's accepting love to shine through you.

Did wolves become mean right after sin, or did it take a while?
—*Lori, 16, Indiana*

I believe it took a while. (But note that wolves have a worse reputation than they deserve. Wolves that attack people have usually been driven that way by severe circumstances.

In Eden there was harmony and peace among all living creatures. Nothing hunted or killed anything else. There was food and housing for everyone. In other words, the *need* for being mean didn't exist.

Sin changed everything, but not immediately. Even today we find remnants of God's perfect creative touch in nature, although we may have to do some serious looking to find them. Good outlasts bad. Always has. Always will.

The average life span of a person took many generations to drop to the level it was when Christ walked the earth. Adam lived 930 years (Genesis 5:5). David used the number threescore and ten (70 years) to identify how long the average person could hope to live in his time (Psalm 90:10). Yes, it's a big drop, but it took several thousand years to get there.

Over the centuries, as habitat and food supplies diminished, and people's attitude toward nature changed, wolves found themselves in a growing battle for survival. They became mean because they needed to be in order to live from day to day. How very sad, and how very sinlike.

I'm looking forward to the day when *"the wolf will live with the lamb, the leopard will lie down with the goat, the calf and the lion and the yearling together; and a little child will lead them"* (Isaiah 11:6, NIV). Won't that be wonderful, Lori?

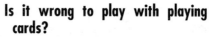

Is it wrong to play with playing cards?

—*Christopher, 12, Ontario*

There's nothing wrong with playing cards, just as there's nothing wrong with a handgun. They're just objects, one made of paper, the other of steel. We could even say there's absolutely nothing wrong with Christopher. He's just a guy made of flesh, blood, a bunch of squishy organs, and a smart brain.

But sin has a way of taking innocent objects and turning them into things that are very, very wrong. If Christopher picks up the handgun and kills someone with it, the pistol has become a lethal weapon, and the guy with the squishy organs is suddenly a murderer. *How* something is used makes a big difference.

Poker and other such games are proven time-, money-, and life-wasters. They've been known to destroy families, bankrupt risk-takers, and even lead to loss of life. I've never owned a pack of playing cards for the same reason I've never owned a handgun. There's danger there—not in what they are, but in where they can lead. And since you've got a smart brain, you'll leave them alone too.

Jesus says: *"For the waywardness of the simple will kill them, and the complacency of fools will destroy them; but whoever listens to me will live in safety and be at ease, without fear of harm"* (Proverbs 1:32, 33, NIV).

Find other ways to amuse yourself, Christopher. Leave playing cards to the simple, and the fools.

I was wondering why, when people talk about God, they always make excuses for Him. I believe in God, but sometimes people just make excuses.
—*TJ, 15, Alaska*

God certainly doesn't want anyone making excuses for Him. He has told us who He is, what He does, and His desire for our future. But, for some people, that's not enough.

What happens is this: Folks try to interpret what God says to fit what's happening in their lives. They attempt to explain divine activity with human insight. It doesn't work.

When people say "It was God's will that . . ." or "God caused this to happen so . . ." or "God must've had something in mind when He . . ." or "The Lord brought this upon me so that I would . . . ," they're walking on shaky ground, trying to second-guess God. That's not possible.

Our heavenly Father gets blamed for stuff He didn't do, and praised for stuff with which He wasn't even involved. When life doesn't fit the mold we've created by our interpretation of Scripture, we begin making excuses. "God knows best," we sigh when the world falls down around our ears.

So where *is* God in all this mess? The same place He's always been—loving us and longing for the time when He can destroy all sin and its consequences. In the still small voice of reason and hope we hear Him above the noise of discouragement and fear. *"God is our refuge and strength, an ever-present help in trouble. Therefore we will not fear, though the earth give way and the mountains fall into the heart of the sea. . . . Be still, and know that I am God"* (Psalm 46:1-10, NIV). Don't make excuses. Listen and learn.

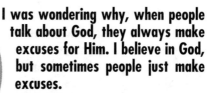

I was wondering why, when people talk about God, they always make excuses for Him. I believe in God, but sometimes people just make excuses.

—*TJ, 15, Alaska*

There's a cliché from the olden days that says "Don't put the cart before the horse." Can you imagine how useless it would be to harness a horse *behind* a cart? Not only would the animal be really confused, also you wouldn't go anywhere.

That saying reminds me of the well-meaning people who insist "God brought this problem, or sorrow, or hurt, or sickness, or challenge into my life to teach me something." That's like hitching up ol' Paint behind the buckboard.

Wouldn't it be more realistic to say "When that bad thing happened to me, God was right there with encouragement and hope. I came out of it with a new understanding of His love and power"?

TJ, God doesn't *cause* bad things to happen. Sin does. But when bad things do take place—and they always will because we live in a sin-filled world—we can know Jesus is right there by our side, offering unlimited wisdom and mental power to overcome the results of our misfortune.

"The Lord is good, a refuge in times of trouble. He cares for those who trust in him" (Nahum 1:7, NIV).

When pain, sickness, hurt, sorrow, and problems pop up, don't make excuses for God. Don't say it's His fault. Get busy and invite your heavenly Father to be a part of the solution. And then listen as He directs your thoughts to new plans for action and fills your life with hope.

If, right before Jesus comes, someone orders you to do something bad or else you'll die, and you know you already have some kind of sin in your life, do you not do the bad thing and die, or do you do it? Either way, you won't be going to heaven so what difference does it make?
—*Jason, 14, West Virginia*

What I think you're saying, Jason, is that heaven isn't worth fighting for. You already think you're lost, so why not do the bad thing and live a little longer? Right?

First of all, you're not the judge of you. God is. And He thinks your being in heaven is worth everything, including the life of His only Son Jesus. He doesn't give up, even if it means making you feel guilty for that "kind of sin" in your life.

Second, you've got to decide whether you're a sinner or a citizen of heaven. Sinners couldn't care less about a future life with Jesus. But when citizens of heaven sin, they say, "Wait a minute. That was stupid! Looks like I need God's help."

Citizens of the heavenly kingdom aren't perfect. They're constantly doing battle with evil, and will be until Jesus comes. When Jesus returns, He's not expecting to find a bunch of people who have never sinned. He'll be looking for those who have given their hearts to Him and, through the Holy Spirit, are learning, growing, overcoming hurtful habits, and preparing themselves to live in heaven. People just like you.

"For the grace of God that brings salvation has appeared to all men. It teaches us to say 'No' to ungodliness and worldly passions, and to live self-controlled, upright and godly lives in this present age" (Titus 2:11, 12, NIV). Always say no to sin.

I would like to know more about the Bible. Maybe a few stories, too.

—*Jeremy, 11, Alabama*

The Bible is a love letter. You heard me right. It's God's way of saying "I love you" to millions of people. It's also a rule-book, filled with good advice on how to live healthier, happier, more productive lives.

Even though the Bible, as we know it, was written by many authors over several hundred years, each book, chapter, and verse agrees with the others. It doesn't contradict itself. Why? Listen: *"All Scripture is God-breathed [inspired by God] and is useful for teaching, rebuking, correcting and training in righteousness, so that the man of God may be thoroughly equipped for every good work"* (2 Timothy 3:16, 17, NIV).

It's also a book of stories, reviewing the adventures of earth's inhabitants from Creation to their future life in heaven. For juniors, parts of the Bible are fascinating. Others are boring. But every word is important.

You don't have to understand *all* the Bible for it to help you. Some readers have discovered three or four texts that bring them encouragement and hope. They write them down and post them on refrigerators and the walls of offices. These mini-Bibles remind them of God's love and interest in their lives. Texts such as: *"I will say of the Lord, 'He is my refuge and my fortress, my God, in whom I trust'"* (Psalm 91:2, NIV), or *"He gives strength to the weary and increases the power of the weak"* (Isaiah 40:29, NIV). Why don't you find a favorite and post it on your wall?

I would like to know more about the Bible. Maybe a few stories, too.
—Jeremy, 11, Alabama

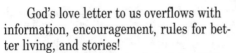

God's love letter to us overflows with information, encouragement, rules for better living, and stories!

Sometimes whole books of the Bible tell just one story, such as Ruth, Esther, and Job. Others tell collections of adventures such as Genesis, Exodus, Samuel, and Daniel.

But the stories I like the best are found in Matthew, Mark, Luke, and John. In these books I find Jesus walking dusty roads in places with beautiful names such as Judea, Samaria, and Galilee. I see crippled men leap for joy, children raised from the dead, and I learn how to pray.

Each of these books ends with a resurrected Saviour who with love compels His followers to go out and prepare people for the coming kingdom of heaven.

Jeremy, the best way to know more about the Bible is to pick it up and read it. Begin with Luke. Then check out portions of Psalms and Proverbs. Don't think you have to start at Genesis and read straight through to Revelation. God has lessons for you *anywhere* in the Bible. And don't forget to invite Him to sit by your side as you explore.

Never, *ever* think Bible reading is for sissies or perfect people. It was written for you and me so we could learn more about our friend Jesus. *"For I am not ashamed of the gospel of Christ: for it is the power of God unto salvation to every one that believeth" (Romans 1:16).* Put that power in your life today!

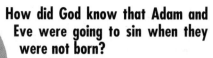

How did God know that Adam and Eve were going to sin when they were not born?
—Lindsay, 9, Oklahoma

God knows everything. Somehow He can bend time and peek into the future. How? I haven't a clue.

But don't forget some of the other things God knew before Adam and Eve were created—things terrifying and sad. The Father saw His precious Son suffering with disease, hunger, and loneliness on this earth. He saw Him ridiculed and rejected, tormented and hurt. And imagine the horror He felt as visions of Christ's death filled His perfect, sinless mind.

Knowing what He knew, He went ahead and created Adam and Eve anyway. Why? Because He wanted Lindsay to live with Him forever in heaven. That's right. The same powerful eyes that could see what sin would do also witnessed what the plan of salvation was capable of. And by peering just a little further into the future, God saw you and me running up to Him in heaven, thanking Him for allowing us the opportunity to live forever.

"For God so loved the world, that he gave his only begotten Son, that whosoever believeth in him should not perish, but have everlasting life" (John 3:16).

Before we were born, God knew *we* were going to sin. But He also knew how lonely He'd feel without us in His kingdom. So here we are, struggling with this old world because God peeked into the future and saw how happy we'd be living with Him in heaven.

In heaven, will people still have babies?
—Collene, 11, California

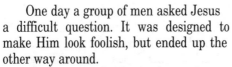

One day a group of men asked Jesus a difficult question. It was designed to make Him look foolish, but ended up the other way around.

They reminded Christ of an ancient law Moses wrote stating that if a man's brother died and left a wife with no children, the man was supposed to marry the grieving widow.

"Let's say," they suggested, "that the man had seven brothers, and one by one each died right after marrying the widow, leaving the next brother to take his place, exactly as Moses directed."

Wow. Talk about a streak of bad luck!

"Then," they pressed, "after all the brothers had married the woman and died, she died too. At the resurrection, whose wife will she be, since all seven were married to her?"

Jesus answered their question—and yours. *"Are you not in error because you do not know the Scriptures or the power of God?"* He asked them in Mark 12, verse 24, NIV. *"When the dead rise, they will neither marry nor be given in marriage; they will be like the angels in heaven"* (verse 25, NIV).

The answer to your question is no. But keep in mind another statement from God's Book: *"No eye has seen, no ear has heard, no mind has conceived what God has prepared for those who love him"* (1 Corinthians 2:9, NIV). As exciting as having a baby may be, heaven holds even greater mysteries—and joys.

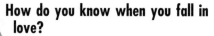

How do you know when you fall in love?

—*Justin, 13, New Mexico*

Ah, love! That wonderful experience filled with chirping birds, puffy clouds, and living-happily-ever-after feelings. It's so simple, everyone does it. At least, they think they do.

Love is kind of complex—like spaghetti. If all the ingredients are there, yummy. But leave out the tomato sauce and the cooking part, and all you have is a pile of cold noodles.

You see, love requires many things. It has lots and lots of ingredients, such as trust, commitment, honesty, a forgiving and accepting spirit, and humor. If one or more of these are missing, well, cold noodles.

You know you're falling in love when all the ingredients come together in your life. You're willing to trust someone; to commit your life to him or her; to be honest, forgiving, and accepting; and to laugh off mistakes.

Can a 13-year-old fall in love? Yes, in the chirping-bird, puffy-cloud, living-happily-ever-after version. But that's not the lasting love you'll enjoy someday, because many of the ingredients are still missing. Only time, experience, and God's shared wisdom can provide the rest. Be patient. It'll happen. And you'll know when it does because you've taken the time to gather and prepare all the ingredients.

"A new commandment I give you: Love one another. As I have loved you, so you must love one another" (John 13:34, NIV).

Is it good to go with the crowds?

—*Girl, 10, Maine*

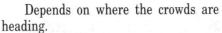

Depends on where the crowds are heading.

Juniors hate being considered different or weird. They like being included in whatever's going on. So when many in the crowd pull out cigarettes, or joints, or smuggled copies of tomorrow's math test, there's a problem. Should you go along with them, or be labeled as weird?

First, allow me to introduce you to some pretty off-the-wall people. How about the guy who built a boat when no one had ever seen rain, or the woman who was willing to give up her life for her people? Noah and Esther stood out in the crowd. They were different.

Or did you hear the one about the boy who insisted that with God he could successfully face a giant that an army had refused to fight? Then there was this woman who raised quite a stir by pouring expensive perfume on Christ's feet, attempting to show her appreciation for how He'd changed her life for the better. David and Mary ignored the crowds and demonstrated true bravery all by themselves.

What I'm trying to say is "Don't be a crowd follower. Be a crowd leader!" If your friends are heading in directions you know to be wrong, remember Noah, Esther, David, and Mary. Be different. Be weird. Be right.

"Whether you turn to the right or to the left, your ears will hear a voice behind you, saying, 'This is the way; walk in it'" (Isaiah 30:21, NIV). Stick with crowds whose goals include heaven.

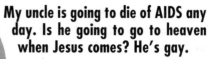

My uncle is going to die of AIDS any day. Is he going to go to heaven when Jesus comes? He's gay.

—*Girl, 11*

Your uncle must make that decision. You see, God loves everyone. He wants *all* people to go to heaven. As a matter of fact, if your uncle chooses not to become a citizen of the new earth, God will be lonely for him throughout the ceaseless ages of eternity.

Let's stop for a minute and think this through. Heaven will be a re-creation of Eden. The animals live peacefully together, flowers never die, there's no violence or pain, no anger and sadness. Everything is as it was in the beginning, including God's ideal for human relationships. Homosexuality didn't exist before sin entered the world. It will not exist in heaven. It's simply not a part of God's eternal plan for our happiness.

So, as things are now, your uncle would hate heaven. He'd be lonely, feel like an outcast, be uncomfortable around God—the very same feelings he's lived with on this earth. People who maintain a gay lifestyle will not be in heaven because God knows they'd be miserable there. And misery, loneliness, and uncomfortableness cannot exist in God's new earth. Those are the results of sin, and sin will have been wiped from the universe.

But if your uncle chooses to accept the future as God has designed it, and asks his loving Saviour to make some changes in his life, heaven *will* be his home when Jesus comes. He'll find it a joyous place, filled with thousands who've fought the same battle he's fought and won their own victories with Jesus' help.

Are we going to see all the things they mention in Revelation, or will God take us?
—Jorge, 11, California

The book of Revelation brims with very vivid images of high-flying angels, thrones, scrolls, a dragon, a lamb, a beast, terrible plagues, strange horses, a lake of fire, and a beautiful city made of gold. Are we going to see all these things?

Jorge, Revelation is a written account of a dream or vision given to John by God. In order for John to understand what was going to happen in the future, God used symbols to illustrate important points. For instance, the woman clothed with the sun in Revelation 12 represents God's church. The dragon is, of course, the devil.

These symbols show what's happening behind the scenes while we struggle to overcome Satan on this earth.

If we live long enough, we will witness *some* of the events foretold in Revelation, such as the plagues, the Second Coming, and best of all, the New Jerusalem and the re-created world. However, Christians have no reason to fear what is to come. Sadness? Yes. Careful preparation to withstand evil forces? Certainly. Fear? Absolutely not.

Remember the story of Noah? God warned of a terrible flood to come. So Noah built an ark. Have you ever noticed that the ark had only one window? When the Flood came, the boat rocked, the thunder roared, the earth shook. But Noah remained safely inside, out of reach and out of sight of the terror.

Why do guys get to show up at church wearing jeans and a sweater or a nice shirt but girls get looked down on if they don't dress up?

—*Tara, 14, New York*

Hold on a minute! You're not suggesting that just because guys don't show respect for God you shouldn't have to either, are you?

What we wear to church isn't supposed to be a reflection of our independence. It's an indication of our love for God.

How would you feel if you had a birthday party coming up and invited all your friends? You spent hours cleaning the house, decorating the living room, cooking delicious food, and blew your entire savings account on a new hairdo and lovely dress, and then your friends showed up in beach wear, gardening clothes, or soiled football uniforms? Something tells me you'd be a little hurt. Not only would they be showing lack of respect for your house, hard work, and invitation, they would be saying in essence, "My freedom to choose how to dress is more important to me than anything else. I'm here, aren't I? That should be enough."

It's not enough, Tara. Not for you. Not for God. When you go to church, you choose from your closet what you believe shows respect for the God you're worshiping. What other people do, guys or girls, is their business. What you wear to church is between you and God. Choose the best you have.

"In that day a man will look to his Maker, and his eyes will have respect for the Holy One of Israel" (Isaiah 17:7, NKJV).

How tall will we be when we go to heaven?

—*Marcus, 10, Oklahoma*

Throughout the Bible and the writings of our friend Ellen White, heaven is pictured as an "Eden restored." In other words, when God makes all things new again, our world will be as nice as the original Garden of Eden.

So perhaps we can catch a glimpse of the new earth and its inhabitants by studying the world right after God created it.

Listen to these words written by Mrs. White: "As Adam came forth from the hand of his Creator, he was of noble height, and of beautiful symmetry. He was more than twice as tall as men now living upon the earth, and was well proportioned. His features were perfect and beautiful. His complexion was neither white nor sallow, but ruddy, glowing with the rich tint of health. Eve was not quite as tall as Adam. Her head reached a little above his shoulders. She, too, was noble—perfect in symmetry, and very beautiful" (*Spiritual Gifts*, vol. 3, p. 34).

Let's say the average height of today's male is approximately 5 feet 10 inches. That would make Adam about 12 feet tall! How'd you like to have him on your basketball team?

So it looks like we're all going to do some serious growing when we reach heaven. For those juniors who aren't as tall as they'd like to be, relax. You've just found another reason to look forward to your home in the new earth.

Why do we have curfews?
—Lisa, 14, Alaska

Makes you feel like no one trusts you, doesn't it? Most parents say they do trust their children but it's the other people's kids that make them nervous.

They have a point. You they've lived with, raised from a diaper-dumper, taught lessons of safety and health, prayed with, cried with, argued with. They have a pretty good idea of your values and motivations.

But then this stranger shows up on their doorstep wanting to whisk you away to who knows where to do who knows what. Oh, sure, you know everything's cool. But they don't, and it makes them nervous. "Be home by 9:30," they demand, hoping against hope that you'll live through the evening.

I'm not being overdramatic here. Parents worry. It's their job.

So here's what you do. Replace concern with knowledge. Introduce your friends to your parents. Let them get to know each other. Then be *very* specific about where you're going and what you'll be doing as you head out with the gang. Build your parents' trust slowly. You might be surprised at the results.

One word of warning. If a friend, especially a guy, doesn't like this system, run—don't walk—to the nearest exit. If that person doesn't respect your parents' wishes, he won't respect yours, either. The Bible tells moms and dads to *"Discipline your son, and he will give you peace"* (Proverbs 29:17, NIV). Earn your parents' trust, and the same thing will happen to you.

Why does God let us get discouraged?
—Girl, 12, West Virginia

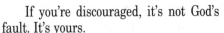

If you're discouraged, it's not God's fault. It's yours.

I'm not talking about a sadness over the loss of a friend, the hurt that comes when someone treats you badly, or the occasional feeling of frustration over a persistent problem. These are legitimate reasons to feel down in the dumps.

What I'm referring to is the act of feeling sorry for yourself to the point of wanting to give up. That's discouragement, and God hates it as much as you do. He's done everything He can to keep you from feeling that way. As a matter of fact, He even died so you'd never have to spend one minute under the cold blanket of discouragement.

So who's giving you those feelings of hopelessness, worthlessness, and doubt? That's right, the father of discouragement—Satan himself. He wants you to forget how valuable you are, how important you are to God's cause and to other people. If he can keep you discouraged long enough, all the good stuff you could do won't get done. Then others will suffer. And they'll get discouraged, and so on, and so on.

Fight it! Don't give into it. Pick up your Bible and read texts such as *"Do not fear, for I am with you; do not be dismayed, for I am your God. I will strengthen you and help you; I will uphold you with my righteous right hand"* (Isaiah 41:10, NIV). Show Satan who's in charge of your life, then get on with it.

Will God forgive Adam and Eve?

—Antoinee, 11, California

He already did, a long, long time ago, even before Jesus created this world.

Forgiveness is the most powerful element of what's called the "plan of redemption." This plan, created by God, makes it possible for us to look forward to a home in heaven. It's the wonderful process of instruction, encouragement, and hope that can take us from a sinful world to a perfect earth made new.

When was this plan developed? Listen to our friend Ellen White: "The purpose and plan of grace existed from all eternity. . . . Redemption was not an afterthought, a plan formulated after the fall of Adam, but an eternal purpose, . . . not only of this atom of a world, but for the good of all the worlds that God had created" (*Signs of the Times*, Dec. 15, 1914).

You and I, along with Adam and Eve and everyone else who's lived or will live on this earth, have already been forgiven. Trouble is, most people don't know that. They think they have to beg God to pardon them when they make mistakes.

Instead, we all should be thanking our Creator for the forgiveness He's already freely and lovingly placed in our lives. Forgiveness is something we *accept*, not cause to happen. It's already there waiting for us.

Adam and Eve will be in heaven for the same reason we'll be there. We've been forgiven. It's part of the plan. Always has been.

Why did God make the tree of good and evil?

—*Galan, 12, Oklahoma*

It looked like any other tree in the Garden of Eden. It had leaves and fruit, branches with birds nesting among them. At its base was found cool shade just right for snoozing, or dreaming wild and wonderful daydreams.

There was absolutely nothing special about the tree, except what God said concerning it. *"You are free to eat from any tree in the garden; but you must not eat from the tree of the knowledge of good and evil, for when you eat of it you will surely die" (Genesis 2:16, 17, NIV).*

Strange. Why would a God of love make such a silly rule? It's just a tree! That's exactly what Satan said to Eve when he appeared to her as a beautiful flying serpent. *"'You will not surely die,' the serpent said to the woman. 'For God knows that when you eat of it your eyes will be opened, and you will be like God, knowing good and evil'" (Genesis 3:4, 5, NIV).*

Satan was right about one thing. Adam and Eve did discover evil that day. They also found out about its *results,* too. Even before the sweet taste of the fruit washed from their tongues, they felt a troubling sensation deep in their hearts. For the first time ever, Adam and Eve experienced painful feelings of guilt and shame.

God placed the tree in the garden so human beings could choose which power they wanted leading their lives—good or evil. They chose evil. The world has never been the same since.

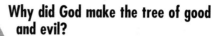

Why did God make the tree of good and evil?
—*Galan, 12, Oklahoma*

Adam and Eve made their choice. They ate the fruit and proved both God and Satan right. They did discover evil. They did die.

Galan, did you know there are trees just like that in our world today? No, they don't have branches and leaves and fruit. These "trees" are loaded down with ink and electrons and sound. Anything that can increase our knowledge of evil, such as trash-filled literature; violent, perverse television shows; and music blasting hurtful, unrespectful lyrics should be considered off-limits to the Christian, just like that tree in the Garden.

Think of all the beauty remaining in this world. Think of the good, kind, helpful, and uplifting experiences we can share with others. Don't be attracted by the fruit of evil hanging all around you. Say no to Satan. Do what even Adam and Eve failed to do—resist temptation and choose the eternal life God offers, not the death Satan makes so inviting.

"Do not be overcome by evil, but overcome evil with good" (Romans 12:21, NIV). When faced with a choice, choose life; leave evil fruits to rot in the warmth of God's forgiving love.

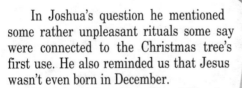

Is it good to celebrate Christmas?
—*Joshua, 11, California*

In Joshua's question he mentioned some rather unpleasant rituals some say were connected to the Christmas tree's first use. He also reminded us that Jesus wasn't even born in December.

Many people refuse to celebrate Christmas for a variety of reasons. I honor their dedication to their beliefs and respect their wishes to not be included in such things as gift-giving, holiday parties, and so on. And I hope they'll be just as respectful to my desire to remember the birth of Jesus in the way and time I choose.

Satan has done a pretty good job of tainting all celebrations having to do with God. On the day we remember Christ's resurrection, kids are running around millions of backyards looking for bunny eggs. And buried somewhere under all the tinsel and wrapping paper, credit card receipts and brightly colored greeting cards hides the image of a Baby lying in a manger.

Is it good to give gifts? Sure. Is it good to look for eggs in the backyard? Why not? But when these fun activities leave us little time to think of the *real* reason for Christmas and Easter—Christ's birth, death, and resurrection—that's bad.

"When you have eaten and are satisfied, praise the Lord your God. . . . Be careful that you do not forget the Lord" (Deuteronomy 8:10, 11, NIV). Enjoy the fun, but remember the reasons.

How do you get to heaven?

—Lyle, 13, New Mexico

When I was a little boy, I used to stand in our backyard in Tennessee waiting for Jesus to come. I'd gaze up into the sky, watching the clouds drift by, wondering if *that* one, or *that* one, was filled with holy angels and Jesus Himself.

One summer afternoon, tired of playing Superman with my friend Roger, I sat down and began watching the sky when suddenly a terrible feeling swept over me. *What if I'm not ready?* I thought. *What if I have sinned and don't even know it? What if Jesus comes and refuses to take me back to heaven with Him?* I ran and found my mother loading clothes into the washing machine. "Am I going to be saved?" I gasped. "Hurry. I've gotta know."

Mom smiled. "Of course you are," she said.

"How can you be sure?" I asked.

"Because Jesus loves you very much and wants you to be with Him in heaven," Mom said softly, looking at me with eyes that always quieted my fears.

How do you get to heaven? By believing God loves you so much that He's willing to forgive your sins and help you prepare to be a citizen of His new earth. Then you allow Him to lead you, correct you, and finally save you.

I still occasionally scan the sky and wonder. But I'm never afraid. *"Now there is in store for me the crown of righteousness, which the Lord, the righteous Judge, will award to me on that day—and not only to me, but also to all who have longed for his appearing"* (2 Timothy 4:8, NIV).

How do you ask a boy out?

—Girl, 10, Maine

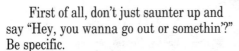

First of all, don't just saunter up and say "Hey, you wanna go out or somethin'?" Be specific.

I was not much older than you when I went on my first official, this-is-going-to-cost-me date. There was this really neat girl who lived about five blocks from my house in Syracuse, New York. She was the older sister of one of my sister's friends. I liked her because she was smart and funny—a combination I've always enjoyed in other people no matter what gender they happen to be.

I planned our date carefully and made sure I had enough money to cover it. Then I called and said, "Hi, Mary. This is Charles. Would you like to go play miniature golf with me? We can get an ice cream afterward."

"What flavor?" she asked.

Together we rode our bikes to a nearby shopping center. I bought the tickets, and we played two games. She beat me both times, but I didn't care. I was on a *date!* It was fun being in charge of making sure another person was having a good time.

When you ask a boy out, make sure (1) you've got the money to cover expenses if there are any; (2) you outline exactly what you're going to do on the date; and (3) you keep your parents or guardians informed of who, where, what, when, and how. If you play miniature golf, let the guy win once.

And remember: *"He who walks with the wise grows wise, but a companion of fools suffers harm"* (Proverbs 13:20, NIV). Pick your dates carefully. Then have a safe and wonderful time!

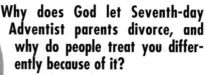

Why does God let Seventh-day Adventist parents divorce, and why do people treat you differently because of it?

—Christina, 13, Indiana

God did not create divorce. He created marriage, and happiness, and love. Divorce goes contrary to everything He had in mind when He formed earth's first husband and wife.

One day a group of Pharisees asked Jesus, *"Is it lawful for a man to divorce his wife for any and every reason?"* *(Matthew 19:3, NIV).* Jesus had a quick and ready answer. *"'Haven't you read,'* he replied, *'that at the beginning the Creator made them male and female, and said, "For this reason a man will leave his father and mother and be united to his wife, and the two will become one flesh?" So they are no longer two, but one. Therefore what God has joined together, let man not separate'"* *(verses 4-6, NIV).*

Jesus wanted to make sure His hearers understood that divorce was not supposed to be an option. Then Christ revealed the *only* acceptable reason for two people to end their marriage. *"I tell you that anyone who divorces his wife, except for marital unfaithfulness, and marries another woman commits adultery"* *(verse 9, NIV).* According to the Bible, marital unfaithfulness, which means having sex with someone who isn't your wife or husband, is just cause for divorce in God's eyes.

Why this divine loophole? Because marriage binds two people together with God-ordained bands of trust and commitment. Sex outside of marriage breaks these bands, and the beautiful "one flesh" condition ceases to exist.

Why does God let Seventh-day Adventist parents divorce, and why do people treat you differently because of it?

—Christina, 13, Indiana

God hates divorce as much as you do. But He did allow husbands and wives the option of ending their marriage if someone breaks the "one flesh" condition of their union by having sex with another person.

Seventh-day Adventists enjoy a deep understanding of God's Holy Word. We've learned specific truths that set us apart from other Christians. But even while being unique, we share a common trait with our friends and neighbors. We're human beings living in a sinful world and, sadly, totally capable of making terrible mistakes.

God created His laws of love for all people in all churches. But I'll have to admit that when I see so many Adventist marriages ending in divorce it makes me sad. "They should know better," I say to myself. "They should spend more time with their Bibles and less time with their lawyers."

Adventists get divorces for the same reasons other people do. We've allowed sin to enter our homes. We've turned our eyes away from Jesus and become self-centered and unforgiving. We've stepped out of bounds in our relationships and permitted Satan to make choices for us.

But God says, *"Do not be overcome by evil, but overcome evil with good"* (Romans 12:21, NIV). Thoughts of divorce fade away when married couples let God back into their homes and lives.

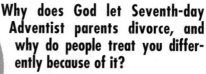

Why does God let Seventh-day Adventist parents divorce, and why do people treat you differently because of it?

—Christina, 13, Indiana

Let's say you have a friend whose parents have recently divorced. She's probably feeling frightened, confused, and angry. Perhaps she's blaming herself for what happened!

Your friend's emotions are all mixed up because her world just got blasted out from under her. She shows up at school and sits down beside you. You know the situation, and you want to help, but you're not sure how. Certainly you don't want to say something stupid—something that might make matters worse.

So what do you do? You might try to keep out of her way, ask friends for advice, smile and attempt to make her feel better when you know deep in your heart you don't have a clue how to handle the situation. You may even feel a little embarrassed and frustrated yourself as you attempt to work through *your* feelings about *her* feelings.

And what does your friend see? She sees you acting strangely, keeping at a distance, treating her differently.

Many people don't know how to deal with someone in a divorce situation. In frustration they turn away, removing their love at a time when the person needs them most. But with God at your side you don't have to withhold attention, no matter what your friend is facing. *"Whoever loves his brother lives in the light, and there is nothing in him to make him stumble" (1 John 2:10, NIV).* Forgive people their weaknesses and show them God's strength.

Where did God come from, besides always being there? Is there something better than God?
—*Leslie, 14, Ontario*

In humanity the life cycle consists of three stages: (1) before existence; (2) existence; (3) after existence. Everything has a beginning, middle, and end.

Then God comes along and says, *"I tell you the truth. . . . Before Abraham was born, I am" (John 8:58, NIV)!* Notice He didn't say "I *was*." He said "I *am*."

Prior to that, He asked Job, *"Where were you when I laid the earth's foundation?" (Job 38:4, NIV).*

Everything we see didn't exist at one time or another. And everything we see will, somewhere down the line, die, fade, vanish, be absorbed, change into something else, or be consumed—including ourselves. So the idea of an "I AM" doesn't fit into our human thinking at all, because we haven't experienced it.

So if I say to you, "God didn't *come from* anywhere, because He always existed," you won't understand, and I don't expect you to. I don't either. But it's true. We simply have to admit there are things about God we don't know.

Is there something better than God? I truly don't think so. He is *"one God and Father of all, who is over all and through all and in all" (Ephesians 4:6, NIV).* And that's all we'll ever need.

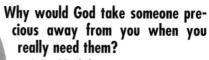

Why would God take someone precious away from you when you really need them?
—*Lacey, 15, Alaska*

Has this happened to you recently, Lacey? I'm so sorry. Losing someone we love is terrible and lonely, and hurts very deep inside.

But God didn't take that person away from you. Satan did. Before sin entered this earth, there was no death or dying or loneliness. There was only life, joy, and endless love.

Please make sure you place the blame for death where it belongs— squarely on Satan's evil shoulders.

"God could've kept it from happening!" you say with a touch of anger in your voice. That's true, and someday He will. Satan and sin will be erased completely from the universe. Until then, death will continue to be a part of life on this earth.

By the way, Lacey, God knows how you feel. He watched as His own Son was nailed to a Roman cross. He heard Him cry out in pain. He was there when the last breath was taken. Why didn't He stop that horrible scene? Because He knew His Son's death was necessary so you and your family could live again without pain.

There are a couple texts you need to read. *"I will not leave you comfortless: I will come to you" (John 14:18). "For the Lord comforts his people and will have compassion on his afflicted ones" (Isaiah 49:13, NIV).*

You have three friends ready to help you through your sorrow, Lacey. Jesus, who experienced death; the Holy Spirit, who's even called the Comforter; and Christ's loving Father, who watched it happen. Ask Them to comfort you right now.

Is it a sin to be boyfriend and girlfriend at age 12?
—*Girl, 12, West Virginia*

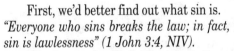

First, we'd better find out what sin is. *"Everyone who sins breaks the law; in fact, sin is lawlessness" (1 John 3:4, NIV).*

Whether you're 12 or 20, any relationship that breaks the law is sin. What law? God's everlasting law of love as proclaimed from Mount Sinai and spoken from the lips of Jesus.

Each of the "rules for better living," as I like to call them, serves one unchanging purpose—to protect God's people from the heartbreaking results of sin. Rules such as: don't love something or someone more than you love God; don't forget to keep the Sabbath holy; honor your parents; don't murder or steal; don't lust after someone else's husband or wife; love your neighbor as yourself. Other rules guard against hurting your own body with unhealthy habits and unclean foods.

What's that got to do with having a boyfriend or girlfriend? Everything. You see, sometimes, in order to please the person we like, we lose sight of God's laws. We break them. We do things we shouldn't, go places we shouldn't, harm our bodies with impure thoughts and actions—all in an attempt to keep the attention of the guy or girl we're interested in.

"For it is not those who hear the law who are righteous in God's sight, but it is those who obey the law who will be declared righteous" (Romans 2:13, NIV).

If boys and girls, men and women, keep their relationship safely within the boundaries set by God's laws, there's no sin.

"What's up, man?"
—Dan, 12, Alabama

Just hangin', Dan, trying to answer a few questions from my junior friends.

A few months ago I wrote an article for *Guide* magazine about a 13-year-old girl named Raven Rowbottom who goes around to schools in her neighborhood teaching kids about the dangers of drugs and alcohol. She makes her own props and everything. Sends out a monthly newsletter, talks to bigwigs in the town where she lives, and wrote a book called *An Easy Way to Stop Smoking,* using information she gathered at her local library.

Last week I watched a report on television about some kids who volunteer their time at a home for disabled children, helping them learn to do stuff such as get coordinated and read. Impressive!

It's amazing what juniors can do if they set their minds to a task. Listen to this beautiful description of a Kid we all should get to know better: "His willing hands were ever ready to serve others. He manifested a patience that nothing could disturb, and a truthfulness that would never sacrifice integrity. In principle firm as a rock, His life revealed the grace of unselfish courtesy" (*The Desire of Ages,* pp. 68, 69).

Yes, I'm talking about the child Jesus, as described by our friend Ellen White. I've seen many illustrations of that type of caring, loving attitude in the lives of today's young people, too. I hope you will always try to be like Jesus in all things.

Are dinosaurs going to be in heaven?
—Patrick, 12, Oklahoma

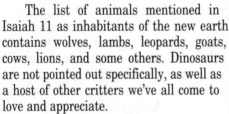

The list of animals mentioned in Isaiah 11 as inhabitants of the new earth contains wolves, lambs, leopards, goats, cows, lions, and some others. Dinosaurs are not pointed out specifically, as well as a host of other critters we've all come to love and appreciate.

I have a feeling that if God had listed *all* the animals waiting for us in the new earth, our Bibles would be so large we couldn't lift them.

We worship a *Creator* God, a Being who loves to make things for His and our enjoyment. If you enjoy dinosaurs, then check your backyard when you take up residence in heaven.

But don't expect the meat-eating, flesh-tearing, evil-eyed creatures we see in movies or museums. Listen to this quote from our friend Ellen White: "Every species of animal which God had created were preserved in the ark. The confused species which God did not create, which were the result of amalgamation [crossbreeding] were destroyed in the flood" *(Spiritual Gifts*, vol. 3, p. 75). Only nonmutated, pure forms of each species survived in the ark. Since there were no dinosaurs after the Flood, we must conclude that they didn't make the passenger list. But the beautiful, peace-loving creatures from which they came, did. And those animals will also roam the new earth.

When we get to heaven, bring your favorite critter over to my place. Then we'll head to the tree of life for a little fruit snack. It'll be fun!

Is heaven above the world or galaxy, or is it higher? And if you sin once, will you still go to heaven?

—*Pleshonna, 11, California*

In space there's no up or down, high or low. There's just vast emptiness. But don't think everything's in confusion out there. Our friend Ellen White says all worlds and galaxies circle God's throne in an orderly, well-planned manner (*The Great Controversy*, pp. 677, 678).

Since we can't see heaven even with our most powerful telescopes, I'd have to say it's far from this earth and way beyond any galaxies we've gazed at. That's why I'm so glad Jesus offers to live right in my heart where I can talk to Him instantly, and He can be a constant part of my life.

As for your second question, you need to hear a text written by the apostle Paul—a man who devoted all his life to the God he loved. Listen: *"I do not understand what I do. For what I want to do I do not do, but what I hate I do"* (Romans 7:15, NIV). Poor Paul—he wanted to be good, to be sinless, but he kept blowing it, and hating himself for it.

Christians aren't perfect. They make mistakes, just as Paul did. But when they sin, they feel terrible about it and immediately ask God to forgive them and help them do better next time.

People who sin and don't let it bother them will never enjoy heaven. But those of us who slip now and then, are truly sorry, and accept God's forgiving love can look forward to the joys waiting in the new earth where there'll be no temptation and sin.

Can you get AIDS at this age?
—*Danielle, 13, New Mexico*

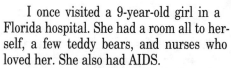

I once visited a 9-year-old girl in a Florida hospital. She had a room all to herself, a few teddy bears, and nurses who loved her. She also had AIDS.

Seems her mother had used an infected needle to shoot drugs when she was pregnant. Now this sweet, innocent girl was going to die because she'd shared her mother's blood before she was born, as all babies do.

You can get AIDS at any age. But researchers agree that this terrible condition is one of the most preventable plagues there is. AIDS is transferred from one person to another through sexual intercourse and/or the exchange of blood—such as when two people use the same needle when shooting drugs.

The disease is *not* transferred through saliva, tears, sweat, urine, or fecal matter. In other words, you *can't* get it by kissing, comforting a crying infected person, playing a rousing game of softball, or using a public restroom. If you're careful and use good, common sense AIDS is not a big concern.

Hospitals continually check their blood supplies, and doctors and nurses are carefully trained in keeping the problem from spreading.

If you run across someone with AIDS, respond as God did in 2 Kings 13:23: *"But the Lord was gracious to them and had compassion and showed concern for them"* (NIV).

How do you let somebody know you really like them?
—*Girl, 12, Maine*

Something tells me that our questioner has her eye on a certain young man and this certain young man makes her heart go pitter-patter. I know how you feel. My heart's done the same thing. Everyone's has.

May I suggest some caution here? Finding someone you *really* like is not too difficult. One day you look up and *POW*, the guy who punched you in the arm the day before suddenly looks like the answer to all your dreams. And he may be, someday. Who knows? But a problem arises if he doesn't feel the same way about you that you feel about him. So if you fall all over yourself letting him know just how wonderful he is, he may reject your well-intentioned advances, or, worse yet, laugh in your face. (Some guys never learn that girls' hearts can break too.)

So I'd recommend a more careful approach. Ask for his help with a particularly challenging piece of schoolwork. Write him a note complimenting him for something he did, such as earning a high score on a test or hitting a home run during a ball game. Include an extra dessert in your lunch and offer it to him discreetly. Believe me, truthfully playing to a guy's ego or his digestive tract is a sure winner when it comes to catching his attention. If he backs away, you're only out a few honest compliments and a cupcake.

"Dear children, let us not love with words or tongue but with actions and in truth" (1 John 3:18, NIV). Good luck!

Why is the world so evil?
—*Sarah, 10, Indiana*

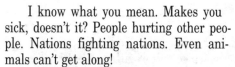

I know what you mean. Makes you sick, doesn't it? People hurting other people. Nations fighting nations. Even animals can't get along!

The world is evil because God gave humanity a choice. He didn't want folks to love and obey Him because they were afraid of Him. He didn't want men and women to keep His laws for fear of punishment. God desired that all people live according to His heavenly standards because they *chose* to.

Well, Adam and Eve made their decision. And that's why we're in the mess we're in.

Guess what? There are some people who blame God for pain and suffering, hate and death. They blame *God!* But wasn't His newly created world overflowing with joy and love, peace and harmony? Of course it was. Evil has even made people think that bad stuff is God's fault. How unfair!

But don't despair. Until Jesus comes to vanish sin forever, there are many things we can do to lessen its influence in our lives. With God's help we can be kind when others are mean. We can love when others hate. We can forgive when others hold grudges. And we can hope when others despair.

"Trust in the Lord and do good; dwell in the land and enjoy safe pasture. Delight yourself in the Lord and he will give you the desires of your heart" (Psalm 37:3, 4, NIV).

Sarah, make your own choice. Choose to love and obey God.

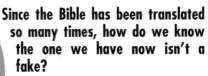

Since the Bible has been translated so many times, how do we know the one we have now isn't a fake?

—Corinne, 13, Ontario

Have you ever played the game in which someone whispers something to someone, then that person whispers to the next person? By the time the message reaches the last player, it's completely changed. Did that happen to the Bible? Did all those writers, rewriters, translators, updaters, and transcribers create such a mixed-up mess we can't trust it anymore?

Since earliest times the books of the Bible have been considered sacred to those who collected and copied them. The individuals who did this work took great pains to make sure every letter, word, paragraph, and chapter was identical to the original. If a new translation was in order, those who did the actual writing worked from preserved manuscripts written in the original Bible languages—Greek and Hebrew. They wanted to be absolutely certain of maintaining the purity of every single truth and life-enriching doctrine. Our Bibles *can* be trusted.

But here's the greatest test. If, when reading, you feel closer to heaven and find comfort in its pages, then God is still at work, changing lives through the power He placed in the Bible long ago. *"And we also thank God continually because, when you received the word of God . . . you accepted it not as the word of men, but as it actually is, the word of God, which is at work in you who believe"* (1 Thessalonians 2:13, NIV).

Will we stop at other planets as we travel to heaven, or will we go straight there?
—*Derick, 12, Alaska*

God showed our friend Ellen White tiny glimpses of the journey we'll take after Jesus comes the second time. Although she didn't include any details in her brief account, she did say the expedition would last seven days (*Early Writings*, p. 16).

What do *you* think any trip would be like with Jesus Himself in the lead? Will He want us to ignore passing worlds? Will our Creator God try to hide the mysteries of the universe from us?

Or will we swoop low over incredible scenes of cosmic beauty and pause to get acquainted with the perfect, sinless beings of other worlds? If the angels can travel from God's throne to our side faster than a prayer, why is it going to take seven *days* for us to get to heaven?

I believe the answer lies in the very character of Jesus. He's been waiting a long time for this and wants even our first week with Him to be worth the sacrifices we've made to maintain our readiness for the journey. Remember, this is the God who loved us so much He was willing to die for our sins. Now we're together, no longer separated by sin.

Derick, our journey to heaven will be such an amazing event, such an incredibly exciting occasion, that whatever happens will bring us joys beyond imagination. *"Behold, I come quickly,"* announces Jesus in Revelation 22:7. Like John, I say, "HURRY!"

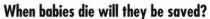

When babies die will they be saved?
—Haani, 12, West Virginia

My brother Bob and his wife had a tragic experience many years ago. While serving as missionaries in Ethiopia, they had a baby. But it was born dead.

On that terrible day the rain was coming down hard. Bob carried the tiny, still form out of the hospital and took it to a quiet place on a hillside where he buried it deep in the ground. The rain brushed the tears of anguish from his cheeks and gently laid them on the grave.

When I heard that story for the first time, it broke my heart. It still does.

Someday that faraway grave will open and a little baby's heart will start beating. His eyes, so long closed by death's silent sleep, will blink, and he'll see Jesus smiling down at him. And he won't be afraid.

The baby's parents are looking forward to a joyous reunion on that day. This time it won't be raining, and the tears staining their cheeks will spring from unspeakable joy.

Babies can't knowingly disobey God. They don't understand right from wrong. But they do know when they're loved. Heaven will be filled with children, like my brother's baby, who'll never know anything but love. *"Do not be amazed at this, for a time is coming when all who are in their graves will hear his voice and come out" (John 5:28, 29, NIV).* I hope today's the day.

Do you have many missionary stories?

—*Summer, 9, Alabama*

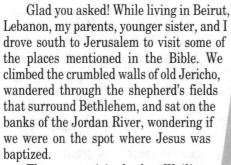

APRIL
4

Glad you asked! While living in Beirut, Lebanon, my parents, younger sister, and I drove south to Jerusalem to visit some of the places mentioned in the Bible. We climbed the crumbled walls of old Jericho, wandered through the shepherd's fields that surround Bethlehem, and sat on the banks of the Jordan River, wondering if we were on the spot where Jesus was baptized.

Then we visited the Wailing Wall—a section of the rampart encircling the site of Solomon's Temple.

One cold morning I got up before anyone else and discovered that during the night a blanket of snow had fallen, covering the ground with soft, white folds. Slipping into my warmest clothes, I quickly hurried to the Damascus Gate and entered the quiet, narrow streets of the Old City. It was so peaceful.

Before long, I found myself roaming across the Kidron Valley and began climbing the Mount of Olives. With deep reverence, I slipped through the front gate of the Garden of Gethsemane and found a place to rest beneath gnarled and twisted olive branches. Suddenly I heard footsteps approaching. A man, probably in his early 20s, shuffled up beside me, a friendly smile lighting his weather-tanned face.

"Hello," I said in my best Arabic.

He nodded, then motioned for me to follow.

"Where are we going?" I asked. He just smiled, and began walking, his worn boots crunching in the new-fallen snow. (Continued April 5.)

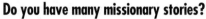

Do you have many missionary stories?
—*Summer, 9, Alabama*

The stranger didn't look back to see if I was coming. He just continued walking through the snow, out of the garden.

We climbed the hill in silence. Each time I attempted to begin a conversation with him, he'd just smile and nod, his threadbare coat blowing in the cold wind whispering through the Kidron Valley. *My Arabic must be pretty awful,* I thought to myself. I tried English. No luck. He continued leading me along the winding road.

Before long we came to a small church perched on the hillside. He pointed up at it and tilted his head questioningly.

Inside the little structure were display cases filled with handwritten portions of scripture. I recognized names such as Isaiah, Jeremiah, Psalms, and others. But it was the stranger's expression that captivated my attention. He'd run his hand along the smooth glass that separated him from the sheets of faded parchment as though he was touching something of great value. Such reverence. Such deep affection for those ancient writings.

He motioned to me again. We left the little church and soon were standing at the very top of the mountain, gazing down at the walls encircling old Jerusalem.

"It's beautiful," I said pointing. "Look how the snow makes everything so clean and—" My words faltered. The man beside me was crying. (Continued April 6.)

Do you have many missionary stories?

—*Summer, 9, Alabama*

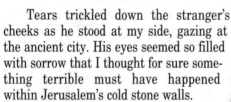

Tears trickled down the stranger's cheeks as he stood at my side, gazing at the ancient city. His eyes seemed so filled with sorrow that I thought for sure something terrible must have happened within Jerusalem's cold stone walls.

"Why are you crying?" I asked softly.

The stranger looked over at me, and I saw the anguish had passed, replaced by a tired and kindly smile. Once again he motioned for me to follow.

He led me to a small cafe in an old building by the edge of the road. The warmth inside felt good to my face and hands as we entered, the room's dim recesses a welcome relief from the early-morning brightness outside.

"I see you've met my brother," an older man called as I sat down near the window. "He's the best guide in Jerusalem. Been taking tourists up and down the Mount of Olives for years."

"But he doesn't ever say anything," I sighed. "Doesn't he know any English at all?"

The older man took a seat across from me as my happy guide busied himself preparing some cups of hot chocolate at the counter. "You're not the first visitor to ask that," he said. "You see, my little brother doesn't talk because he can't. He's never said a single word. Doctors call it a birth defect. They say he'll never be able to speak. Not ever." (Continued April 7.)

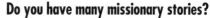

Do you have many missionary stories?
—*Summer, 9, Alabama*

With a satisfied grin, my guide placed a steaming cup before me, then hurried to the door. With a wave he was gone.

"Going out to look for someone else to lead up the mountain," his brother announced with pride lifting his words. "Works from sunup to sundown."

"But," I protested, reaching into my pocket, "I didn't pay him yet."

"Wouldn't do any good to try," the man said, raising his hand. "He never asks for money. You see, my brother's a Christian, and believes God wants him to spend his life showing visitors the beauties of the mountain. It's like his witness. His silent witness."

Today, whenever I think of Jerusalem, I picture two men climbing the Mount of Olives. One is Jesus, the Son of God, walking those narrow paths, knowing full well He'll be betrayed and crucified by the very people He came to save.

The other is a kind, weatherworn stranger with a threadbare coat and friendly smile who demonstrates daily that the sacrifice of the first Man still changes lives today, and brightens the way for anyone willing to listen to the silence of redeeming love.

107

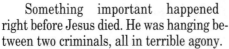

Will those who believe in Christ, but not in the seventh day as the Sabbath, go to heaven?

—*Holly, 9, Oklahoma*

APRIL

8

Something important happened right before Jesus died. He was hanging between two criminals, all in terrible agony.

"Hey! Aren't you the Christ?" one called with an angry, sarcastic voice. "Why don't you save yourself, and us too?"

The other thief had been watching Jesus carefully. He'd seen Him give comfort to His weeping mother even while pain racked His bruised and bleeding body. He'd heard Him ask God to forgive the guards for their cruel actions. Not one curse had he heard Jesus hurl at the crowd. Not one murmur of anger or hate had escaped the stranger's parched lips.

"Don't you fear God?" he asked, addressing the other criminal. "We deserve to die. But this man is sinless."

At that moment the second thief fully believed what he'd heard about this Stranger from Nazareth. As his body trembled in pain, he called out, *"Jesus, remember me when you come into your kingdom"* (Luke 23:42, NIV).

Christ answered him immediately, *"I tell you the truth . . . you will be with me in paradise"* (verse 43, NIV).

The thief didn't have time to learn all that is involved in becoming a Christian. But he was saved anyway, because he believed in Jesus. We, on the other hand, have time. Obeying all of God's laws keeps us safely within the boundaries of His saving power. With us, belief must be combined with obedience.

How did angels become angels?
—*Victoria, 11, California*

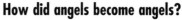

Our friend Ellen White wrote the answer to your question while describing Satan before his rebellion in heaven.

"A special light beamed in His countenance and shone around Him brighter and more beautiful than around the other angels; yet Christ, God's dear Son, had the preeminence over all the angelic host. He was one with the Father before the angels were created" (*The Faith I Live By*, p. 67).

Angels, like everything else in the universe, came directly from the powerful, loving hand of the Creator.

Why were they brought into existence? For the same reason we were—to enjoy the friendship and companionship of a loving God.

It's reassuring to know that we all have an angel assigned to our side. In times of sickness I feel my angel close to me. When tempted to do something I shouldn't, knowing such a glorious being is standing at my side gives me the motivation to resist.

Someday, when Jesus returns, I'm going to meet my angel face-to-face. I think we'll become close friends. Together we'll enjoy eternity, worshiping the God who made us both.

Why do you get hiccups?
—*Rachel, 12, New Mexico*

Mr. Funk and Mr. Wagnalls, two guys who probably suffered from occasional bouts of this awkward condition and who also wrote an encyclopedia, offer this explanation: "Hiccups are involuntary contractions of the diaphragm that occur with contractions of the larynx and closure of the glottis, arresting the inflow of air. They are commonly induced by minor stomach upset. Mild cases usually disappear without treatment."

One time I saw a third grader cure her hiccups on the spot, using a very peculiar method. She filled a cup half full of water, then bent over and drank the liquid from the *opposite* side of the rim, across from where people normally drink. This "upside down" sipping not only got her chin wet; it also ended her hiccups.

Not being one to believe without experiencing, I tried my young friend's cure the next time I had "involuntary contractions of the diaphragm." Sure enough, I got a wet chin and stopped hiccupping immediately. Don't ask me why it works. Even my wife has found it a quick and painless way to get her larynx and glottis to behave in a more civilized manner.

Eating too fast, eating while under stress, or even laughing hard seems to be enough to get things jumping. Although I've never heard of anyone dying of hiccups, I've seen some dying of embarrassment while fighting a nasty attack.

I'm looking forward to heaven, where all of our body parts will behave themselves.

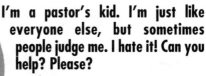

I'm a pastor's kid. I'm just like everyone else, but sometimes people judge me. I hate it! Can you help? Please?
—*Girl, 12*

First, you need to know something important. Those people aren't judging you. They're judging your parent. And that's not fair either.

Some church members insist that the preacher's kid be a shining example of a perfect Christian boy or girl. After all, a spiritual leader in the community should know how to raise children, right?

Well, perhaps. But boys and girls have minds of their own. They make choices, sometimes good ones, sometimes not so good.

But that doesn't keep unthinking churchgoers from being totally shocked when a preacher's kid doesn't live up to the high standards they've set. They suddenly become judge and jury for the church family, condemning the poor child for actions they'd more readily accept in someone else's kid.

Strange. We don't expect a doctor's young son to be able to perform open-heart surgery, or an artist's daughter to paint a masterpiece. Why should we assume that a preacher's child is going to live a perfect life based on the fact that his or her parent pounds the pulpit once a week?

Don't despair. *"The Lord works righteousness and justice for all the oppressed"* (Psalm 103:6, NIV). That includes preachers' kids who must grow up under other people's standards.

111

I'm a pastor's kid. I'm just like everyone else, but sometimes people judge me. I hate it! Can you help? Please?
—*Girl, 12*

Should a preacher's son or daughter be "better" than, say, the offspring of a plumber?

We certainly have ample opportunity to *learn* how to be better. My childhood as both a preacher's and missionary's kid was filled with spiritual activities such as evangelistic meetings, prayer bands, community services, Ingathering, Sabbath school programs, Bible studies, and tons of sermons—many preached by my own dad.

Did all that make me "better" than my friends? No. But it did take away any excuse I had to be worse. I knew what sin was. I knew how much it hurt my heavenly Father when I turned my back on His love. All those meetings, programs, and sermons left impressions on my young mind. Later in life those impressions came in handy.

So, in one sense, you're *not* like everyone else. God has given you the opportunity to learn even deeper lessons about His love. All you have to do is open your eyes and ears to the many church activities around you. Watch your parent at work. Pay attention to the sermons. Get to know the God your parent represents.

And never let judgmental people stand in your way. *"Blessed are they which are persecuted for righteousness' sake: for theirs is the kingdom of heaven" (Matthew 5:10).* Do something to really get their tongues wagging: forgive them.

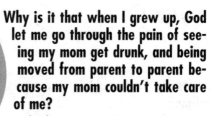

Why is it that when I grew up, God let me go through the pain of seeing my mom get drunk, and being moved from parent to parent because my mom couldn't take care of me?

—*Girl, Indiana*

Your question breaks my heart. I can't think of anything worse than seeing parents willingly give up control of their lives and actions to alcohol or drugs, especially when they have children in need of love and attention. I'm so sorry for what you're going through.

You *must* understand something. God is not the cause of your suffering. He doesn't make mothers get drunk. He doesn't start the fights moms and dads have. The last thing in this world He wants to see is for kids to be shuffled from one parent to another.

Sin brings suffering and pain. *Sin* splits families. *Sin* causes the hurt we all face.

People live by the choices they make. As you've discovered, parents are perfectly capable of making horrible mistakes. Unfortunately, their bad choices usually affect more than themselves. They affect their children as well.

Will you do me a favor? Promise yourself, right now, that you won't repeat your mother's errors. Determine *never* to surrender control of your actions to alcohol or drugs. You've seen the results. Instead, with Samuel's mother, Hannah, say, *"I have drunk neither wine nor strong drink, but have poured out my soul before the Lord"* *(1 Samuel 1:15).*

Satan may have torn your family apart, but God promises to help you put your life together. Ask Him to begin this moment.

Why is it that when I grew up, God let me go through the pain of seeing my mom get drunk, and being moved from parent to parent because my mom couldn't take care of me?

—*Girl, Indiana*

I think Jesus must have been thinking of all the boys and girls who would face broken homes in the future when He spoke to His disciples one evening.

They were eating supper in a Jerusalem upper room. Only Christ knew this would be their last meal together, for that very night Judas would betray Him to the killing mob.

"I'm going away," Jesus said.

"Where?" Peter asked.

"It's a place you can't come just yet," the Master stated.

The disciples became sad. They loved Jesus and couldn't bear the thought of being separated from Him. That's when He spoke the words you and I, and everyone who has felt lonely or betrayed, need to hear. Listen: *"I will not leave you as orphans." "I will ask the Father, and he will give you another Counselor to be with you forever"* (John 14:18, 16, NIV).

The King James Version of the Bible records Jesus' words as "he shall give you another Comforter." Something tells me you need a comforter—someone to listen to you, cry with you, dream with you.

When sin tears families apart, most children find themselves facing days, and even years, of fear and uncertainty. God sees the tears. He feels the hidden pain. He hears the whispered calls for help. You are not alone. You have the Comforter waiting to bring warmth back into your heart. Ask for Him now.

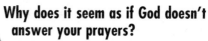

Why does it seem as if God doesn't answer your prayers?
—*Lindsay, 14, Ontario*

Ever have days when everything goes right? I have. Many times. My work flows along effortlessly, everyone's friendly, I feel good about my life.

On days like that, I have no problem believing God answers prayers.

Then the bad times come. Work commitments drag me down, people aren't kind or understanding, and my life seems like it's not worth the effort.

On those days I think God *never* answers prayers.

How we feel physically, mentally, even socially, has a lot to do with how we feel about God. In our depression and frustration, we plead with Heaven for relief. We ask God to come up with answers, and make it quick. When nothing seems to happen, we say to ourselves, "Humph! God isn't listening. He doesn't care about me."

Lindsay, sometimes we've just got to believe that God answers prayers whether we feel like it or not. When our minds or bodies or social life can't seem to get a grip, that's the time for our faith to kick in—faith in a prayer-hearing and prayer-answering God.

Just what kind of God are we talking about here? Listen to this incredible text. *"Before they call I will answer; while they are still speaking I will hear"* (Isaiah 65:24, NIV). God does hear and answer prayers, even though we sometimes feel He doesn't.

Why does it seem as if God doesn't answer your prayers?

—Lindsay, 14, Ontario

It might be wise for us to consider exactly what we're asking for. Here's an example. When I was teaching at a little church school in Georgia, one of my third graders would always pray before taking a test. He also prayed before coming up to bat, at the start of a race, whenever he faced a challenge.

While I love to see children talking to their heavenly Father, I was curious about why this young fellow prayed so much.

"I'm asking God for a good grade," he explained. "Or for a home run, fast feet—whatever I need."

I quickly explained that God doesn't answer prayers all by Himself. He needs help.

"God needs help?" my little friend gasped.

"That's right," I stated. "He needs *your* help to answer your prayers. Want to get an A? Study harder. Want to hit a home run? Practice longer. You'll be surprised at how many more prayers get answered when you work in partnership with God."

Sure enough, when my student got busy and worked toward his goals, his grades, ball playing, and outlook on life improved.

God isn't Santa Claus. He doesn't pass out answered prayers like party favors. He listens to our sensible requests and creates a plan of action for us to follow. Then it's our responsibility to do our part in making the answers possible.

"The prayer of a righteous man is powerful and effective" (James 5:16, NIV). But only when we work in partnership with God.

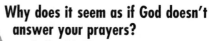

Why does it seem as if God doesn't answer your prayers?
—Lindsay, 14, Ontario

When I was a kid, I wanted a horse. I could see myself racing down our street, holding tightly to the reins, feeling the wind on my face, and hearing the thunder of four hooves carrying me wherever I wanted to go.

Yup, a horse would fulfill all my dreams. There could be nothing better on earth. That's what I told God every night before I went to sleep.

One day my aunt Dorothy called and said her dog had had puppies and asked if I would like to have one. Wait a minute. You can't ride a dog! A puppy doesn't have hooves!

That's when Toodles came into my life. He was part fox terrier and part beagle, but mostly he was wagging tail and slurpy tongue. It took about three seconds for Toodles to become the answer to all my prayers.

Sometimes when we ask God for stuff, we need to stop and think about our requests. I wanted a horse because I wanted a friend. And *that's* what I should have prayed for.

You see, God's answers cut beneath the surface of our prayers. They fulfill the deeper desires of our heart. Never think God didn't answer if you didn't receive *exactly* what you were praying for. *"He will fulfil the desire of them that fear him" (Psalm 145:19).* Anytime I question that verse, I remember Toodles.

Why does it seem like God doesn't answer your prayers?
—Lindsay, 14, Ontario

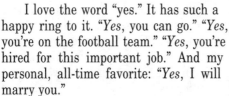

I love the word "yes." It has such a happy ring to it. "*Yes*, you can go." "*Yes*, you're on the football team." "*Yes*, you're hired for this important job." And my personal, all-time favorite: "*Yes*, I will marry you."

Wouldn't it be nice if God said yes to all our prayer requests? We could ask for anything we want, knowing what the answer would be. But there's a problem. God loves us. And sometimes yes is the worst answer He could possibly give.

When it comes to God and our prayer life, we've got to learn to appreciate the word "no." When God says no, He's demonstrating as great a love for us as when He says yes.

"Please, Mommy. *Please!*" I heard a child pleading in Wal-Mart the other day. His finger was pointing at the candy rack. I'm sure he could almost taste the sweet treats resting in neat, colorful rows just out of reach.

"No," the mother stated firmly. Now, I'm sure you could list four or five good reasons that she answered his request with that word. Perhaps dinnertime was approaching. Maybe the child was developing cavities, or was diabetic, or was fighting a cold. Did that mother say no because she hated her son? Hardly. Her response sprang from a heart of love. And that's exactly where all of God's answers come from.

"He will be very gracious unto thee at the voice of thy cry; when he shall hear it, he will answer thee" (Isaiah 30:19).

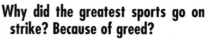

Why did the greatest sports go on strike? Because of greed?
—Stefan, 13, Alaska

Something tells me you're a baseball or hockey fan. Both of these games suffered greatly, starting in 1994.

Why the strikes? Because the players and owners said to each other, "If you're not going to do things my way, I'm not going to play with you anymore." Sounds kind of childish.

If only the players and owners were affected, it wouldn't be so bad. But what about the guy who sells souvenirs, or the woman who cooks the hot dogs? How about the motel workers, taxi drivers, photographers, radio announcers, and even the folk who clean up the stadiums after the games? Shouldn't the owners and players have considered how their actions would affect them, too?

Greed drives most businesses and sports organizations to do unkind or unthoughtful deeds. But that shouldn't surprise us. Listen to what the Bible says. *"For the love of money is a root of all kinds of evil. Some people, eager for money, have wandered from the faith and pierced themselves with many griefs"* (1 Timothy 6:10, NIV).

So when you see a national sport such as baseball topple and fall, just shake your head and sigh. You're witnessing another example of what evil can do to those whose lord is printed in the United States mint.

"But you, man of God, flee from all this, and pursue righteousness, godliness, faith, love, endurance and gentleness. Fight the good fight of faith" (verses 11, 12).

How do you know when you meet the right guy to marry?
—Girl, 12, West Virginia

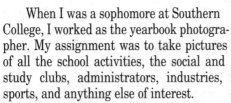

When I was a sophomore at Southern College, I worked as the yearbook photographer. My assignment was to take pictures of all the school activities, the social and study clubs, administrators, industries, sports, and anything else of interest.

One day my editor told me to go over to A. W. Spalding Elementary School to record the activities of the college's student teachers as they practiced instructing real, live classes.

The image that appeared in the yearbook shows a teacher-in-training standing before a group of eighth graders, textbook in hand, imparting great amounts of knowledge to his semiattentive pupils. If you look closely at the picture, you'll see a young girl's right eye and a strand of dark hair just sticking into the frame. Little did I know it, but the owner of the eye and hair would someday become my wife.

My wife? In eighth grade? I was a sophomore in college! I wouldn't be caught dead with such a child.

Ten years later we met again. Today I wouldn't be able to live without her.

What made her "right" for me? In this case, time. Never underestimate its value when searching for someone with whom to spend the rest of your life.

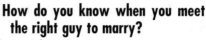

How do you know when you meet the right guy to marry?
—*Girl, 12, West Virginia*

Many years ago a popular song was making its way up the music charts. In sweet, tuneful notes the words went "It's so sad to belong to someone else when the right one comes along."

Boy, I sure didn't want to be in that situation! From then on, every time I got involved with a young lady that silly song would start playing in the back of my mind. It made me wonder. Is this girl the right one? Or will someone even better come along?

Then I was reintroduced to Dorinda, the girl I'd photographed years before (see yesterday's story), and suddenly that song vanished from my thoughts like echoes in a cave. I didn't care who else came along. I wasn't looking anymore.

True love doesn't leave room for doubt. It doesn't attempt to compare, to judge, to hold romantic contests. True love is the simple decision that this person *is* the right one. And that decision is joyfully made every day and every night for the rest of your lives together.

"But what if . . ." *No!* There cannot be any "what ifs." That's what destroys marriages. That's what tears homes apart.

Love and marriage aren't games. They're beautiful experiences that God created for our happiness. But millions of couples keep singing that old song, because they haven't allowed God to put a new tune in their hearts. *"He will take great delight in you, he will quiet you with his love, he will rejoice over you with singing"* (Zephaniah 3:17, NIV). That's God's number one hit!

How do you know when you meet the right guy to marry?

—Girl, 12, West Virginia

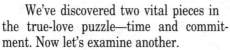

We've discovered two vital pieces in the true-love puzzle—time and commitment. Now let's examine another.

Somewhere, I'm not sure exactly where, people got the idea that to get through any trouble, to overcome any obstacle, to conquer any foe, all you need is love.

Wait a minute. Most couples love each other when they get married. But then along come crying babies, mortgage payments, unkind bosses, sudden layoffs, sickness, temptations, and a swarm of other distractions. Quickly they discover that loving each other doesn't pay the bills. Being committed doesn't keep illness or injury from rearing its ugly head.

The awful truth is that love never has been nor ever will be enough. Any of the "distractions" mentioned above can damage a relationship terribly, sometimes permanently.

It takes more than love to keep two people together. It takes God. Where human love fails, God's love prevails. The "right guy" you're looking for either knows this fact or is willing to accept it. A marriage without God simply cannot stand against Satan's angry attacks. The divorce rate proves that.

Anyone who wants to succeed in marriage must begin by studying and practicing God's brand of love as found in 1 Corinthians 13. Here's a sample: *"Love is patient, love is kind. It does not envy, it does not boast, it is not proud" (verse 4, NIV).* All "right guys" try to love like that.

Why do girls always watch you?
—*Jason, 14, Alabama*

Girls watch guys for the same reasons guys watch girls—because we're all very, very weird.

Actually, watching is a great way to learn. That's how I discovered something fascinating about girls when I was a junior. While I was trying to muscle my way through challenging situations, my female schoolmates were quietly using their brains. They usually ended up with a solution. I usually ended up with sore muscles.

Girls watch guys because they're trying to figure them out. They want to understand them, believe them, trust them. They're also trying to determine how they can best fit into their lives. After all, God created men and women to someday live together in a happy, loving, caring home.

There was this one girl in school I liked. Her name was Kay. For fun, I used to write her name as Kay Mills, just to see what it looked like. See what I mean? Even juniors know that someday they may marry one of those creatures sitting across the aisle from them, strange as it may seem at the time.

So we watch each other. And we learn, and grow, and mature.

I remember the first time I saw my wife's name combined with mine. I liked it. Still do.

Since girls are watching you, why not give them something pleasant to look at? Show them with your actions that you can be as trustworthy and believable as they want you to be. Then they'll want to be friends, and *you'll* have something to watch.

Do people who don't know God get to go to heaven?

—Lindsay, 9, Oklahoma

Being a missionary's son made it possible for me to visit many countries of the world. Sometimes I'd see whole towns filled with hardworking, kind, helpful people who'd never heard of Jesus, or Adam and Eve, or heaven. If Christ were to come right now, would these nice men, women, and children die forever simply because you or I never told them the story of salvation?

Of course not. We worship a fair and wise God. He judges us on what we know, not what we don't know. Listen to this text: *"Anyone, then, who knows the good he ought to do and doesn't do it, sins" (James 4:17, NIV).* Knowledge comes before judgment.

Some people who've never heard of Jesus will be surprised when He returns and invites them to go to heaven with Him. *"I was hungry and you gave me something to eat,"* Jesus will say as recorded in Matthew 25:35 (NIV). *"I was thirsty and you gave me something to drink, I was a stranger and you invited me in, I needed clothes and you clothed me, I was sick and you looked after me, I was in prison and you came to visit me" (verse 36, NIV).*

These people, along with many followers of Christ, will ask, "When did we do all these things for You?"

Jesus will reply, *"Whatever you did for one of the least of these brothers of mine, you did for me" (verse 40, NIV).*

What a wonderful opportunity we have to introduce unbelievers to their Saviour *before* He comes. Then they, too, can live their lives looking forward to their new home in heaven.

What does Jesus mean when He says you will live forever and ever?
—*Michael, 10, California*

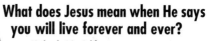

It's hard for us to imagine *forever*. Everything we have, everything we know about, has a beginning and an end.

When your mom or dad buys a new car, they know someday it'll wear out and have to be shipped to the junkyard. Where's that really cool shirt you got three years ago for Christmas? Or those superfast cross-trainers Grandma gave you for your birthday? How are they holding up? See what I mean? On this earth, stuff wears out, breaks down, rots, ages, fades, ceases to be useful; in other words, stuff dies.

But imagine a shirt that doesn't wear out. It looks and feels brand-new a week after you get it; a month; a year; 100 years. You give that same shirt to your children. They give it to their children. A thousand years later that shirt is being proudly worn by generation after generation.

That's what God means when He says we'll live forever and ever. We'll never wear out. We'll never be sick, get old, become feeble. We'll feel the same excitement for life tomorrow as we'll feel a million, trillion years from now. This is because all of the forces that harm or destroy life, such as sin and disease, will be totally absent from the universe.

"For God so loved the world, that he gave his only begotten Son, that whosoever believeth in him should not perish, but have everlasting life" (John 3:16). I'm looking forward to living forever with Jesus. How about you?

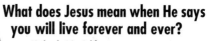
APRIL
25

125

I want to know about the future of the world.

—*Levi, 13, New Mexico*

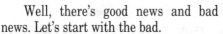

Well, there's good news and bad news. Let's start with the bad.

One day the disciples asked your question to Jesus. Do you know what the Master said first? *"Be not terrified"* (Luke 21:9). Oh, that must've been helpful! Then He continued: *"Nation will rise against nation, and kingdom against kingdom. There will be great earthquakes, famines and pestilences in various places, and fearful events and great signs from heaven"* (verses 10, 11, NIV).

Now we know why Jesus said, "Be not terrified." His description of earth's future didn't look too inviting. But there was more. *"Men's hearts failing them for fear, and for looking after those things which are coming on the earth: for the powers of heaven shall be shaken"* (verse 26).

Whew! Ready for the good news now? Listen to what Christ said next. *"At that time they will see the Son of Man coming in a cloud with power and great glory. When these things begin to take place, stand up and lift up your heads, because your redemption is drawing near"* (verses 27, 28, NIV).

Earth's future looks kind of rough. Satan isn't about to give up without a fight. But we Christians know that when things look hopeless, our friend Jesus will split the sky with His coming. The earth may tremble, but we won't. We'll see that cloud and jump for joy. *"Jesus is coming! Jesus is coming!"* we'll shout with relief and happiness. That's the good news.

I want to know about the future of the world.

—*Levi, 13, New Mexico*

This old world began as a creation of God. Then sin messed it up terribly, killing off its beautiful plants, animals, and people.

A great flood rearranged the earth's gentle face, leaving deep scars and barren landscapes.

Earth's soil has received the spilled blood of Jesus, felt the pounding of bombs, experienced destruction from overharvesting, and has been choked under layers of man-made chemicals. It's been leveled for cities, burned, drilled, altered by natural disasters, and had its streams, lakes, and rivers poisoned by industry.

But *"the Lord himself shall descend from heaven with a shout, with the voice of the archangel, and with the trump of God: and the dead in Christ shall rise first"* (1 Thessalonians 4:16).

Earth's troubles aren't over yet. *"And I [John] saw an angel coming down out of heaven. . . . He seized . . . Satan, and bound him for a thousand years. He threw him into the Abyss, and locked and sealed it over him"* (Revelation 20:1-3, NIV).

The abyss mentioned in the text represents this world. Satan will be imprisoned here after Jesus comes.

Is our world doomed to darkness forever? What happens at the end of the thousand years? The answer is terrifying and wonderful all at the same time. We'll discover it tomorrow.

I want to know about the future of the world.

—*Levi, 13, New Mexico*

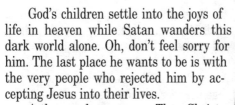

God's children settle into the joys of life in heaven while Satan wanders this dark world alone. Oh, don't feel sorry for him. The last place he wants to be is with the very people who rejected him by accepting Jesus into their lives.

A thousand years pass. Then Christ brings the redeemed back to earth to witness the last scenes of our old world's horrible history. Two things happen in quick succession. The evil dead (those who weren't raised at Jesus' second coming) come to life. And, *"Satan will be released from his prison and will go out to deceive the nations in the four corners of the earth. . . . They marched across the breadth of the earth and surrounded the camp of God's people, the city he loves"* (Revelation 20:7-9, NIV).

The soil trembles under the tread of a million marching feet. We stand protected behind the walls of God's "camp." Just as the attack by the wicked is about to begin, God's voice is heard. One by one, in words firm, yet spoken from a breaking heart, our Saviour reviews the sins of those who march against the camp. The attackers hear what's being said, and finally, with great anguish, agree God is just and that they deserve their coming punishment.

Fire suddenly bursts from the earth and falls from the sky. *"If anyone's name was not found written in the book of life, he was thrown into the lake of fire"* (verse 15, NIV). It ends quickly, leaving our world a smoking ruin. But there's more.

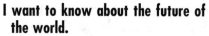

I want to know about the future of the world.

—Levi, 13, New Mexico

The future of our world contains scenes of utter despair and unspeakable joy. After the destruction of the wicked in the lake of fire, something wonderful, glorious, unimaginable happens, and we'll be there to see it!

"Then I [John] saw a new heaven and a new earth, for the first heaven and the first earth had passed away. . . . I saw the Holy City, the new Jerusalem, coming down out of heaven from God, prepared as a bride beautifully dressed for her husband. And I heard a loud voice from the throne saying, 'Now the dwelling of God is with men, and he will live with them. They will be his people and God himself will be with them and be their God. He will wipe every tear from their eyes. There will be no more death or mourning or crying or pain, for the old order of things has passed away'" (Revelation 21:1-4, NIV).

Our old, tattered, burned, and bruised world will be re-created. The same voice that called it into existence at Creation will speak again, transforming it from the home of sin to the palace of redemption. Unfading flowers will burst from purified soil. Birds will fill the unpolluted skies with song. Animals, no longer afraid, will walk the forests and fields together. And you and I, along with our families, will make our home on an earth free from sin, where we'll all live in peace.

The future of the world is bright, just like ours.

If the wages of sin is death, why isn't Satan dead by now?
—Girl, Maine

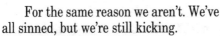

For the same reason we aren't. We've all sinned, but we're still kicking.

Let's travel back in time for a moment. We're in the Garden of Eden and God the Creator (Jesus) is talking to Adam. *"You are free to eat from any tree in the garden; but you must not eat from the tree of the knowledge of good and evil, for when you eat of it you will surely die"* *(Genesis 2:16, 17, NIV).*

But when Eve and then Adam ate from the tree, they didn't drop over dead on the spot. You see, what the sin of disobedience to God's law does is separate us from the life-sustaining power of heaven. When earth's first inhabitants allowed sin to enter their lives, they began the dying *process.* Years later, they did die, and every generation since Eden has fallen victim to that deadly pattern.

When Jesus died on the cross, He became a painful example to the universe of what that terrible separation can do. But when He rose from the dead, He showed what can happen when men and women choose to end their separation from God by accepting His forgiveness and saving grace.

When you invite God into your heart, you close the gap, allowing Jesus to save you from that endless separation brought on by sin. You may die an earthly death (as Jesus did), but you'll live again in heaven. Those who remain separated, such as Satan, will experience a death from which there is no resurrection.

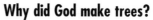

Why did God make trees?
—Shelby, 10, Indiana

Consider these two Bible verses: *"Then God said, 'Let the land produce vegetation: seed-bearing plants and trees on the land that bear fruit with seed in it, according to their various kinds'"* and *"Then God said, 'I give you every seed-bearing plant on the face of the whole earth and every tree that has fruit with seed in it. They will be yours for food'"* (Genesis 1:11, 29, NIV).

I don't know about you, but I'm sure glad God made trees. Think about it. Without these magnificent giants scattered about the world, where would birds sit?

Can you imagine a summer without sweet apples, tangy oranges, juicy peaches, or mushy bananas? I can't. God knew what He was doing when He made trees.

And what would warm afternoons be like without leafy branches to snooze under while the lawn goes unmowed?

Another reason God made trees is to provide the oxygen in the air we breathe.

Also, God made trees for the same reason He made everything—for our pleasure. So the next time you hear the wind rustling the leaves of a tree, or bite into a delicious fruit plucked from its branches, or dream in the shade cast by its sturdy trunk, remember to thank God for His thoughtfulness and love. And be glad birds have somewhere to sit!

Do you think Jesus will come in our lifetime?

—Amanda, 13, Canada

I must be careful how I answer your question, Amanda. If I say yes, I'm suggesting I know as much as God, which I certainly don't. *"No one knows about that day or hour, not even the angels in heaven, nor the Son, but only the Father"* (Mark 13:32, NIV).

Be very wary of those who say they've figured out the month or year of Christ's return. They're trying to play God.

If you'll rephrase your question and ask "Do you *want* Jesus to come?" or "Are you *preparing* for Jesus to come in our lifetime?" my answer is a resounding *yes!* Why? Because all the biblical signs are pointing to a soon return. All the prophecies concerning the Second Coming have been or are being fulfilled. The conditions for His return are just as Jesus said they'd be. Besides, I'm sick and tired of living in a world rotting away because of sin and selfishness, aren't you?

When Jesus comes is His business. Getting *ready* to meet Him—that's our business. Let's both prepare!

"Behold," announces Christ in Revelation 22:12, *"I am coming soon! My reward is with me, and I will give to everyone according to what he has done"* (NIV).

With John I shout, *"Amen. Come, Lord Jesus"* (verse 20, NIV).

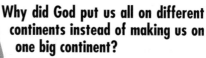

Why did God put us all on different continents instead of making us on one big continent?

—Josh, 14, Alaska

When I was a kid, my family and I lived in the Philippines, where my father worked as a missionary. From our little house, I used to dream of what America was like.

Finally we boarded the ship that would take us to the United States for a visit. During the next 40 days I discovered just how much water separates continents. It was a *long* journey.

At Creation God told Adam and Eve, *"Be fruitful and increase in number; fill the earth and subdue it"* (Genesis 1:28, NIV). The Creator wanted us to enjoy all of the earth and marvel in the beauties of other countries. He asked us to watch over every corner of the globe, acting as His caretakers.

This command also gave men and women the opportunity to choose where they wanted to live. My wife and I built our house in West Virginia—a state filled with gentle hills and peaceful valleys. Our parents prefer Tennessee, with its warmer climate and many lovely waterways. We have friends in busy Los Angeles, California; hot, dry Arizona; and picturesque Idaho. Each place is different. Each has special qualities all its own.

As much as we like West Virginia, we're looking for a new home with Jesus. *"Thine eyes shall see the king in his beauty: they shall behold the land that is very far off"* (Isaiah 33:17). In heaven people *will* live together on one big, beautiful continent—if they choose to.

MAY 3

There's this guy I really, really like, but he doesn't feel the same about me. He doesn't even know I'm alive, and when he does notice me, he treats me like dirt. I've tried to give him up, but I can't! Please help.

—*Girl, 12, West Virginia*

I can offer all kinds of suggestions, such as don't stop trying; he's not good enough for you; try finding someone else. But that advice is hard for a hurting heart to hear.

Liking someone and not having that person like you in return strikes at the very core of our human pride. We might even end up saying to ourselves, "Man, there must be something wrong with me. I must not be attractive, talented, or smart enough."

If there's one thing I've learned, it's this: things change. When I look back on my past relationships, I'm amazed at how many strong feelings I thought would never fade. But they did. Sensations of romantic love I just knew would last a lifetime have vanished. As for those times when my pride took a beating, I find my old heart has healed quite nicely.

Anytime you choose to care for someone, you take a risk. Sometimes you win; he likes you back. Sometimes you don't; he turns out to be a real jerk and treats you like dirt. That's life. But don't stop trying to love just because a guy doesn't have the courtesy or intelligence to respond maturely. Just lift your sights, and give your heart time to heal.

"Beloved, let us love one another: for love is of God; and every one that loveth is born of God, and knoweth God" (1 John 4:7). Ask for heaven's help as you learn to love successfully.

Why do boys torment girls? Why are they so gross?
—Kendra, 13, Alabama

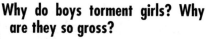

Of course, not *all* boys are tormenters or act gross. Some show more confidence in themselves by behaving like gentlemen.

Boys who torment girls, or do stuff that's disgusting, want attention, plain and simple. They've discovered effective ways to make people drop whatever they're doing and focus, even for just a moment, on their strange actions.

As children grow up they find a rather disturbing trend taking place in their lives. They're no longer the center of attention. While their cute antics used to bring a joyful response from friends and family, now no one seems to be interested. Youngsters find they have to be more disturbing to get a rise out of anyone. Some guys entering their teens get carried away, making life miserable for others.

Add to this the uncertainty boys feel about girls and, well, you seem to be familiar with the results.

Here's an effective way to deal with this situation. When a guy does something to torment you, just say, "Please don't do that." Then ignore him. If he acts gross, turn away and concentrate on something else. When guys don't get the attention they're craving, they usually give up.

The apostle Paul suggests that we *"run with patience the race that is set before us" (Hebrews 12:1).* Life is filled with people who like to torment or gross us out. Get used to it.

135

God had asked William Foy to be His prophet. He refused. Will he be in heaven?

—Heather, 11, Oklahoma

William Foy, a Freewill Baptist preparing to be an Episcopal minister, was given two or three visions relating to the second coming of Jesus and other last-day events.

The man felt reluctant to tell anyone about what he'd seen, even though the Lord told him to do so. William Foy was prejudiced against anyone who claimed to have divine revelations. Also, Foy was a mulatto—a person of White and Black heritage—and kept asking himself, "Why should these things be given to me to bear to the world?"

He finally agreed to become a witness for Jesus. But a third vision proved too confusing, and he gave up, turning to farming, although he continued serving as a spiritual leader in his community.

During one of his early meetings a certain member in his audience found his witness especially amazing. Her name was Ellen White. Later, after the Lord had given her a few visions of her own, she was telling a gathering what she'd seen. This time it was Foy who was amazed. He jumped to his feet and praised God, saying, "That's the same vision He gave to me!"

Apparently God was searching for a person to be His partner in giving the end-time message to the world. One rejected the responsibility; another didn't. But both understood that God sometimes overlooks our weaknesses, and saves us in spite of our not doing the good we could have done if we'd only followed His gentle leading.

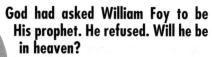

God had asked William Foy to be His prophet. He refused. Will he be in heaven?

—Heather, 11, Oklahoma

The Foy experience raises a question. In 1912, long after his death, Ellen White labeled the man's experience with Jesus as "genuine" (Arthur L. White, *Ellen G. White: The Early Years*, p. 490). Nowhere does she consider her one-time acquaintance as lost or abandoned by God.

But didn't he refuse to do what God wanted him to do? Yes. Wasn't his life less effective for Jesus because he was unsure of himself or found it hard to overcome certain prejudices? Yes. And isn't it safe to say that *we* are more like William Foy than Ellen White? Again, sadly, yes.

We can't earn our way to heaven by doing good works or by holding evangelistic meetings or by serving as a missionary in some far corner of the world. We will live in heaven because God forgives our sins and our errors in judgment. Jesus knows we're weak and afraid. He understands how our minds and attitudes can be damaged by sin. And He doesn't give up on us, either. He keeps bringing us new opportunities to make our lives meaningful.

God says, *"I will heal their waywardness and love them freely, for my anger has turned away from them"* (Hosea 14:4, NIV).

Don't ever think that because you missed an opportunity to do something great for God, He has rejected you. Just get yourself ready for the next chance He'll bring your way. Then do your best, thankful for the persistence of His powerful love.

Is it a sin to play a game called truth or dare? One Sabbath I played it, and the others dared me to kiss this boy, and so I did. Is it really a bad sin?

—*Debbie, 10, California*

Sin is any activity, thought, desire, or habit that separates you from Jesus.

Playing a game, any game in which you wouldn't want Jesus to sit by your side, should be considered off-limits. Whether truth or dare fits into that category is up to you.

Don't get the idea that Jesus doesn't like fun and games. I'm sure He'd enjoy a close matchup in baseball, table tennis, or wholesome parlor games, especially if these activities help develop mind and body skills. And don't think Sabbath is a day for sitting around with a long face feeling frustrated. It's a day designed for joy—as long as the end result of each activity keeps you snug as a bug by Jesus' side.

I certainly don't consider kissing a sin as long as it results in genuine smiles and feelings of friendship. When kissing becomes a simple thrill to fool around with, it saddens the God who invented it. He wants kissing to mean something, to bring hearts closer together in love.

Here's an easy test for whether something is sinful. Ask yourself, "Would I do this with my friend Jesus standing next to me?" If the answer is yes, enjoy. If not, find another way to spend your time. *"Now that you know these things, you will be blessed if you do them"* (John 13:17, NIV).

MAY 8

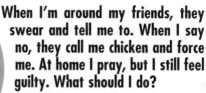

When I'm around my friends, they swear and tell me to. When I say no, they call me chicken and force me. At home I pray, but I still feel guilty. What should I do?
—*Girl, 11, Maine*

Kids swear, or take God's name in vain, for two reasons. First, it makes them feel grown up. They probably hear adults swearing all the time, as on television. Since the last thing a kid wants to be is a kid, they allow irreverent words to pass through their lips.

Second, some preteens and teens like to challenge God. They've heard such verses as *"Thou shalt not take the name of the Lord thy God in vain; for the Lord will not hold him guiltless that taketh his name in vain" (Exodus 20:7).* What's the first thing a little child does when you tell him or her not to do something? That's right. He or she does it, just to see how serious you were.

As for wanting to be grown up, adults who use the Lord's name without reverence are just as guilty of breaking the third commandment as their young friends. Swearing doesn't prove you're grown up. It proves you're still a child needing control.

Challenging God isn't a great idea, either. Not because He'll bring fire and brimstone down on your head, but because your actions separate you from Him. He doesn't feel welcome in your life. And God doesn't stick around where He's not considered a valuable member of the family. It's not His style.

"The thoughts of the wicked are an abomination to the Lord: but the words of the pure are pleasant words" (Proverbs 15:26).

MAY 9

When I'm around my friends, they swear and tell me to. When I say no, they call me chicken and force me. At home I pray, but I still feel guilty. What should I do?
—*Girl, 11, Maine*

In today's society, it's hard to stand up for what you know to be right, especially when your friends are taunting you.

The fact that you still feel guilty after you get home and pray doesn't mean that God hasn't forgiven you. *"If we confess our sins, he is faithful and just to forgive us our sins, and to cleanse us from all unrighteousness" (1 John 1:9).*

Perhaps you haven't made the decision to really do what you know to be right. Maybe you're not allowing Jesus to work in partnership with you to overcome the temptations your friends toss your way. Guilt doesn't just highlight sin. It serves as God's persistent reminder that you've still got work to do, even after He's forgiven you.

The next time someone tells you to use God's name without proper reverence, say, "Jesus is my friend. So is God. I want to show Them the same courtesy I show you by not using *your* name disrespectfully." If this person laughs, he or she is probably embarrassed. But you've stood up for your right to honor your heavenly Father. And that night, when you bow in prayer, you'll find the load of guilt gone, replaced by a growing confidence in yourself.

"Be strong and take heart, all you who hope in the Lord" (Psalm 31:24, NIV). And always speak God's name with reverence.

Is it wrong for girls to be pastors?

—*Jenniffer, 14, Indiana*

There may be more to this question than meets the eye. If you're asking whether girls (or women) should serve as spiritual leaders in churches or communities, I say, "Absolutely."

Whether these women should be *ordained as ministers* is up to the church organization to which they belong. In other words, if a woman wants to serve as an ordained minister of the Seventh-day Adventist Church, the General Conference, which is the governing body representing Adventists worldwide, would have to make that decision.

Scripture doesn't pay much attention to this matter because in Bible times women's ordination wasn't a concern.

Personally, and I'm speaking for myself only, I'd like to see my church do whatever it takes to hasten Christ's return. If ordaining women as ministers would mean more people would learn of God's love, then let's do it! If not, then we've got more important challenges to worry about.

Jenniffer, do you feel God calling you to the ministry? Then don't let anyone stop you. *"All things can be done for the one who believes"* (Mark 9:23, NRSV). God will show you the way.

If you want to go to heaven, and you don't think you're going to make it, what will happen?

—Fernando, 15, New Mexico

The Bible gives a beautiful description of those who will be saved when Jesus comes. Listen: *"Here are they that keep the commandments of God, and the faith of Jesus" (Revelation 14:12).*

Heavenbound people "keep" two things: the commandments (God's law), and faith (God's grace). In other words, they obey while accepting Christ's forgiveness.

I assume you want to go to heaven, Fernando. That means you're on your way! But then you do something stupid such as tell a lie, cheat on a friend, mistreat your body, speak disrespectfully to or about those in authority, or basically act like a jerk. You get to thinking, *No way will God let me into heaven.*

But you're forgetting the faith part of the Revelation description. It's time for your faith in Jesus to kick in. Christ uses His never-ending grace to forgive you, and offers powerful help for overcoming your bad habits or secret sins. He makes you feel lousy about yourself so you'll get down to business correcting your faults.

"No discipline seems pleasant at the time, but painful. Later on, however, it produces a harvest of righteousness and peace for those who have been trained by it" (Hebrews 12:11, NIV). When doubts come, it's probably Jesus reminding you that you've got work to do. *"God disciplines us for our good" (verse 10, NIV).*

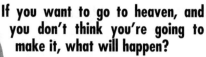

If you want to go to heaven, and you don't think you're going to make it, what will happen?

—*Fernando, 15, New Mexico*

MAY
13

Doubts about heaven can come from two sources. First, it may be Jesus gently reminding you of the high standards you're supposed to be shooting for. When He comes, He wants to find you actively involved in fighting sin and temptation, not just sitting back with an I-give-up attitude.

Second, Satan loves to make us believe we're totally unworthy of being saved. He does this by constantly throwing temptations in our path, making the world of sin seem so inviting, leading us into body and mind-destroying habits, and keeping us so busy we don't have time for spiritual activities such as Bible study, worship, and prayer.

Fernando, the journey to heaven isn't a joyride. It doesn't just happen. There's a lot of work, real work, on your part. But you don't make the trip alone. Jesus walks beside you, whispering encouragement and correction in your ear. Listen to what Paul said about his highway to heaven: *"I know what it is to be in need, and I know what it is to have plenty. I have learned the secret of being content in any and every situation, whether well fed or hungry, whether living in plenty or in want. I can do everything through him who gives me strength"* (Philippians 4:12, 13, NIV).

When feelings of doubt come up, ask God to give you strength, and tell Satan to bug off!

How do you get girlfriends?
—Boy, 12, Montana

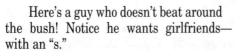

Here's a guy who doesn't beat around the bush! Notice he wants girlfriends—with an "s."

To get a girl to like you more than all the other guys isn't difficult. Just be more. More what, you ask? More thoughtful, forgiving, understanding, gentle, trustworthy, clean, respectful, encouraging, even-tempered, helpful, and generous (very generous), and like the girl's dad a *lot*.

Notice, nowhere did I say more strong, handsome, smart, or talented. Any girl worth getting would rather have a kind, thoughtful boyfriend than one who looks like a movie star and treats her like dirt.

And don't use TV or magazines as your guide to catching a girl's attention. They'd have you believing you're a loser unless you drive a certain car, wear certain clothes, or smell like a Colorado tree.

Girls like to be treated with respect and courtesy. Boys, too, for that matter. So if you want girlfriends, make yourself attractive, starting on the inside and working your way out.

When I was your age, I had lots of girlfriends. We'd pass notes in class, share lunches, and do science projects at the same table. To this day I remember their laughter and sweet smiles. Girlfriends are a beautiful part of growing up.

The Bible says, *"My little children, let us not love in word, neither in tongue; but in deed and in truth"* (1 John 3:18). Always make sure your actions speak louder than your words.

When Jesus comes back, what will happen to all the aborted babies? Not that I've had an abortion, I just wanted to know.

—Girl, 14, West Virginia

Abortion is a hot topic in the world today. Pro-life and pro-choice contestants battle over one main question: When does life begin—at conception, when the male sperm fertilizes the female egg, or at birth?

Ever since sin reared its ugly head, unborn babies have been dying for a lot of reasons—an accident kills the mother, the woman has a miscarriage, the child is stillborn, or disease destroys the life forces necessary to maintain the developing embryo in the womb.

What you're really asking is "How soon is a human being *savable*? Are fetuses (babies growing inside the mother) subject to God's loving judgment? If not, when *does* God begin to hold people accountable for their actions?

First, let me remind you that all life is precious in God's sight, whether it's in the form of an eighth grader studying for a math exam, a full-grown adult hurrying off to work, a toddler stumbling over his feet as he runs down the hall, or a fetus attached to the wall of a mother's uterus.

Our friend Ellen White says, "All things, animate [living] and inanimate [not living], express to man the knowledge of God" (*Counsels on Health*, p. 202). So whether you consider a fetus a child or a mass of dividing cells, it's still a direct expression of God's creative power and deserves our respect and care.

When Jesus comes back, what will happen to all the aborted babies? Not that I've had an abortion, I just wanted to know.

—*Girl, 14, West Virginia*

MAY 16

Our friend Ellen White has much to say about God's love for children. She fills chapters in her books with instructions to parents, suggestions to church members, and reminders to church leaders of the awesome responsibility everyone carries for the salvation of young people.

Realizing abortion wasn't an issue in her day, let's see just how far back she suggests a person can expect God's loving judgment. "I know that some questioned whether the little children of even believing parents should be saved, because they have had no test of character and all must be tested and their character determined by trial. The question is asked, 'How can little children have this test and trial?' I answer that the faith of the believing parents covers the children, as when God sent His judgments upon the first-born of the Egyptians" (*Selected Messages*, book 3, pp. 313, 314).

Wow! God loves kids so much that He'll let the faith of their parents get them to heaven. Isn't that wonderful?

But what about children whose parents don't love God? What about the infants of moms and dads who could care less about salvation, forgiveness, and the hope of Christ's soon return? What will happen to these little ones?

We'll find out tomorrow.

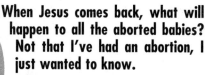

When Jesus comes back, what will happen to all the aborted babies? Not that I've had an abortion, I just wanted to know.

—*Girl, 14, West Virginia*

We're trying to discover just how far back in a person's life God's loving judgment reaches.

Yesterday we learned that God will use the faith of parents to open heaven's doors for their children. But what about the tiny sons and daughters of nonbelieving moms and dads? Listen to what our friend Ellen White says, describing scenes God showed her of our future home. "As the little infants come forth immortal from their dusty beds, they immediately wing their way to their mother's arms. They meet again nevermore to part. But many of the little ones have no mother there. We listen in vain for the rapturous song of triumph from the mother. The angels receive the motherless infants and conduct them to the tree of life" (*Selected Messages*, book 2, p. 260).

It seems babies are savable all on their own. What a wonderful and hopeful discovery!

I think we can safely say that if life does begin at conception, heaven will be filled with aborted babies nestled in the arms of angel parents. If life begins at birth, God joyfully saves those children too, even if their moms and dads choose to reject heaven's offer of eternal happiness.

We can leave the fate of aborted babies in the hands of a God whose love knows no limits, whose saving power knows no bounds.

Why do most Seventh-day Adventist adults always say what not to do?

—*Adrian, 12, Alabama*

It's sad but true. Adults do tend to dwell on the negative instead of the positive when dealing with juniors. That's not the way Jesus taught us to love.

His sermon on the mount overflows with the encouraging phrase "blessed are." There's not one "thou shalt not" in it. Christ continually challenged sinners by telling them what they *should* do, not what they *shouldn't* do.

Maybe adults lean toward the negative because they see dangers lurking in certain activities juniors are drawn to. If you see a friend running onto a busy highway chasing a ball, you don't shout, "I think you'd better turn around now." No. You scream, "*Stop! Don't go any farther!*" Negative, but effective.

When God-loving adults see young people heading full speed into what they believe to be sinful or damaging situations, they get all nervous. "Don't do that," they say. "Don't listen to such mindless music. Don't wear such revealing clothes. Don't go out with such reckless classmates. Don't ruin your health."

I heard a TV comedian say, "It's not that we lie to each other. It's just that the truth takes so long to explain." Perhaps we can translate that to adult talk. "It's not that I mistrust you. It's just that the reasons for my saying 'don't' take so long to explain." Adrian, kids deserve more than a quick "don't." When time allows, ask for a thorough explanation. You might be surprised at what you discover.

148

How bright will my angel be?
—*Jessica, 10, Oklahoma*

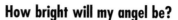

Angels are interesting creatures. The Bible describes them as traveling strangers (Genesis 19:1), speakers in dreams (Genesis 31:11), giving instructions from a burning bush (Exodus 3:2), appearing as a pillar of cloud and pillar of fire (Exodus 14:19, 24), guards with drawn sword (Numbers 22:22, 23), acting as waiters (1 Kings 19:5, 6), lion tamers (Daniel 6:22), stone movers (Matthew 28:2), choir members (Luke 2:10), prisoner rescuers (Acts 5:19), and heavenly messengers (Revelation). I think I can safely say your guardian angels are just as bright or not so bright as you need them to be.

Listen to this beautiful description recorded by our friend Ellen White: "I have seen the tender love that God has for His people, and it is very great. I saw angels over the saints with their wings spread about them. Each saint had an attending angel. If the saints wept through discouragement, or were in danger, the angels that ever attended them would fly quickly upward to carry the tidings, and the angels in the city would cease to sing. . . . But if the saints fixed their eyes upon the prize before them and glorified God by praising Him, then the angels would bear the glad tidings to the city, and the angels in the city would touch their golden harps and sing with a loud voice, 'Alleluia!'" (*Early Writings*, p. 39).

MAY

19

The Bible says no man knows the day or time when Jesus will come. But why do people say He's coming at midnight?

—*Tasha, 11, California*

The Bible announces that *"no one knows about that day or hour, not even the angels in heaven, nor the Son, but only the Father" (Matthew 24:36, NIV).*

To drive home this point, Jesus told the parable about the 10 virgins who fell asleep while waiting at a wedding for the bridegroom to show up. They couldn't keep their eyes open a moment longer. Problem was, the oil in their lamps burned away while they slept, leaving them in darkness.

"At midnight the cry rang out: 'Here's the bridegroom! Come out to meet him!'" (Matthew 25:6, NIV).

Those who had not brought extra oil couldn't properly greet the guest of honor.

In another verse, Christ describes the time of His second coming like this: *"It's like a man going away: He leaves his house and puts his servants in charge. . . . Therefore keep watch because you do not know when the owner of the house will come back—whether in the evening, or at midnight, or when the rooster crows, or at dawn. If he comes suddenly, do not let him find you sleeping" (Mark 13:34-36, NIV).*

At midnight people are usually not concerning themselves with important matters. Christians use the phrase "He's coming at midnight" simply to get the idea across that Jesus will return when we least expect it and, for some of us, when we're not prepared to welcome Him.

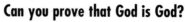

Can you prove that God is God?

—*Girl, 10, Maine*

This young lady has asked an important question. How do I know that the God I'm trying to tell you about really exists? How can I be sure He does what He says He does, and will do what He says He'll do?

Perhaps someone has asked you the same question, only he or she would say, "Why do you go to church on Saturday? God doesn't care on which day you worship." Or someone might ask, "Why do you believe the Bible? It's just a bunch of old stories, right?"

Here's the only answer I can offer: I know God is God because of what He has done and is doing in and for me. When Jesus lives in my heart, I find greater joy and satisfaction in life. I treat people better. I love my wife more. I look forward to the future.

But when I chase Jesus away by being stubborn or selfish, I quickly become depressed, frustrated, angry, impatient, and grow resentful of life and the things that happen to me.

I know God is God because He changes me from sad to glad again and again. Nothing on earth can do that. No person has that kind of power. Only a loving, forgiving God can make such a difference in me.

"Delight yourself in the Lord and he will give you the desires of your heart. Commit your way to the Lord; trust in him and he will do this: He will make your righteousness shine like the dawn, the justice of your cause like the noonday sun" (Psalm 37:4-6, NIV). God proves Himself to *me* every day.

MAY
21

Why did people change God's way of eating?

—Michael, 12, Indiana

In the Garden of Eden, the Creator arranged the perfect menu for Adam's and Eve's health. It consisted of fruits, grains, nuts, and vegetables. Good, clean, refreshing water rounded out the list. "Enjoy!" God said.

I wonder what He'd say if we took Him to McDonald's.

People changed God's menu in more ways than just adding dead animals to it. Cooking oils, refined sugars, heavy spices, and fermented foods wreaked havoc on our ancestors' minds and bodies. They continue to do the same to us today.

Why do most people eat foods so different from what God intended? Because most of these unhealthful concoctions taste good. Our sin-weakened taste buds insist on being stimulated by heavy doses of sweet, sour, spicy, salty, or oily dishes.

I've been very fortunate to have a mother and then a wife who can make God's simple, nourishing ingredients taste absolutely delicious. But it takes extra work on their part. Cooking healthfully is more than nuking a frozen dinner, adding water to a mix, or opening a can. It requires planning, skill, and dedication to prepare meals our bodies need.

Our friend Ellen White suggests, "To every one who is tempted to indulge appetite I would say, Yield not to temptation, but confine yourself to the use of wholesome foods. You can train yourself to enjoy a healthful diet" (*Counsels on Diet and Foods*, p. 35). In my house, that training takes about two seconds!

Where do you live? Do you have a cat or dog? What do you like? Are you happy all the time? Do you have a family? How many books did you write? How did you find out about our school?

—*Angel, 11, New Mexico*

Whew! My wife, Dorinda, and I live in West Virginia in a pretty little house overlooking a valley. We don't have dogs or cats, but we did have 10 ducks until they flew south for the winter. I like listening to music and watching birds munch lunch at our backyard feeders.

I'm not happy all the time because I'm not in heaven yet. When I get to feeling sad, I remind myself that tomorrow will be better, and then I just keep on working. This text jumps into my mind when things aren't going too good: *"Wait for the Lord; be strong and take heart and wait for the Lord"* (Psalm 27:14, NIV).

We don't have a family yet. This is my twenty-second book. I found out about you by calling the education office in your conference and asking for the telephone number of a church school where the students love Jesus and are very, very smart.

When I was your age, I attended a little church school in Syracuse, New York, and had lots of girlfriends because I was the only boy in the upper grades. If a girl wanted to go steady with someone at school, there was just me, so that worked out quite nicely.

One more thing. I like it when kids ask questions. Don't ever stop, because God will always have answers for you, sometimes in the strangest places. Keep your eyes and ears open!

MAY 23

When did people get the idea that Sunday was the Sabbath?
—*Erika, 10, Montana*

It all began soon after Jesus left this earth and returned to heaven. The most powerful Christian church at that time was based in Rome, Italy. Most of its members were Gentiles (people who weren't Jewish and were proud of it). These people grew more and more to hate their Jewish neighbors and decided to drop some of the religious practices they shared in common, such as keeping Saturday as the Sabbath.

For a time one group observed the Bible Sabbath while others attended services on Sunday. Why Sunday? Because, they reasoned, Christ rose from the dead on that day.

Pagan Romans, who worshiped almost everything *except* God, had for centuries kept one day a week as a special day to worship the sun. You guessed it. Sun-day.

It didn't take long before everyone agreed that the first day of the week made a much better Sabbath than Saturday. In the fourth century after Christ's birth, Sunday laws were issued telling everyone how to worship. "Honor Sunday," proclaimed the Roman Catholic Church, "and if possible, do no work on that day." The law also commanded not to "be idle on Saturday, but work" (Council of Laodicea [c. A.D. 364], Canon 29).

Old Testament prophets said such a situation would be coming. *"He will speak against the Most High and oppress his saints and try to change the set times and the laws" (Daniel 7:25, NIV).* Yup. Satan made it happen just as Daniel predicted.

When did people get the idea that Sunday was the Sabbath?

—*Erika, 10, Montana*

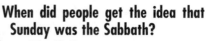

The change from Saturday to Sunday observance began soon after Christ walked this earth. Guess what? Satan's not finished with this issue. Listen to what our friend Ellen White says will take place right before Jesus comes:

"As the crowning act in the great drama of deception, Satan himself will personate Christ. . . . In different parts of the earth, Satan will manifest himself among men as a majestic being of dazzling brightness, resembling the description of the Son of God given by John in the Revelation. . . . The shout of triumph rings out upon the air: 'Christ has come! Christ has come!' The people prostrate themselves in adoration before him, while he lifts up his hands and pronounces a blessing upon them, as Christ blessed His disciples when He was upon the earth. His voice is soft and subdued, yet full of melody. In gentle, compassionate tones he presents some of the same gracious, heavenly truths which the Saviour uttered; he heals the diseases of the people, and then, in his assumed character of Christ, he claims to have changed the Sabbath to Sunday, and commands all to hallow the day which he has blessed. He declares that those who persist in keeping holy the seventh day are blaspheming his name by refusing to listen to his angels sent to them with light and truth" (*The Great Controversy*, p. 624).

We'll know better. Bible-believing Christians always have.

How do you win a boy's love?
—*Girl, 14, West Virginia*

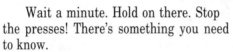

Wait a minute. Hold on there. Stop the presses! There's something you need to know.

The love you have in your heart for anything, whether boy, girl, aardvark, or gila monster, is a precious gift. It's not a prize. You don't win someone's love. You accept it.

Every day of my life I'm thankful for the love that my wife, Dorinda, has for me. It's the most amazing, valuable, meaningful gift I've ever received. That love motivates her to care for me, put up with me, forgive me, sacrifice for me, even scold me.

Don't think of a guy's love as a prize to be won. Rather, think of it as something you'd be happy to accept if he chooses to share it with you. If he doesn't, nothing has been "lost."

And if he refuses your offer of love, he may not be able or willing to take on the responsibility of accepting such a beautiful gift.

With this in mind, here are some suggestions. Be aware of his likes and dislikes. Don't be overly anxious to please. Act interested, not desperate. Be intriguing, but not a show-off. Don't confuse sexual attraction for genuine love. If you use tight jeans and revealing blouses to catch a guy's eye, be prepared to deal with the rest of his anatomy.

Love is a God-given emotion, filled with powerful, protective elements. Treat it with respect, and demand the same from those with whom you share it. Then everyone wins.

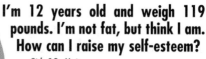

I'm 12 years old and weigh 119 pounds. I'm not fat, but think I am. How can I raise my self-esteem?

—*Girl, 12, Maine*

Twelve-year-old boys and girls are supposed to have a few extra pounds stored away because they're about to begin a rather rapid growing period. So unless you're having trouble walking through an open door, I wouldn't worry.

You've got to realize that excess fat doesn't mean "ugly" or "failure." It may mean it's time to get wiser. Carrying a *significant* amount of fatty tissue under your belt causes the body to overwork most of its systems. Usually, a smarter choice of foods (more raw and less packaged items) and an increase in exercise will, over time, solve the problem.

Some people can eat like a horse and not show it. Others claim air is fattening. No matter where you may fall on the fat line, a return to God's ideal for diet and exercise is the first step toward good health and resulting self-esteem.

If you're watching what you eat, keeping sweets and oily foods to a minimum, munching down lots of raw fruits and an appropriate amount of properly cooked vegetables, while drinking healthy quantities of water each and every day, your body is happily making the decision on how much fat it needs to keep you going.

But, if you're dumping pizzas by the panful, ice cream by the gallon, colas by the case, and candy by the box down your throat, your appetite is telling your body how much fat to store. Not a good idea. Your body knows best. God planned it that way.

I'm 12 years old and weigh 119 pounds. I'm not fat, but think I am. How can I raise my self-esteem?
—*Girl, 12, Maine*

Once you've decided to treat your body with the respect and care it demands, trying your best to follow God's laws of health, it's time to turn your attention to self-esteem.

Some days, when I look in the mirror, I say to myself, "I'm supposed to love *that?*" I don't look as young as I used to, my body seems to be satisfied with its weight when I wish I could lose a few pounds, and my hair decides it doesn't like the way it's been combed for 40 years and tries out styles never seen before.

Self-esteem is a much-battered emotion. On Monday it's up and you like everything about yourself. On Tuesday it's way down, and you feel like a real loser.

Because self-esteem is an emotion, not a cold, hard fact, don't be too concerned about it. Instead, create in your mind something far more valuable: self-confidence. This handy little mind-set will see you through many more challenges than its weaker brother. You build self-confidence in the real world, not in front of a mirror. It can be strengthened by being faithful to your duties, doing *all* your homework, treating people with respect, and keeping your word *no matter what*.

When self-confident people look in the mirror, they say, *"I can do all things through Christ which strengtheneth me" (Philippians 4:13).* Does wonders for your self-esteem, too.

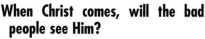

When Christ comes, will the bad people see Him?
—*Holly, 10, Oklahoma*

John the revelator, sitting alone on the little island of Patmos, near Italy, was shown many great and terrible visions by God. Like a video projected on a wide screen, last-day events seemed to fill the sky, revealing the future in startling detail. Listen to what he said describing the end-time:

"The sky receded like a scroll, rolling up, and every mountain and island was removed from its place. Then the kings of the earth, the princes, the generals, the rich, the mighty, and every slave and every free man hid in caves and among the rocks of the mountains. They called to the mountains and the rocks, 'Fall on us and hide us from the face of him who sits on the throne and from the wrath of the Lamb! For the great day of their wrath has come, and who can stand?'" (Revelation 6:14-17, NIV).

To make sure we get the picture clearly, John also states, *"Look, he is coming with the clouds, and every eye will see him, even those who pierced him; and all the peoples of the earth will mourn because of him. So shall it be!"* (Revelation 1:7, NIV).

Yes, Holly, even the bad people will see Jesus coming, and it will frighten them terribly. But will *we* be frightened? Listen: *"In that day they [God's people] will say, 'Surely this is our God; we trusted in him, and he saved us. This is the Lord, we trusted in him; let us rejoice and be glad in his salvation'"* (Isaiah 25:6, NIV). We have nothing to fear.

Why did God make people different colors?

—Ruben, 11, California

From my home office I look down on a peaceful valley and a mountain ridge beyond.

Something always strikes me as interesting. See if you catch what I mean. I see a blue sky, green and yellow grasses, brown earth, and white clouds. The green-backed tree swallow perched atop our martin house boasts different hues than the bluebird and goldfinches flying around the hickory tree. I spot black-and-white cows, gray squirrels, a tan whitetail deer, inky crows, rusty-crowned chipping sparrows, and a couple bright red cardinals squabbling over a nesting site. I notice my wife's yellow daffodils, red and pink pansies, a scattering of bluebells, and a collection of white dogwood blossoms.

Nature bursts with color because God loves beauty and variety. It was only natural for the Creator to design people to show off a variety of colorful shades, too. In His eyes, all hues and tints are beautiful, whether on feathers, fur, or faces.

Guess what? The new earth will be filled with color, too. *"With your blood you purchased men for God from every tribe and language and people and nation. You have made them to be a kingdom and priests to serve our God, and they will reign on the earth"* (Revelation 5:9, 10, NIV).

God gave us each a different color to wear proudly on our skin. It's His way of saying "You're special and beautiful to Me."

Why is baptizing important?
—*Heather, 11, Indiana*

First of all, we must believe it *is* important because Jesus was baptized. If it didn't matter, He would've found something better to do on that sunny afternoon by the Jordan River.

What does our friend Ellen White say? "Baptism is a most sacred and important ordinance, and there should be a thorough understanding as to its meaning. It means repentance for sin, and the entrance upon a new life in Christ Jesus" (*Child Guidance*, p. 499).

Baptism is important because it's a symbol of something deep inside your heart. It's a way of saying to your whole church family, "I love Jesus so much I'm willing to do what He did. I'm publicly showing I'm a Bible-believing, Bible-obeying Christian."

You're also reminding those who attend your service what the apostle Paul said: *"We were therefore buried with him through baptism into death in order that, just as Christ was raised from the dead through the glory of the Father, we too may live a new life"* (Romans 6:4, NIV).

When you come up out of the water after your baptism, you're telling everyone, "This is what Jesus can do for you. He can wash away your sins and let you begin a brand-new life with Him by your side."

Can you get to heaven without being baptized? Yes. But the Saviour hopes you'll share what you've learned with others. By this simple act, your friends can witness a demonstration of God's saving grace in action.

How did you become a writer? How do you learn? Do you like being a writer?
—*Kristie, 10, New Mexico*

I wish I could say I became a writer because there was a great, powerful, driving desire in my heart to be one. Or that I felt God calling me to put words on paper for people to read.

The simple truth is, I became a writer because I wanted to work from home where I could watch the birds and the seasons drift past my window and *not* sit in endless committee meetings playing office politics.

Since I'd always enjoyed reading, I thought I'd try writing. It worked! People published my manuscripts and bought my articles. Then a funny thing happened. I began to feel a great, powerful, driving desire to put words on paper so God could bless the people who read them.

Learning to be a writer isn't hard. Read, study, observe, imagine, write. And, have a good spell-checker on your computer.

Yes, I like being a writer, because I get to sit in my home office by the window and watch the birds and seasons drift by. I also get to answer important questions from Kristie and other juniors all across North America. And I know God will take my humble words and bless others with them, because He has promised He would.

"In his heart a man plans his course, but the Lord determines his steps" (Proverbs 16:9, NIV). No matter what you want to become, no matter what work you choose to do, ask God to be with you; ask Him to guide you each step of the way.

What should I do if my parents aren't fair?

—*Girl, 12, Montana*

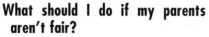

I assume we're talking about God-loving, honest, trying-to-do-the-best-they-can parents.

Sometimes moms and dads issue rules or demands that don't seem to make a lot of sense. "That's not fair," you moan, or whimper, or do whatever you do to show frustration.

Here's a little secret that can save you tons of anger and sadness down the road. Don't expect fairness from other people, because they don't see things the way you do. They don't think like you think. What's important to you may not be important to them. When a decision must be made, parents decide based on *their* values, *their* fears, *their* hopes.

Are they being selfish? No. They truly believe they're doing what's best for you. If you think they're being unfair, don't get all hyper and stomp around like a spoiled brat. Get over it, and move on.

When I was young and my mom or dad did something I thought wasn't fair, I determined that when I was an adult, I'd make some mighty big changes in my life. And I did. Some changes worked. Some didn't. And I also learned a lot about my parents and why they'd acted so "unfairly." In most cases, they were right!

"Children, obey your parents in all things: for this is well pleasing unto the Lord" (Colossians 3:20). If your parents aren't fair, forgive them. Then patiently share your values, hopes, and dreams. Work together to make life more pleasant for all.

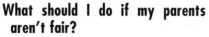

JUNE 2

How can someone change bad habits or the way they are?
—*Veronica, 13, Florida*

Several years ago my church had a Five-Day Plan to Stop Smoking for the employees of a large factory. We set up our equipment, straightened the chairs, and waited.

Soon the room was filled with hard-working, honest, dedicated men and women who shared a very bad habit—smoking. Five days later most of them had changed their lives for the better. How?

First we educated them about what they were doing to their bodies and minds. Next we offered an alternative way to live that didn't include their destructive habit. Then we provided a support system to help them overcome the effects of change.

For someone to become different than they are, they have to clearly see the value of the switch. Then that value has to become the *most* important thing in their lives.

If you want to be a better student, that has to become your most important goal. Want to conquer a bad habit? Place in your mind an image of yourself without that habit, and don't let *anything* stand in your way as you make the change. Ask God for help. Some bad habits can be overcome only when He adds His loving, forgiving power to the process.

"In all these things we are more than conquerors through him who loved us" (Romans 8:37, NIV). Many of the people who stopped smoking in our clinic are alive today because they recognized their need for change and courageously made it happen.

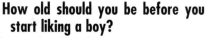

How old should you be before you start liking a boy?
—Girl, 14, West Virginia

My wife's first best friend was a boy. They did everything together, and missed each other terribly when they were apart—which wasn't very often. He was 3. She was 2.

Yes, I know what you meant by your question. But I'm trying to establish something important in the minds of all my junior readers—boys and girls should like each other, enjoy being together, treat each other with respect and Christian love from the cradle to the grave.

Juniors who've learned to be honest, forgiving, and protective of other people's feelings will find they slip naturally into love with those certain "someones" who move in and out of their lives during their teen years.

So don't try to put an age limit on when you should begin liking a guy. Instead, concentrate on becoming a solid, courageous Christian teenager filled with a strong desire to create happy, meaningful relationships with everyone—male and female.

A couple years ago my wife and I were visiting the Midwest. She tried to get in touch with that young friend, now grown up. Was I jealous? Hardly. It was their friendship that taught her how to love so sweetly and unconditionally. Now she's *my* best friend. We do everything together and miss each other terribly when we're apart—which isn't very often.

See what I mean?

Why didn't God come to earth in 1844?
—Kenny, 9, Oklahoma

If you and your family are ever in New York State, take a day and travel to the little town of Low Hampton, near the border with New Hampshire.

Drive down a few country roads to the William Miller farm. You'll find it tucked away behind some towering oak trees and surrounded by apple orchards and deep-green pastures.

Behind the house, past the old wooden barn, and up a small tree-shaded path, you'll stumble onto the place where a group of people stood waiting for Jesus to come on October 22, 1844. They waited all day and into the peaceful, autumn evening. Finally, at midnight, they knew the awful truth. They'd been wrong. Jesus wasn't coming that day.

Why didn't He return? Because it wasn't time yet. And I'm glad because there were people in faraway lands who'd never heard of Jesus. And Kenny, and I, and all the question-askers in this book hadn't been born. God's family wasn't complete, wasn't warned, wasn't ready.

"Behold, I am coming soon! My reward is with me, and I will give to everyone according to what he has done" (Revelation 22:12, NIV). Is it time for Jesus to return to earth? We must live our lives so we won't be terribly disappointed when He doesn't, and when He does.

Does God love everyone, like the poor or sick people?
—Lillian, 10, California

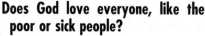

One Christmas Day, a few years before I found my wife, I was living in your home state in a town called Angwin. I was feeling kind of lonely and sad because it was Christmas and I couldn't afford to fly all the way to Ohio to visit my parents.

After opening the gift I gave myself, I jumped into my car and drove down the mountain to St. Helena Hospital. I figured there might be some sad or lonely people there, too. As they say, misery likes company.

After getting permission from the head nurse, I began going from room to room, visiting with anyone who looked as though he or she could use some cheering up. I found one lady crying softly to herself.

"What's the matter?" I asked.

She looked at me with such hopelessness in her dark eyes. "I'm dying," she said, "and I don't know who'll take care of my little daughter when I'm gone."

I stopped feeling sorry for myself really fast! For the next hour I listened to her sob out her life's story, filled with images of pain and poverty. When she finished, I said, "Don't worry about your child, because Jesus will take care of her." Then I read a verse from the Bible I found resting on her nightstand. Listen to the words of hope she heard: *"I will not leave you as orphans; I will come to you"* (John 14:18, NKJV).

I know Jesus loves the sick and poor because, on that Christmas Day, I saw a dying woman smile, and heard her pray.

What do you really think about wearing jewelry?

—*Tara, 14, New York*

I really think it's an awful waste of money. And I really think that those who believe that hanging something made out of gold, silver, diamonds, or whatever on their bodies makes them more beautiful or handsome haven't spent enough time reading their Bibles.

God leaves no room for doubt. He says, *"Your beauty should not come from outward adornment, such as braided hair and the wearing of gold jewelry and fine clothes. Instead, it should be that of your inner self, the unfading beauty of a gentle and quiet spirit, which is of great worth in God's sight"* (1 Peter 3:3, NIV).

One Adventist gentleman told me he wears a wedding ring because he wants to protect women from getting the wrong idea. Excuse me? I've been married for 14 years, and not one woman in my presence has ever needed protection. They know I'm married because I act and talk married. Either that, or the day I said "I do" I became so ugly that women are frightened by me. Whatever the case, not one female has ever gotten the "wrong idea" in her dealings with me.

So if God isn't pleased with our trying to be more beautiful by wearing jewelry and wedding rings, and they aren't necessary as long as married people act married, why bother? Buy something useful with the money, such as a computer for your church school. It'll make God, and a bunch of kids, extremely happy.

168

Why isn't there a pot of gold at the end of the rainbow?

—Candice, 12, Indiana

I know what you're asking, Candice. You're saying "Why aren't we rewarded for following our dreams? Why doesn't this world deliver when we've worked so hard for what we want?"

That fabled pot of gold dwells in a world of make-believe and children's nursery rhymes. In reality, where you and I live, pots of gold and rainbows hide in other people's checking accounts and beneath stormy skies. If we want gold, we have to earn it. If we want rainbows, we might have to weather a shower or two.

But don't worry. There's a pot of gold, of sorts, waiting at the end of a very special rainbow. Listen as John the revelator describes it. *"And the voice . . . said, 'Come up here. . . .' At once I was in the Spirit, and there before me was a throne in heaven with someone sitting on it. And the one who sat there had the appearance of jasper and carnelian [quartz]. A rainbow, resembling an emerald, encircled the throne"* (Revelation 4:1-3, NIV).

The only rainbow worth following is the one that leads to Jesus. The only pot of gold worth having is waiting for us in heaven, where dreams come true and hard work is rewarded for eternity.

Why is there sin?

—*Derek, 11, New Mexico*

One beautiful Sabbath morning my dad and I were on our way to a church where he was to speak. My 11-year-old mind was full of its usual questions, and my father was doing his best to answer them.

Suddenly, without warning, a barn swallow flew into the path of the car. There was nothing we could do to avoid it. The little bird hit the front bumper with a soft thud.

Quickly stopping the car on the side of the country road, we jumped out to see if maybe, just maybe, we'd only stunned the bird. But the little swallow was dead, feathers bent and broken. Overhead, her mate circled, waiting for his partner to fly up to meet him. He was still circling when we drove away.

"Why is there sin?" I asked my dad through angry tears.

He thought for a long moment, then said, "I don't know. No one knows. But one thing is for certain: Jesus is going to put an end to it when He returns the second time."

Derek, some questions have no answers. At least, not now. But someday we'll understand. Someday we'll look into the eyes of the God who has watched a million birds die, who has heard the cries of generations of people, and who hid His face in agonizing sorrow while His only Son hung on a cruel cross.

"God made him who had no sin to be sin for us, so that in him we might become the righteousness of God" (2 Corinthians 5:21, NIV). When we get to heaven, let's ask Jesus your question. I believe He'll have the answer we need to hear.

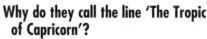

Why do they call the line 'The Tropic of Capricorn'?

—Boy, 11, Montana

This junior must've written his question right after geography class.

The Tropic of Capricorn is a parallel line of latitude south of the equator marking the southernmost point where the sun appears directly overhead at noon. This event happens one day a year (around December 22) and is called the winter solstice.

The line *north* of the equator where the sun shines vertically down on earth one day a year is called the Tropic of Cancer. This happens during the summer solstice. The area between these two lines is called the Torrid Zone.

Both get their names from the constellations that the sun enters (as viewed from earth) during their solstices—Capricorn and Cancer.

Whew! Class dismissed.

On warm summer evenings my wife and I like to sit out on our front deck and gaze into the night sky, watching the stars move slowly through the inky blackness of space. We wonder what it would be like to visit those tiny blinks of lights so far away. Someday that's exactly what we plan to do.

"The heavens declare the glory of God; the skies proclaim the work of his hands. Day after day they pour forth speech; night after night they display knowledge" (Psalm 19:1, 2, NIV).

Whenever you study geography or science or nature, or gaze at the night sky, remember who spoke everything into existence.

Why do we need to go to school?
—*Vanosdale, 11, Florida*

If you lived on a tiny island where food grew wild, where there were caves in which to set up housekeeping, and watching the waves wash onto the shores was your idea of a good time, you wouldn't have to go to school.

Living any other way takes money. To earn money, you get a job. To get a job that pays a half-decent salary, you need an education. To get an education, you go to—you know where.

School can take you from where you are to where you want to be. If you plan on living at home, sponging off Mom and Pop for the rest of your life, drop out of school. If all you desire to know is what television throws in your face, forget your studies. And don't even think about owning anything such as a car or clothes.

Christians regard attending school as good stewardship. God gave us brains, talents, and dreams. Learning new things expands our minds, sharpens our skills, and makes realistic dreams come true. Knowledge is a great weapon for fighting Satan, too.

So sit yourself down, Vanosdale, pull back your shoulders, sharpen your pencil, turn off the television, and crack open a few books. Choose a subject you're interested in and learn, learn, learn. Surprise your teacher by turning in your homework on time, every time.

"Study to shew thyself approved unto God, a workman that needeth not to be ashamed" (2 Timothy 2:15). Hang in there!

What year was Jesus born?
—*Joshua, 11, Maryland*

Here's what the Bible says: *"Jesus was born in Bethlehem of Judea in the days of Herod the king" (Matthew 2:1). "And it came to pass in those days, that there went out a decree from Caesar Augustus, that all the world should be taxed" (Luke 2:1).*

From these two verses we find two names linking Christ's birth to the flow of time. He was born during the reigns of King Herod in Jerusalem, and Caesar Augustus in Rome. It was also during a time when the Roman Empire felt a budget crunch and taxed its citizens.

From this information Bible scholars and historians place Christ's birth somewhere around 1 B.C., but they're not sure of the exact date. There's about an eight-year spread in present thinking on this subject.

We can safely say that God's Son was born approximately 2,000 years ago.

When He was born isn't half as important as *that* He was born. His birth heralded the beginning of the end of Satan's rule on this earth. His life proved we can overcome any evil in our lives. His death and resurrection broke the bonds of the grave so we don't have to fear it.

Joshua, Jesus lived so that you can enjoy the hope of heaven to come. And He demonstrated that not even death can separate you from your bright heavenly future. At your next birthday, remember to thank God for bringing you one year closer to your glorious new life.

Will the 144,000 people that go to heaven and the ones who have red on the bottom of their robes be put in the holy place together?

—Jessica, 10, Oklahoma

believe Jessica is referring to several verses in Revelation 7. Listen: *"Then I heard the number of those who were sealed: 144,000 from all the tribes of Israel" (verse 4, NIV). "After this I looked and there before me was a great multitude. . . . They were wearing white robes." "And he [the angel] said, 'These are they who have come out of the great tribulation; they have washed their robes and made them white in the blood of the Lamb'" (verses 9 and 14, NIV).*

This great multitude, made up of the 144,000 and many, many more, represents the saved of all the ages standing before God and worshiping Him. Some died for their faith. Some passed through great troubles. But all turned their back on Satan and chose to live God's way.

As for the holy place, Jessica, after all this happens and we're safely in heaven with Jesus, there won't need to be a holy or Most Holy Place as mentioned in the Old Testament. Jesus no longer has to be our high priest and do the duties of that important office. We're *saved!* Sin has been vanished forever. Jesus the Lamb has given His life to redeem us. The Temple system is not required anymore.

Instead, heaven will be one big holy place, with Jesus and us living together in joy. Christ's job will change from priest to friend, from Saviour to neighbor. Won't that be *wonderful*?

13

On what day was Jesus crucified?
—Andy, 13, California

We find the answer to your question hiding within an act of kindness by a man with the same name as Jesus' father.

"Now there was a man named Joseph, a member of the Council, a good and upright man, who had not consented to their decision and action [to crucify Jesus]. . . . Going to Pilate, he asked for Jesus' body. Then he took it down, wrapped it in linen cloth and placed it in a tomb cut in the rock, one in which no one had yet been laid. It was Preparation Day, and the Sabbath was about to begin" (Luke 23:50-54, NIV).

We keep the same Sabbath as the Jews did (and still do). When does our Sabbath begin? That's right, Friday afternoon at sundown. That means Jesus died earlier that day.

Each year at Easter, Christians remember that awful weekend so long ago. In our mind's eye we see Joseph gently place Jesus in his tomb as the sun is about to set on Friday afternoon. We think of the Sabbath sadness those who knew Him personally felt.

And then. *And then!* *"On the first day of the week, very early in the morning, the women took the spices they had prepared and went to the tomb. They found the stone rolled away from the tomb, but when they entered, they did not find the body of the Lord Jesus"* (Luke 24:1-3, NIV). Why? *"He is not here; he has risen!"* announced the angel sitting nearby (verse 6, NIV).

Andy, whenever you think of that terrible Friday, remember the glorious Sunday morning that followed, when after resting on Sabbath, Jesus rose, and made our eternal life possible.

Why does it say in the Bible that a woman shall not wear what a man wears? Why doesn't it say a man shouldn't wear what a woman wears?

—Ashley, 11, New York

Oh, but it does, in the very same verse. Check it out. *"A woman must not wear men's clothing, nor a man wear women's clothing, for the Lord your God detests anyone who does this"* (Deuteronomy 22:5, NIV).

What does this mean? Moses and the children of Israel were camped at the very edge of the Promised Land. This was a whole new generation of travelers—the sons and daughters of the original group who'd left Egypt many years before. Moses called them all together and said, *"Hear now, O Israel, the decrees and laws I am about to teach you. Follow them so that you may live and may go in and take possession of the land that the Lord, the God of your fathers, is giving you"* (Deuteronomy 4:1, NIV).

What followed was a history lesson and a long list of do's and don'ts—everything from forsaking idolatry to what foods to eat. Included was the passage about clothes.

We know God wants men to be men and women to be women. It's part of His divine plan. But it seems some men back then didn't like being men and were trying to pass themselves off as women. And some women wanted to be men, so they dressed like them. This wasn't done as a joke, to get laughs. These were acts designed to draw sexual attention for immoral purposes. God did not *and does not* appreciate such disregard for the holiness of our bodies. So He made a rule, one we should follow today.

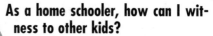

As a home schooler, how can I witness to other kids?
—*Jenniffer, 14, Indiana*

One of the beauties of homeschooling is that you get to choose your own "extracurricular activities."

Students in traditional schools must follow a schedule as outlined by the governing board or individual teachers. Because of the size of most schools, witnessing projects may be difficult to carry out on a regular basis. But you aren't so limited.

Here's an avenue for witnessing that I've found works in both home and traditional schools: letter writing.

Juniors aren't exactly the most mobile group in the world. They don't drive cars. Parents don't want them wandering around doing stuff after classes. And their bank accounts are kind of lean (sort of like mine). But for the price of a postage stamp and a few minutes of their time, they can witness in a most wonderful way to friends, family, and even total strangers.

It begins with lists: addresses, birthdays, anniversaries, special occasions, and holidays. Add to this a sharp eye for scanning the local newspaper or church newsletter, and there are many opportunities for sending someone a helpful hint, word of encouragement or congratulation, or just a happy thought.

Imagine receiving a note from a junior you don't know who reports he or she heard about something you did and just wanted to say he or she thought you were cool. And imagine a lonely shut-in getting a colorful, hand-drawn card wishing him or her a happy birthday with a "God loves you" attached. Powerful witness!

Is it a sin to get divorced?

—Tracy, 11, New Mexico

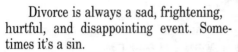

Divorce is always a sad, frightening, hurtful, and disappointing event. Sometimes it's a sin.

The Bible reveals only one acceptable reason for two people to end their marriage by divorce. Listen carefully to this story found in Matthew 19: *"Some Pharisees came to him [Jesus] to test him. They asked, 'Is it lawful for a man to divorce his wife for any and every reason?' 'Haven't you read,' he replied, 'that at the beginning the Creator "made them male and female," and said, "For this reason a man will leave his father and mother and be united to his wife, and the two will become one flesh?" So they are no longer two, but one. Therefore what God has joined together, let man not separate.' 'Why then,' they asked, 'did Moses command that a man give his wife a certificate of divorce and send her away?' Jesus replied, 'Moses permitted you to divorce your wives because your hearts were hard. But it was not this way from the beginning. I tell you that anyone who divorces his wife, except for marital unfaithfulness, and marries another woman commits adultery'"* (verses 3-9, NIV).

Notice three things: 1. Divorce wasn't in God's original plan for His earthly children. 2. Moses allowed divorce because of people's stubbornness. 3. marital unfaithfulness is the *only* acceptable reason for getting a divorce.

Having an affair breaks the sacred bond formed at marriage between the husband, wife, and God. In this case, the affair is sin, while the divorce is not.

Is it a sin to get divorced?
—*Tracy, 11, New Mexico*

Yesterday we discovered the only acceptable reason that the Bible reveals for two married people to divorce each other. That is *marital unfaithfulness*—a husband or wife having a sexual relationship with another person.

Let me quickly add that while there's only one Biblical excuse for divorce, there are hundreds of reasons that two married people should not live under the same roof with each other. Physical and mental abuse, alcoholism, drug addiction, sinful behavior, unkind or dangerous demands, child molestation, all these are acceptable reasons for a wife or husband to get out of the situation *fast!* But they are not cause for divorce.

Why? Because God's healing and forgiving power is available to all men and women. Our Creator can fix things. He can change lives, heal broken hearts, make forgiveness possible. Even the one excuse for divorce we talked about doesn't *have* to bring about a final separation of two people who used to be in love.

Divorce becomes a sin when the husband and wife turn their backs on the power God offers them for rebuilding their crumbling relationship. I'm sure tears of sorrow flow in heaven when two people reject the most effective tool for saving a marriage—God's healing touch.

If two adults you know are getting a divorce, pray for them. Their hearts are hurting. And determine that when you marry, you'll make God a *permanent* part of your new home.

If God talked to us back when He lived on this earth, why doesn't He talk to us now?
—*Girl, 11, Montana*

The apostle Paul must have been asked that very same question. I can imagine him standing before a group of faithful believers. They've had a good meeting, and many hearts have been warmed by the message he presented.

Then a junior sitting in the back of the room timidly raises her hand. "Pastor Paul," she says, "when my parents were young, Jesus Himself talked to them. But He's gone back to heaven, and *I've* never seen Him. Why doesn't He talk to me now?"

Paul must've liked the answer he gave, because he wrote it down in Hebrews 1. Listen: *"In the past God spoke to our forefathers through the prophets at many times and in various ways, but in these last days he has spoken to us by his Son" (verses 1, 2, NIV).*

"But," the girl presses, "I don't hear Him speaking to me."

I can see Paul smile and tenderly begin to unroll an ancient scroll that is nearby. "Don't you remember when Moses was afraid to go to Egypt?" he asks. "Here's what God said about him and his brother Aaron. *'I will be with thy mouth, and with his mouth, and will teach you what ye shall do'" (Exodus 4:15).*

"God does speak clearly to us," Paul continues, "through the sermons we hear, the Bible stories we read, and sometimes, believe it or not, in the very words we say ourselves."

Want to hear God talk to you? Dedicate your ears and lips to Jesus. Then listen for, and speak about, His love.

When we go to heaven, do we necessarily need to play an instrument?
—*Danny, 13, Florida*

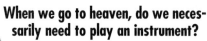

Not into harps, eh, Danny? I'm not either. Guitar, maybe. Perhaps a piano. But I couldn't play a harp if my eternal life depended on it.

I'm not sure who came up with the idea that when we get to heaven we'll all sit around on clouds strumming a stringed instrument. Probably someone who likes doing that on earth—except for the cloud part, of course.

The Bible records a whole orchestraful of instruments being used for praise, such as *"sing for joy to God our strength; shout aloud to the God of Jacob! Begin the music, strike the tambourine, play the melodious harp and lyre. Sound the ram's horn at the New Moon"* (Psalm 81:1-3, NIV). And *"praise him with the sounding of the trumpet. . . . Praise him with the strings and flute, praise him with the clash of cymbals. . . . Let everything that has breath praise the Lord"* (Psalm 150:3-6, NIV).

No, Danny, the ability to play an instrument isn't a requirement for going to heaven. And there'll be plenty else to do besides making music while sitting on your cumulus nimbus.

But when you've finished exploring the universe, when all the mysteries of life you've studied, when your love for God overflows from your thankful heart, you might try *humming* a few praise songs for Jesus. He'll understand.

When did Moses receive the Ten Commandments?

—*Joshua, 11, Maryland*

It's one of my favorite Bible stories.

Moses and the children of Israel had left Egypt and were camped at the base of a mountain called Sinai. Here's how our friend Ellen White describes the event: "Never since man was created had there been witnessed such a manifestation of divine power as when the law was proclaimed from Sinai. 'The earth shook, the heavens also dropped at the presence of God: even Sinai itself was moved at the presence of God, the God of Israel.' Psalm 68:8. Amid the most terrific convulsions of nature the voice of God, like a trumpet, was heard from the cloud. The mountain was shaken from base to summit, and the hosts of Israel, pale and trembling with terror, lay upon their faces upon the earth" (*Patriarchs and Prophets*, p. 340).

Ever wonder why God made such a show of things on this occasion when He was perfectly willing to speak to His followers with the "still small voice" mentioned in 1 Kings 19? The children of Israel were so deep in sin and rebellion, God decided that this demonstration of power just might get their attention. It did.

God gave the Ten Commandments from Sinai when the people needed them most. They were destroying their futures with selfish acts and endless complaining.

What do you think, Joshua? Maybe it's time for God to shake a few mountains again, to get our attention, to help us see our sins.

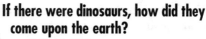

If there were dinosaurs, how did they come upon the earth?

—*Holly, 10, Oklahoma*

The same way puppies, birds, and whales got here. God created them, or at least He created the perfect animals from which they mutated.

Modern scientists make two basic errors when they talk about history: (1) Where things came from, and (2) how long they've been around.

Dinosaur remains were first uncovered in England in the 1820s. A complete skeleton was discovered in the western United States during the late 1800s.

Because the bones looked like nothing alive on earth, the diggers figured these animals must have lived millions of years ago and were part of the evolutionary chain. They were and continue to be wrong on both counts—according to the Bible. Scripture insists *God* created the heavens and the earth, and it places the age of this world somewhere between 6,000 and 10,000 years.

Dinosaurs form a "decision point" for juniors. Either you believe the Bible, or you believe what many scientists say. Either they just happened to end up looking like they did, or they were formed by the loving hand of a powerful Creator. Of course, He didn't design them to eat each other, just like He didn't design *us* to eat animals. But they were part of His creation, as we are.

JUNE

22

Should we love our stepparents the same as our own parents?
—*Erin, 11, California*

Love is the most wonderful, most powerful, most rewarding emotion God placed in our hearts. We, like Jesus, have enough love built into us to cover every person on earth. And that includes stepparents.

But don't think you have to love them the *same* as your own mom or dad. After all, they're not part of you physically, as your birth parents are. You didn't come from their bodies. You weren't built with their chromosomes and other genetic building materials. And you don't share the same family history.

However, it's perfectly all right to love them *as much* as you love your own parents—if you choose to. After all, they've accepted the responsibility to raise you, protect you, and love you just as if you'd come from their bodies.

So don't hold back, thinking you're being unfaithful to your original mom or dad. You'll always love them in a special way. Simply create a new type of love, and shower your stepparents with tons of that endless supply of affection and care God placed in your heart. You'll have more than enough.

"But the stranger that dwelleth with you shall be unto you as one born among you, and thou shalt love him as thyself" (Leviticus 19:34). This rule worked for the children of Israel. It can work for stepparents and stepchildren, too.

What will happen if I don't go to heaven?
—Dori, 12, New York

The day has arrived. In the sky you see a dark cloud coming closer and closer. It gets brighter and brighter. Then you see Jesus sitting on His throne, surrounded by millions of angels. You hate Him. You hate the very sight of Him. So you run and hide with a bunch of other people who despise the Lord.

Suddenly it's 1,000 years later. You see Satan calling great crowds of people together, urging them to join his battle against God. In the distance you see a city made of gold, and you laugh. "We can take that city for ourselves," you shout.

Just as you and the others rush forward, guns and knives in hand, you hear a voice speaking to you. It reminds you of all the times you refused to listen to Jesus. You see images of yourself turning your back on God again and again and again until you didn't care what He wanted you to do.

"Yes," you finally agree, "I don't deserve to be in the city with God. I don't want to be there anyway. I hate Him."

With those words on your lips, fire flashes all around and you die, this time forever.

Dori, that's not you. You love Jesus and accept His forgiveness for your mistakes. When He comes, you'll be so glad to see Him you'll jump up and down and shout, "Here I am, here I am!" And He'll shout back, "Well, come on, Dori. I want to take you to your new home where you won't be bothered by the devil anymore." And away you'll go, your hand safely in His.

What will happen if I don't go to heaven?
—*Dori, 12, New York*

One afternoon when I was a junior, I sat alone thinking about life and God—important stuff like that.

Suddenly a thought crossed my mind that made me feel cold inside. I asked myself, "Have I committed the unpardonable sin? Have I done something that made God so angry at me that He'll refuse to take me to heaven when He comes back?"

The idea was so terrible, so frightening, I quickly ran to find my dad. "What if I've committed the unpardonable sin?" I gasped. "What if God doesn't love me anymore?"

My father took me in his arms and gave me a hug. "Charlie," he said, "the fact that you're worried about it should tell you something. People who've allowed themselves to commit the unpardonable sin couldn't care less about what God thinks, or about their future life in heaven. They don't want Jesus in their hearts. They don't try to make themselves better, more loving and kind. They don't even feel guilt anymore because they've closed their ears to God's gentle voice."

Looking into my father's eyes, I said, "I *do* want to live in heaven. And when I make a mistake, I feel awful."

"That means Jesus is still living in your heart," Dad said with a smile.

Juniors, never think you've committed the unpardonable sin. Never think you're unsavable. As long as you allow God's Spirit to speak to you, to guide you, you're on the road to heaven.

How can I help people get ready for Jesus' second coming?
—*Jenniffer, 14, Indiana*

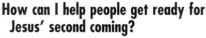

Now, here's a young lady who is missionary-minded. What do I mean by that? She's concerned about others—a trait she shares with the greatest missionary ever—Jesus Christ.

What can missionary-minded juniors do to help people get ready for the Second Coming? The very same things Jesus Himself did when He walked the dusty paths of this earth.

Acts 10:38 reports, *"God anointed Jesus of Nazareth with the Holy Ghost and with power."* Then Jesus *"went about doing good, and healing all that were oppressed of the devil."*

Notice the two steps needed to become missionary-minded. 1. You need the Holy Ghost as your partner. 2. You begin going about doing good and healing the oppressed.

How do you get the Holy Ghost to join your team? It's easy. Just ask for Him. The very first thing He'll do is point out any habits or character traits in your life that would hinder your missionary work—such as selfishness, dishonesty, lack of patience, or prejudice. Then He helps you overcome these problems.

Next, you're ready to "heal the oppressed," which means showing people a better life. This is accomplished by "doing good." Doing good might mean preaching, teaching, singing a song, offering a friendly smile, helping a neighbor, collecting food for the hungry, befriending a new classmate, or simply praying for someone. Missionary-minded juniors, in partnership with the Holy Spirit, find many ways to witness. Get started today!

JUNE 26

187

I go to a Christian school, but most of the kids are not Christians. I never really knew what peer pressure was until I moved here. I really love God, but sometimes I just feel like giving up. How can I make the right choices and still have friends?
—*Jessica, 13, New Mexico*

First of all, Jessica, don't ever give up. Life is tough for everyone, whether he or she loves Jesus or not. Giving up is like saying "OK, Satan, you win." Do you really want to lose to him?

Life is an endless series of choices. It doesn't control you—you control it, by the decisions you make. One of the most important choices anyone faces is "Am I going to live God's way, or the devil's way?" There's no middle ground. You can't live part for God and part for Satan. It doesn't work.

Peer pressure is having a bunch of people try to force their choices on you. When you give in to them, you're handing *them* control of *your* life. Not a good idea. They don't know what's best for you. They don't know how you feel in your heart. They don't hear God's still small voice speaking to you, telling you right from wrong, trying to keep you out of trouble.

So, Jessica, make the right choices regardless of whether a few friends turn up their noses. Ask yourself, "Am I willing to give up heaven for their friendship? Am I willing to trade eternal life with Jesus for a short life doing things their way?" I'm sure you've already figured out the answer.

"Those who trust in the Lord are like Mount Zion, which cannot be shaken but endures forever" (Psalm 125:1, NIV).

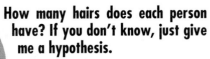

How many hairs does each person have? If you don't know, just give me a hypothesis.
—*Girl, 10, Montana*

Believe it or not, someone actually counted them. It was found that the average adult has about 120,000 hairs sticking out of his or her head. Those with red hair have fewer; blonds have more. Each day 70 to 100 of our beautiful strands fall out.

The Bible has a lot to say about hair. Samson and Nebuchadnezzar grew lots of it. Ezra plucked his out. Solomon said his girlfriend's hair was like a flock of goats. Shadrach's, Meshach's, and Abednego's hair did *not* get singed in the fiery furnace. And Mary, Lazarus' sister, wiped Jesus' feet with hers.

There's a verse in Matthew that might be of interest to you. Telling His disciples not to worry about life and stuff like that, Jesus said, *"And even the very hairs of your head are all numbered. So don't be afraid"* (Matthew 10:30, 31, NIV).

Wow! Jesus knows everything about us—even how many hairs we have. Why would He remind us of such a seemingly unimportant fact? Because our heavenly Father wants us to realize just how important we are to Him. If He knows how many hairs we have, He certainly knows when we're feeling sad, fighting sickness, having a hard time in school, being afraid, or wondering if anyone loves us.

So the next time you comb your hair, stop and think about the God who created it, placed it on your head, and knows how many you have. Amazing!

What is heaven like?
—*John, 11, Florida*

I'm glad you asked that question, because, strange as it may seem, many people have a hard time with the idea of heaven. I know one young man who states bluntly, "Nothing I've heard about heaven makes me want to go there."

Basically, heaven will be what you want it to be. God created this world with the express purpose of making Adam and Eve happy through its beauties and mysteries. Even though sin has messed up much of the original loveliness, some of what remains still can excite and challenge our minds.

God will create the new earth (that is what most people mean when they speak of heaven) to make *us* happy. If you're into nature, you'll study animals who aren't afraid of you. Do you like plants? In heaven they won't die. Enjoy traveling? Set your course for worlds at the very edge of the universe. Are you a homebody? Build a cabin by a mountain lake or take up residence in the City of God, surrounded by kind, loving neighbors. Forget crime and violence. And there won't be a hospital in sight.

I like photography, flying airplanes, tinkering with computers, listening to music, bird-watching. In heaven these interests will continue to grow in ways I can't even imagine. As a matter of fact, that's exactly how God describes our world to come. Through the apostle Paul He says, *"No eye has seen, no ear has heard, no mind has conceived what God has prepared for those who love him"* (1 Corinthians 2:9, NIV).

John, those who don't want to go to heaven aren't good thinkers. Use your imagination. It'll be even better than that!

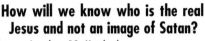

How will we know who is the real Jesus and not an image of Satan?
—*Jonathan, 12, Maryland*

You hear a knock at your front door and when you peek through the little peephole, you see a woman standing in the entry with a big smile on her face.

"What do you want?" you shout.

"What do you mean, what do I want?" she calls back as if her feelings are hurt. "Don't you know me? I'm your mother."

"My mother?" you gasp. Then you notice she has the same hair color and style as your mom. She's wearing a dress just like one your mother wears; white collar, little green stripes. And she's carrying an identical purse to the one you gave your mother on her birthday.

"Open up," the woman pleads with a warm giggle. "I forgot my keys. Silly me. I've got to start fixing supper. You know how your father hates it when supper's not ready, and your brother, Timothy, will be home from his football practice soon."

You don't open the door. Why? Because that's not your mother. No matter how much she knows about your family or how much she looks like the woman of the house, it's not her. How can you tell? Because you know your real mom like you know yourself. You're familiar with every detail of her face, the sound of her voice, the way she moves her head and hands.

The only way to recognize an impostor is to know, beyond the shadow of a doubt, the real thing.

How did God create the earth?

—Justin, 11, Oklahoma

Reading the first chapter of Genesis, which talks about the creation of the world, can really shake you up. At the beginning of each day, when something is about to happen, the Bible simply states, "And God said . . ."

God said? Wait a minute. Don't you mean "God made," or "God built," or "God assembled"?

No. It just repeats seven times, "And God said . . ."

As amazing as it may seem to us poor, sinful earthlings, this world (and everything in it) exists because God *told* it to. His voice is enough to make microscopic molecules come together to form a cat. At His command, a tree appears, fully grown, casting its shade on newly formed grass. One word from the Creator and, where there was a rock, now there's a butterfly.

I don't know how He does it, Justin. I can holler out the word "horse" all day long and, unless there happens to be one standing nearby, no horse pops into view.

Here's a question for you. If God by His words can create a world from nothing, can we trust Him to keep a promise He's spoken to us? Hey, if God says something, *I believe it!* You and I are living proof of His "word power."

"What I have said, that will I bring about; what I have planned, that will I do. Listen to me" (Isaiah 46:11, 12, NIV).

With this glimpse of the power of His word, we, like Samuel, should always say, *"Speak; for thy servant heareth" (1 Samuel 3:10).*

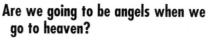

Are we going to be angels when we go to heaven?

—*Ruth, 11, California*

Not exactly. The angels living in heaven right now have never fallen into sin. We have. They didn't need Jesus to die for them. We did. Angels don't know what it's like to be saved from the devil's deadly grip. We do.

Although we're going to be best friends with them, we'll always be just a little different from our heavenly companions. And our past experiences will be the main peculiarity setting us apart from those glorious beings.

Are we going to be angels when we go to heaven? Let's just say, we're going to be angels with a difference. We'll do what they do—fly effortlessly through space, sing praises to God, revel in the beauties of a perfect world, keep our minds active and challenged by studying our Father's creative power. But there will always be a depth to our love for God that no other being can truly understand.

Listen to the words of this beautiful old song: *"Holy, holy, is what the angels sing, And I expect to help them make the courts of heaven ring; But when I sing redemption's story, they will fold their wings, For angels never felt the joys that our salvation brings."*

How can God forgive us when we do such bad things?

—Emily, 11, New York

God's forgiveness seems to know no bounds. He forgave Adam and Eve for their disobedience, Moses for striking the rock in anger, King David for murdering the husband of a woman he was lusting after, the prostitute Mary for committing adultery, and Paul for persecuting Christians. These represent just a tiny sampling of His willingness to forgive.

But you must remember one important thing about forgiveness. It doesn't change the *results* of what we did. Adam and Eve still had to live and die in a sinful world. Moses lost the privilege of leading the children of Israel into the Promised Land. King David couldn't bring the dead man back to life. Mary still had to contend with her reputation. And the apostle Paul spent his whole life fighting the "good fight" of faith, knowing what he'd done before he met Jesus on the Damascus road.

The reason Jesus can forgive so much is that He loves us more than He hates what we do. And He's also providing a clear, powerful example of how *we're* supposed to forgive others. That's right! He expects us to be as forgiving as He is.

Jesus says, *"But I tell you: Love your enemies and pray for those who persecute you, that you may be sons of your Father in heaven. He [God] causes his sun to rise on the evil and the good, and sends rain on the righteous and the unrighteous"* (Mattthew 5:44, 45, NIV). When we forgive others, we're showing God that we got the message.

JULY

3

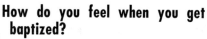

How do you feel when you get baptized?

—*Girl, 10, Montana*

I can't speak for anyone else, but when I got baptized, I felt very, very . . . wet. I also felt (a) happy to be an official member of the Seventh-day Adventist Church, (b) glad that I could, from then on, take part in the Communion service (you know, drink the little glass of grape juice and eat the tiny cracker), and (c) very excited to be up in front of everybody.

The fact that my dad baptized me made the day even more special.

What I didn't feel was . . . different. I was still me, still got tempted a lot, still made mistakes. But I knew my baptism had shown Jesus, and my whole church family, that I was serious about heaven and about trying to live a better life.

Baptism makes you feel like you're doing something important. It makes your mind decide some stuff, such as, you're going to be a better person and fight the devil even harder.

After you hear the bubbles in your ears, you come up from the water and see the pastor smiling at you. Usually the church congregation is singing, or the organ is playing softly. There's a lot of splashing and hugging. It's neat, and not scary at all.

The Bible says, *"Whoever believes and is baptized will be saved"* *(Mark 16:16, NIV).* This simple act of love for God brings us closer to the Source of strength we need to reach heaven. And that always feels wonderful!

JULY
4

Why does God allow bad things to happen to people you love?
—*Eliza, 11, Florida*

This is a common question not only for juniors but for adults as well.

Whenever something bad happens, we look for someone to blame. Most of the time, we blame God. After all, He's the Creator of the universe. He could've stopped it, right?

Then we remember Calvary. In our mind's eye we see Jesus, God's own Son, dying in agony on a Roman cross. "Wait a minute!" we gasp. "Why doesn't He stop *that* from happening? Doesn't He love Jesus?"

Listen. The sinless Man on the cross is speaking, His words recorded in Luke 23:46. With His last breath He whispers, *"Father, into thy hands I commend my spirit."* Then He dies as lightning flashes across the sky.

Here was One who had every reason to be angry at God, to blame Him for the suffering He had to endure. But even at the moment of death He spoke His Father's name with reverence and love, handing over His spirit—or breath—willingly. Why?

Jesus knew what caused suffering and pain. He understood its source. And it wasn't His Father. It was sin.

Eliza, don't think of the bad things that happen as individual events allowed by God. Rather, think of them as terrible results of the sinful *condition* that exists. Fire will burn your fingers, not because God allows it, but because that's what fire does. Same with sin. Blame Satan. Trust God.

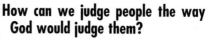

How can we judge people the way God would judge them?
—Jonathan, 12, Maryland

To judge something means to come to a decision about its value.

Let's say you have a favorite jacket. Wearing it makes you feel handsome. People comment on how great you look whenever you slip it on.

How would you judge that jacket? "It's great," you insist. "Nicest one in my closet."

If someone offered you a dollar for it, you'd laugh. "It's worth much more than that." Why? Because you have a *personal* interest in and appreciation for that jacket. Whenever you wear it, you feel good about yourself.

God judges us with the same personal interest. He thinks we're wonderful. He calls us His "children"! In short, He loves us. So when He judges us, He goes *way* out of His way to make sure everything is done for our ultimate happiness.

We need to have that type of love. We, like our heavenly Father, must learn to look beyond a person's bad attitude, sinful habits, rebellion, mistakes, and anger to see the true value hiding inside. Jesus demonstrated this when He loved sinners, while hating their sins.

If your favorite jacket gets dirty or torn, you clean and mend it, just as God gets busy and helps clean and mend our lives before He passes final judgment on us. Our job is to love others and offer to help them in any way we can.

JULY 6

197

How can God be three people: the Son, the Spirit, and the Father?
—Julie, 11, Oklahoma

Let's take a close look at each of these "parts."

The Son, or Jesus Christ, created the world and then later came to this earth as a baby to grow up and show us how to live a loving, unselfish life. He also died for our sins so we could look forward to eternal life in heaven.

The Spirit, sometimes called the Holy Spirit, Holy Ghost, or Comforter, has the important task of guiding our conscience, making us feel lousy when we sin and glad when we overcome temptation. It's His leading that directs us toward heaven.

The Father acts as our judge. Now, I'm not talking about a judge like we see on TV. When the Bible was written, and God the Father was labeled our "judge," that meant He was our lawyer, defender, and jury all rolled into one. Bible judges had to be convinced that a person was guilty because as far as they were concerned, the person was totally innocent. God considers us innocent unless *we* convince Him otherwise.

So, here we have three Gods all working for our salvation. But unlike any three people you'd put together on this earth, there's no differences of opinions here. They think alike, act alike, and work with the very same powerful love for us.

Like Paul, we can confidently say, *"The grace of the Lord Jesus Christ, and the love of God, and the communion of the Holy Ghost, be with you all"* (2 Corinthians 13:14). All three exist and work endlessly for our victory over sin and our future joy in heaven.

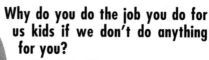

Why do you do the job you do for us kids if we don't do anything for you?
—*Michael, 11, California*

Most people work for rewards. I do. But remember, Michael, some rewards aren't seen. Some are only felt.

When I do what I do for kids, God gives me a feeling of satisfaction down deep in my heart. No, I can't make a car payment with it. It won't make me better-looking, improve my health, or get my face on TV. Writers don't even get to meet most of the people who read their books.

But I know you're out there. And I know God loves you. So each time I sit down at the computer to write, I ask God to choose my words for me so that when you read them He can speak directly to you without you even knowing it. You'll think you're just enjoying an exciting story or gathering some information. I know better. You're hearing God whisper in your ear, giving you some new ideas, making stuff you didn't understand before a little clearer. Perhaps teaching you how to deal with life and its challenges more successfully.

When I was a junior, I read many stories and gathered tons of information from the books I lugged home from the Adventist Book Center. I never met the authors of those books, but I know God spoke to me through their words. And I understand now why they worked so hard for me.

Whenever I read Isaiah 51:16, where God says *"I have put my words in thy mouth,"* I smile because I know it's true. If anything I write makes you love or understand God more, it's *His* words you heard, not mine. I just typed them.

What do you think of wearing makeup?
—Emily, 11, New York

Makeup serves two purposes. First, it can hide blemishes and scars, conceal minor imperfections on our body, and make us look healthier if our natural color needs a little boost.

Second, it can draw attention to ourselves, make us look sexually attractive (by worldly standards), and, in some cases, completely change our appearance.

I believe God wants us to look healthy. After we've been careful about our diet, have exercised faithfully, taken in sufficient amounts of liquid (the watery type), rested enough, and overcome health-destroying habits, a little makeup applied skillfully can "make up" for what our bodies can't do naturally.

No one likes to look at someone who has pale lips, dark, sullen eyes, and blotchy skin. Carefully applied makeup can help lessen the impact of what sin has done to us.

But beware of using makeup as an enticement to attract other people. You're using false bait. If the real you and the made-up you are very different, what's going to happen when someone sees you as you really are? Something to think about.

Personally, I like to meet faces that greet me with a smile rather than an inch of foundation covered by a rainbow of rouges, lipsticks, and powders. Natural-looking skin, lips, and eyes that radiate a healthy glow get my vote every time. Remember, when people look at you, they're supposed to be able to catch a glimpse of Jesus as well. Don't smother Him with makeup.

There are only three people my age in my class. Did everyone else flunk or skip a grade?
—Boy, 12, Montana

Probably not. Kids start school at different ages. Some begin when they're 5. Others wait until they're 6 or even 7. This doesn't indicate they're smart or dumb. They just begin at different ages.

Students who flunk a grade aren't necessarily stupid. They might have a hard time learning in the "traditional" method of teacher teaching and student listening. They might need to see more illustrations. They might be confused or distracted by all the commotion in the classroom. Place them in another learning environment and they just might zoom ahead of everyone!

When I was a schoolteacher I had a student who couldn't keep up with everyone else. I'd see him looking around the room, concentrating on everything but his schoolwork. So I gave him a temporary new place to sit—in our school van, parked outside my window. He got all his work done in record time.

Students who skip grades are probably fast learners, not necessarily more intelligent than those of us who plod along at the normal speed. There's nothing on earth more frustrating than sitting in a classroom listening to a teacher tell you something you already know. Fast learners need constant challenges to keep them interested.

Whatever your "learning style" may be, remember: *"The fear of the Lord is the beginning of wisdom"* (Psalm 111:10).

Would God ever get married?
—*Crystal, 13, Florida*

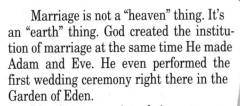

Marriage is not a "heaven" thing. It's an "earth" thing. God created the institution of marriage at the same time He made Adam and Eve. He even performed the first wedding ceremony right there in the Garden of Eden.

Marriage came into being so men and women wouldn't be lonely. *"The Lord God said, 'It is not good for the man to be alone'"* (Genesis 2:18, NIV). Usually God doesn't get lonely, because He's surrounded by millions of adoring angels and a universe full of beings who enjoy His friendship. Right now He is lonely for us because sin has separated us from heaven. But that will soon change.

"I will make a helper suitable for him" (NIV), the Creator continued in the same verse. Wives and husbands were made to be partners together. God has partners: His Son Jesus, the Holy Spirit, plus a million angels and a universe full of beings who enjoy His friendship.

"Be fruitful and increase in number," God told Adam and Eve in Genesis 1:28, NIV. *"Fill the earth and subdue it. Rule over the fish of the sea and the birds of the air and over every living creature that moves on the ground"* (verse 28, NIV). Husbands and wives were supposed to have babies and care for the earth. But God can speak people into existence and create worlds with simple commands. No need for marriage.

Remember, Crystal, marriage is God's gift to us. It creates new homes in which His plans can be carried out in our lives.

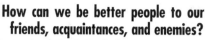

How can we be better people to our friends, acquaintances, and enemies?
—*Jonathan, 12, Maryland*

By not sounding like a clanging brass or a tinkling cymbal. That's how the apostle Paul describes any attempt to be a good neighbor if we don't have love in our hearts.

Becoming more loving is the only way to better ourselves socially. Knowing more facts than everyone else labels you a genius. Winning every race makes you an athlete. Being more handsome or beautiful identifies you as a "hunk," or "babe." But having more love turns you into a friend.

Think about the people you know. With whom do you most enjoy spending time? If you're like me, it's those who share love with every greeting, who genuinely care about you, who listen instead of talk, who sympathize, encourage, freely allow their laughter and tears to blend with yours.

How do you learn to love more? By sitting at the feet of an expert on the subject—Jesus Christ. His friends, acquaintances, and, yes, even His enemies recognized His great willingness to love. This was demonstrated in His spirit of forgiveness, patience, and unconditional kindness.

Paul says, *"And now these three remain: faith, hope and love. But the greatest of these is love"* (1 Corinthians 13:13, NIV).

Jonathan, join me in making a pledge to love more, starting today. Your friends, acquaintances, and enemies will recognize that you're special, and be attracted to the God you reflect.

Will the people who were going to take Bible studies but died before the first study be in heaven?

—Nicholas, 11, Oklahoma

Nicholas, let's take your question a few steps further. What if these people had completed one lesson? Then could they be saved? How about 10 lessons? What if they finished the study course and had decided to get baptized but suddenly died? What if they were baptized but made a mistake, disobeyed God, and their lives ended tragically right after their blunder?

The problem is that we're trying to figure out exactly when a person is saved. Only God makes that decision, and He knows people a whole lot better than we do. *"For man looketh on the outward appearance, but the Lord looketh on the heart" (1 Samuel 16:7).* We can't read people's thoughts, so we're in no position to judge whether a person should or shouldn't end up with us in heaven after Jesus' second coming.

Also, don't think of salvation as a kind of reward for something we do. Salvation is a gift from God offered freely. We're saved when we accept this wonderful gift. From then on, our most important job is to *stay* saved by daily growing in Jesus, letting Him take more and more control of our lives and our thoughts.

"But when the kindness and love of God our Savior appeared, he saved us, not because of righteous things we had done, but because of his mercy" (Titus 3:4, 5, NIV). Anyone who dies walking or even stumbling on the pathway to heaven dies saved.

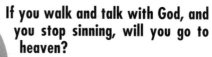

If you walk and talk with God, and you stop sinning, will you go to heaven?
—*Pacell, 11, California*

Jesus described a rather strange scene to His disciples one day. He was talking about His future second coming. Christ and His followers may have been passing a meadow as He spoke.

"When the Son of Man comes in his glory, and all the angels with him, he will sit on his throne in heavenly glory.... He will separate the people one from another as a shepherd separates the sheep from the goats. He will put the sheep on his right and the goats on his left.

"Then the King will say to those on his right, 'Come, you who are blessed by my Father; take your in-heritance.... For I was hungry and you gave me something to eat, I was thirsty and you gave me something to drink, I was a stranger and you invited me in, I needed clothes and you clothed me, I was sick and you looked after me, I was in prison and you came to visit me'" (Matthew 25:31-36, NIV).

Now, consider the surprising response from the sheep—I mean the saved people about to go to heaven. *"Lord, when did we see you hungry . . . thirsty . . . ? When did we see you a stranger . . . needing clothes . . . ? When did we see you sick or in prison . . . ?"* (verses 37-39, NIV). In other words, they didn't even know they'd been doing good. They'd just been living their lives the best way they knew how.

Walking and talking with God isn't a condition for salvation. It's the natural result of choosing Jesus as your friend, and heaven as your goal.

If you walk and talk with God, and you stop sinning, will you go to heaven?

—Pacell, 11, California

Can you stop sinning? Can anyone?

Some say yes, insisting that before Jesus comes, there'll be a group of individuals who are living perfect, sinless lives.

If that's the case, we sure have a lot of work to do. Even Paul, writing to his friends in Rome, lamented, *"For what I do is not the good I want to do; no, the evil I do not want to do—this I keep on doing"* (Romans 7:19, NIV). Then he cries out, *"What a wretched man I am! Who will rescue me from this body of death?"* (verse 24, NIV). Answering his own question he exclaims, *"Thanks be to God—through Jesus Christ our Lord"* (verse 25, NIV).

Stopping sinning isn't possible on this earth *unless* Jesus gives you the power necessary to fight and overcome temptation. And it may take a whole lifetime to learn how to accept and use such a wonderful weapon against sin.

So if you're like Paul and find yourself not doing the good you want to do and doing the bad you don't want to do, don't get discouraged. Just thank God for His forgiveness and try again. The more of your heart that you give the Holy Spirit to control, the more victory you will have over Satan.

I once watched a mother bird build a nest. She worked awfully hard. That night a strong wind blew it down. Did she give up? Did she just sit around and feel sorry for herself? No. She got busy and built again, this time using more mud and stronger twigs. Think of your journey to heaven as being like that nest. When evil knocks you down, get up and keep walking after Jesus!

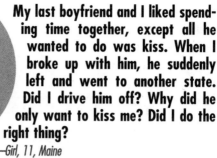

My last boyfriend and I liked spending time together, except all he wanted to do was kiss. When I broke up with him, he suddenly left and went to another state. Did I drive him off? Why did he only want to kiss me? Did I do the right thing?
—*Girl, 11, Maine*

You didn't drive him off, and you did do the right thing. Relationships are supposed to be a whole lot more than kissing. Successful partnerships include having fun with others, going places and seeing new things together, sharing hidden thoughts and fears with someone we trust, and having quiet times, too.

Ask any truly happy couple what the secret to their relationship is, and they'll say, "We're each other's best friend." You see, romantic love must include friendship, or it won't survive very long.

Your companion probably wasn't comfortable with all the other elements that are supposed to go along with love. He may have been embarrassed, uncertain of how to act, what to say, how to be a true friend. So he stuck with what made him feel good and didn't involve a lot of thinking and planning—namely, kissing.

Now, don't get me wrong. Kissing is sweet and good and fine with God *as long as* it strengthens relationships and guides couples toward a meaningful life together. Kissing without friendship and a caring attitude is just a plain, boring, doesn't-do-anybody-any-good brand of sex.

The next time a guy wants to kiss you, tell him that friendship must come first. Then don't settle for less.

Have you ever wondered what it will be like when Jesus comes again?

—*Greg, 10, Montana*

JULY

17

Yes, many times. And I'll let you in on a little secret: It used to scare me.

When I'd hear a preacher telling about how the mountains will shake and the earth will tremble, with people running around screaming, cursing, and asking the rocks to fall on them, I felt fear. And when I'd read about how some would be taken to heaven and some wouldn't, I thought, *Hey, what if my mom or dad don't get to go? What if I suddenly find myself all alone?*

Want to know what changed my fear to joy whenever I think of the Second Coming? I got to know the One who's coming back. I discovered He was a 10-year-old once, too. He knows what it's like to face an uncertain future, sometimes alone. I know He'll take extra-special care of kids when He returns.

And Greg, remember this: Jesus' second coming will frighten only those who have chosen to ignore God all their lives. Those of us who have read about Him, sang songs to Him, prayed every day to Him, won't be scared. Like it says in Isaiah 25, we'll look up and shout, *"Surely this is our God; we trusted in him, and he saved us. This is the Lord, we trusted in him; let us rejoice and be glad in his salvation"* (verse 9, NIV).

So when you're wondering about the Second Coming, think of Jesus tenderly placing children on His lap. For those who love and trust Him, that's what it'll be like.

Why do we die?
—*Jessica, 11, Florida*

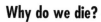

First, I want to make something very clear. Before Adam and Eve sinned, there had never been death in the universe. And after the destruction of the wicked, there will never be death again.

This shows us that death is a direct result of sin. Everything that sins dies, just as God said in Eden. *"You are free to eat from any tree in the garden,"* He told Adam and Eve. *"But you must not eat from the tree of the knowledge of good and evil, for when you eat of it you will surely die" (Genesis 2:16, 17, NIV).*

They ate. They died. With their disobedience they opened the door for Satan to flood this world with evil, pain, and suffering.

Today we live where death stalks the homes of the richest and the poorest. Even people who live good lives, who wouldn't think of hurting anyone or sinning against God, die. Why? Because of the result of sin. And don't go blaming Adam and Eve too much. Do you always resist temptation? Are you living a sinless life? No. None of us are. We make mistakes. We blow it. We sin. And we too will die. Maybe.

Someday soon Jesus will break the death hold on this earth. *"And God shall wipe away all tears from their eyes; and there shall be no more death, neither sorrow, nor crying, neither shall there be any more pain: for the former things are passed away" (Revelation 21:4).* Hurry, Jesus! Please come today.

JULY 18

How can we not let Satan lash out in us, making us hurt others and ourselves?

—Jonathan, 12, Maryland

Our New Testament friend Paul wondered the very same thing. So he came up with a plan of action. He divided himself into two types of personalities, calling half of himself "spiritual" and the other half "unspiritual."

Then he wrote, *"I find this law at work: When I want to do good, evil is right there with me. For in my inner being I delight in God's law; but I see another law at work in the members of my body, waging war against the law of my mind and making me a prisoner of the law of sin"* (Romans 7:21-23, NIV).

Sounds familiar, doesn't it? There's a part of us that wants to do good all the time, and another part just waiting to do evil. Paul's right. It's a war in there! *"What a wretched man I am!"* he cries out in verse 24 (NIV).

The question you've got to ask yourself is, "Which law is going to control my life? Satan's or God's?"

Would you like to save yourself an awful lot of future pain? Then get busy right now and make God's law the controlling force in your life. How? By daily, *daily*, spending time in prayer, telling God about your problems, fears, and temptations; about how you want to do good but keep messing up; and how you're sorry for blowing it so much. Tell Him you need His help. Jesus isn't pushy. He doesn't force Himself on people. He comes into hearts and minds only when invited. *So invite Him!*

Only then can you keep Satan from lashing out.

Why didn't God destroy Satan?

—Benjamin, 11, Oklahoma

For the same reason He doesn't destroy us. He loved him.

What? God loved Satan?

Yes, He did, when Satan was Lucifer. But He absolutely *hates* what Satan does.

"But," you say, "if God had destroyed him, all the pain and suffering in the world would never have happened."

I take that to mean that if God knows your great-grandson or great-granddaughter is going to murder a neighbor, He should come down and destroy you right this minute so it won't happen.

"Wait a minute," you say. "I don't want God to kill me off because of something a future relative is going to do."

Exactly. If He'd destroyed Satan back there in Eden, the whole universe would see how unfair that was. Instead Jesus told His Father, "Let *Me* die. Let Me pay the price for Satan's sin, and for everyone's sin. Then death will be only a sleep, and all those who choose to love and obey You will have a bright future waiting beyond the grave."

Satan will ultimately be destroyed, along with those who follow him and turn their backs on God's forgiving grace. But this will happen only after *everyone*, including you and me, has had a chance to choose which side he or she is on, and which future he or she wants— eternal life or eternal death.

"For sin shall not be your master, because you are not under law, but under grace" (Romans 6:14, NIV). Benjamin, choose grace!

How does a creationist's theory differ from an evolutionist's?

—Jared, 12, Washington

Basically, creationists believe in God, while evolutionists don't. It's not possible to be a Bible-trusting Christian and an evolutionist at the same time.

Here's why.

The Bible informs us in the first chapter of Genesis that God created the heavens and the earth. This is a far cry from the concept that all life evolved from sea slime, as evolutionists insist. Scripture indicates that people have inhabited our world for somewhere between 6,000 and 10,000 years. Our evolutionist friends place humanity's beginnings *millions* of years ago.

But before you dismiss the evolutionary theory as useless to the Christian, consider that in some areas they're correct. People and animals do "evolve" in many ways. There are creatures that have adapted to new environments by changing the way they live and even how they look.

Check out all the different nationalities of people, their skin colors and physical sizes and shapes. These are the results of the evolutionary process that all living beings experience. As Christians, we know God set these processes in motion. They didn't just happen by chance.

"Professing themselves to be wise, they became fools" "who changed the truth of God into a lie, and worshipped and served the creature more than the Creator" (Romans 1:22, 25).

I believe in God and the Bible. How about you?

Why were people born?
—*Xenia, 10, California*

Sometimes I ask that very same question, especially when I hear about someone doing something terrible to another person. "It would've been better if that bad individual had never been born," I say to myself.

But then I pause for a moment. The evil person didn't cause pain and suffering because he or she was born. It was the result of the choices that individual made. Contrary to what Hollywood says, there are no "natural-born killers" or robbers or rapists. Everyone who is born has the same opportunity to live a helpful, unselfish life.

I like the way a shepherd-boy-turned-king summed up his philosophy on why he was born. Listen: "*Since my youth, O God, you have taught me, and to this day I declare your marvelous deeds. Even when I am old and gray, do not forsake me, O God, till I declare your power to the next generation, your might to all who are to come*" (Psalm 71:17, 18, NIV).

Why were people born? Why were *you* born? To enjoy God's unconditional love, and to experience the joy of sharing that love with everyone you meet.

What did God do before He created everything?
—Girl, 13, Maine

There's a photograph I enjoy looking at each time I travel down to Tennessee to visit my parents. It's in an album resting on the top shelf of the closet at the end of the hall.

In beautiful black and white, I see my parents when they were newly married. None of us kids had been born. We were only a hopeful gleam in their eyes. But still, unbelievably, those two people, who would later create me and my sister and two brothers, look happy. Happy without us? Yup.

If we could see a photograph of God before He created this world, we'd see a beautiful Being happily forming fantastic universes and inhabiting them with lovely creatures. We'd see Him smiling with eager anticipation as He, along with Jesus and the Holy Spirit, busily placed planets in orbit, tended to never-dying gardens, communed with beings from the far reaches of space.

Looking closer, we'd see a gleam in His eye. That gleam is for you and me. God was planning us, getting ready to speak our world into existence, preparing to be our Saviour and friend.

"Yea, I have loved thee with an everlasting love: therefore with lovingkindness have I drawn thee" (Jeremiah 31:3).

Before God made us, He did exactly what He does now. He loved.

When will Jesus come?
—*Jason, 10, Montana*

As I'm writing these words, my sweet wife is in another room ironing some curtains. Her mind is filled with the duties of the day and projects we're currently working on. But I know that hidden away under the load of chores and business concerns, there's a sad memory that surfaces from time to time.

Recently her cousin Kenny died of cancer. Kenny was a happy man with a little child and a loving wife. He took comfort in knowing Jesus, even as the disease was eating away his life.

For Kenny, the wait is over. He's asleep. There are no days and months and years in his thoughts. As far as he is concerned, the time between his sad death and joyous resurrection is but the blink of an eye. The next thing Kenny will hear is Jesus calling his name, inviting him to go to heaven with Him.

We can say that in Kenny's case Jesus will come one microsecond from now. But for those of us who must live on, it will seem like such a long time to wait.

"'In a little while I will once more shake the heavens and the earth, the sea and the dry land. I will shake all nations, and the desired of all nations will come, and I will fill this house with glory,' says the Lord Almighty" (Haggai 2:6, 7, NIV).

Jesus will come soon. That fact was enough to bring hope and comfort to Kenny. It can do the same for us, too.

Why do parents always say, "I know my child," and think they know what you're thinking and feeling?
—*Adrian, 12, Alabama*

Probably because they *want* to understand you and help you with your problems.

When a mom or dad says, "I know my child," what they're really saying is "From observing my son or daughter's behavior during the past 12 years, I believe I know how he or she will react to certain situations." One problem: kids, especially teenagers, can change like the weather.

That's why it's important for parents to be a part of their offspring's lives. Then they're in a better position to sense the changes in their children's attitudes, recognize increasing peer pressures, understand fears and uncertainties, and know what their kids are up against.

But most parents have precious little time to spend with their family. So *you* have to become the teacher, filling your mom or dad in on the finer details of your life, letting them know when your attitudes change, allowing them to discover what you're thinking, and what scares you.

Believe me, there's a real advantage to having parents who say they "know their child" and actually do. You can use their experience to your benefit, unless you like messing up your life while they stand by and watch because you refuse to communicate with them.

Give dear ol' mom or dad a break. Tell 'em how you feel. Allow them to really truly know you. You'll like the results!

How can we know that when we see a "vision" it's from God and not Satan?

—*Jonathan, 12, Maryland*

First of all, I want to say that the whole idea of "visions" is kind of overrated in our world right now. We've got people having "out-of-body experiences" left and right, folks "channeling" with the supposed spirits of departed loved ones, movies depicting lost loves rising from the mists, and dozens of books proclaiming close encounters of the supernatural kind.

Even our beloved Bible states that *"it shall come to pass in the last days, saith God, I will pour out of my Spirit upon all flesh: and your sons and your daughters shall prophesy, and your young men shall see visions, and your old men shall dream dreams"* (Acts 2:17).

But which are from God? Listen to these Bible words: *"Dear friends, do not believe every spirit, but test the spirits to see whether they are from God, because many false prophets have gone out into the world. This is how you can recognize the Spirit of God: Every spirit that acknowledges that Jesus Christ has come in the flesh is from God, but every spirit that does not acknowledge Jesus is not from God"* (1 John 4:1-3, NIV).

Why does this test work? Because the last thing Satan wants is for you to draw closer to Jesus. The closer you are to Him, the more obvious Satan's counterfeit becomes. If the vision you hear about, read, or experience stays true to Bible teachings and highlights Jesus and not self, you can rest assured that God is delivering the message. If not, ignore it.

Will snakes have wings in heaven?
—*Scott, 11, Oklahoma*

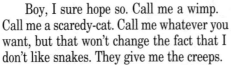

Boy, I sure hope so. Call me a wimp. Call me a scaredy-cat. Call me whatever you want, but that won't change the fact that I don't like snakes. They give me the creeps.

Some juniors I know can pick them up, play with them, wrap them around their neck, even keep them for pets. Not me. Oh, I've picked up a snake or two and played with it. But I was using every bit of bravery I possess, even though I know most are harmless and are perfectly happy to keep out of our way.

If there are snakes in heaven, I can guarantee you that they won't freak me out, or anyone else for that matter. They'll be beautiful and friendly. They might even have wings like the serpent in the Garden of Eden. I'll trust God either to make them appealing or make me braver than I am.

Maybe God created some of us to be a little nervous around snakes because He wanted us to be the same way around Satan whom He calls *"that old serpent, which is the Devil" (Revelation 20:2).* When I picture Satan as a coiled rattler waiting to bite me, it's easy to want nothing to do with him. I guess those who like snakes will have to imagine Satan as something else. A roaring lion or flesh-eating vulture, perhaps?

Rest assured that heaven will be a safe, happy place with nothing creepy in sight. Sounds like my kind of country!

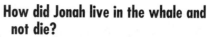

How did Jonah live in the whale and not die?

—Willie, 13, Washington

He must've been one hardy soul. Of course, he had a little help from God. But still, in the belly of a fish for three days? *Yuck!*

The stomach of any mammal is a terrible place to be, unless you're a hot-fudge sundae. Foods love stomachs. In tummies they break down into energy-producing sugars, starches, proteins, and blood-building nutrients. But the stomach is no place to be if you're a person who just happens to still be alive.

Powerful acids start immediately to dissolve your flesh. Bacteria eat into muscles and bones. Contractions move you through dark passageways filled with bile and other body juices. The process gives the phrase "getting wasted" a whole new meaning.

Now, here sits Jonah in a large, dark, smelly stomach, and nothing happens. Nothing! Only God could halt the natural processes of digestion in that sea creature. Only God could place His hand on the animal and guide it to a distant shore. Only God could protect the man as he's vomited onto the sands.

Got something in your life that makes you afraid? Facing a situation for which you can't seem to generate enough courage? Think of stomachs. Think of Jonah. Think of God.

JULY 28

Is there life on the other planets? Are they like us or are they monsters?

—*Reshonna, 11, California*

Whenever our friend Ellen White speaks of the "beings of other worlds" she uses words such as "innocent" and "loyal" *(Messages to Young People,* p. 253), "unprepared to comprehend the nature or consequences of sin" *(The Great Controversy,* p. 498), "intelligent" *(Patriarchs and Prophets,* p. 155), and "all sizes, . . . noble, majestic, and lovely" *(Early Writings,* p. 39).

But here's what I believe to be the most important description of these faraway beings. "They bore the express image of Jesus, and their countenances beamed with holy joy, expressive of the freedom and happiness of the place" *(ibid.).* Mrs. White, in vision, presented a rather pointed question: "I asked one of them why they were so much more lovely than those [people] on the earth. The reply was, 'We have lived in strict obedience to the commandments of God, and have not fallen by disobedience, like those on the earth'" *(ibid.).*

Wow! Perfect beings who haven't sinned. Imagine how smart and beautiful they must be.

So, Reshonna, the next time you're watching a sci-fi flick and some ugly, drooling creature from a distant planet goes around killing people, remember the vision God gave Mrs. White. There are no monsters out there beyond the stars, only loving, perfect beings who worship God and long to be your friends.

Is it OK to color your hair at my age?
—Girl, 10, Maine

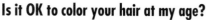

Coloring your hair isn't a *sin,* if that's what you mean. Many women (and men) give their hair a healthier, more pleasing glow because it makes them feel confident about themselves and hides the effects of aging or disease.

Most juniors have little problem with the effects of aging and enjoy an overall healthy glow. If disease damages your hair, coloring it makes sense.

However, if you want to change or enhance your hair color simply because you're tired of it being whatever hue it happens to be, may I suggest some other uses for your money and time, such as buying a good book or visiting a friend.

Hair color should be far down the list of important things in life. The more time we spend worrying about the way we look, the less sensitive we become to the needs of others. What would you think if the Bible reported that Jesus didn't have time to heal the sick one day because He was having a facial?

Yes, we must take care of our bodies and show respect for others by making ourselves as pleasant to look at as possible. But there are limits. Before you color your hair, ask yourself, "Is this really necessary? Am I taking good care of myself or am I being vain?"

"Present your bodies a living sacrifice, holy, acceptable unto God" (Romans 12:1). Don't let the color of your hair become more important than the beauty of your life.

JULY

30

How far does my family go back?
—Paul, 10, Montana

Tracing family roots is quite a challenge and can be loads of fun. You must become a real detective and do tons of research as you move back through the generations.

My wife has been tracing her family history by using a computer program. She can print out names and relationships back into the 1700s.

If you want to discover your roots, begin by talking to your parents, grandparents, and—if they're still alive—great-grandparents. Ask them for names and information about their relatives.

Dig through old albums, Bibles (many people place short family histories in the front pages, recording dates of births and baptisms), and legal documents such as marriage certificates, family-run business records, and land deeds.

The secret lies in your last name. Follow it back through the years. Unless you're a Native American, your ancestors journeyed from countries beyond the oceans. Your last name can give you a hint of whether you have European, Asian, African, or Latin American ties. For instance, if your last name ends in "i-a-n" you probably have some Armenian (Middle Eastern) branches in your bloodline. If you've got an "s-e-n" at the end, check out Western Europe. "L-o-s" may indicate roots in Greece.

Guess what? If you travel far enough back in time, you'll discover that we all share two ancestors. Here's a hint: one built a boat, the other lived in a garden. Neat, huh?

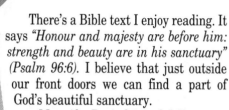

There's a Bible text I enjoy reading. It says *"Honour and majesty are before him: strength and beauty are in his sanctuary"* *(Psalm 96:6)*. I believe that just outside our front doors we can find a part of God's beautiful sanctuary.

My wife, Dorinda, and I live on a hillside overlooking a peaceful West Virginia valley. Behind our house is a wooded area filled with songbirds and buzzing bugs. Beside the woods rests a little pond that we like to visit often.

This pond has all the usual inhabitants. Frogs lullaby each other to sleep at night, fish splash in the morning sun, and sometimes we see a turtle or two perched atop a half-submerged log, catching some rays. There's even a water snake that glides by occasionally, searching for something to eat.

One day we were looking out over the placid waters when an idea surfaced in our minds. As beautiful as this sanctuary was, something was missing—something with webbed feet and soft feathers. Something that could paddle across the ripples or fly among the clouds overhead. Something that quacked.

We hurried back to the house and made a phone call. "Yes, we can order just what you want," the voice on the line assured us. "They'll arrive in about two weeks."

I looked at my wife and she looked at me. We smiled. Soon we were going to become a mommy and a daddy. Little did we know just how accurate that statement was.

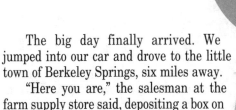

The big day finally arrived. We jumped into our car and drove to the little town of Berkeley Springs, six miles away.

"Here you are," the salesman at the farm supply store said, depositing a box on the counter. "They sound hungry."

We lifted the lid and peeked inside. There, looking back at us, were 10 of the cutest, softest, wiggliest little baby ducks we'd ever seen. They were chirping and squawking and whistling and scolding one another, all trying to get out of the box at the same time.

"Hold on, guys," I said, carefully closing the lid. "We've got to get you home first."

We paid for our purchase and drove back to the house, listening to the constant commotion coming from the cardboard box in the back seat.

Our new family was only 2 days old, and already they were itching to get out and explore the world. But we couldn't just set them free. There were dangers at the pond for baby ducks. Foxes, snakes, raccoons, turtles, stray cats, and hungry dogs couldn't be ignored. No, as parents of those innocent, vulnerable creatures, my wife and I had to protect them until they could learn to look out for themselves.

We thought of the Bible verse that says, *"O Jerusalem, Jerusalem . . . how often I have longed to gather your children together, as a hen gathers her chicks under her wings, but you were not willing" (Matthew 23:37, NIV).*

For now, our new family would live safely under our wings.

"What if they drown?" I asked as I busily filled a basin with fresh, clean water.

"They won't drown. They're ducks," my wife insisted.

I looked at the little, furry balls with their oversized beaks, legs, and feet. They were only 3 days old and had never seen water enough to swim in.

"Ducks like water," my wife continued. "God made them that way."

"OK," I agreed reluctantly. "We'll give it a try. But if I have to do mouth-to-beak resuscitation on one of these little fellows, it'll be your fault."

When the water level in the basin looked about right for a duck to swim in, I turned off the faucet and lifted one of the baby mallards away from the rest. "Now, don't be afraid," I told it. "It's just water and—"

The instant the duckling caught sight of the cool, clear liquid, it jumped right out of my hand and dove headfirst into the basin. *Splash!*

It was all over that tiny pool, swimming, diving, making like a submarine, peeping, squeaking, flapping its tiny featherless wings and raising such a ruckus that all the other ducks suddenly felt left out and almost jumped out of their apple box. One by one I lifted the remaining nine and placed them in the basin. Such a madhouse of joyous ducks I've never seen.

Sometimes our happiest moments come when we simply do what God programmed us to do. Ducks can swim. We can love.

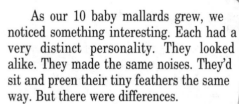

As our 10 baby mallards grew, we noticed something interesting. Each had a very distinct personality. They looked alike. They made the same noises. They'd sit and preen their tiny feathers the same way. But there were differences.

Several were passive and kept to themselves, while others were aggressive and went around trying to get everyone else interested in playing tag, wrestling, or taking part in whatever games baby ducks invent.

Some enjoyed sitting in the sunlight that streamed through the window, while others sought out dark, quiet spots under the straw. Several ducklings took many naps. Others seemed to have an endless source of energy and kept busy hour after hour.

All were mallards. All were hatched on the same day. But all were different.

The next time you're in a crowd of juniors, look around. Notice the many personalities, character traits, and actions of your companions. That's the way God intended. If we were all the same, think how boring life would be.

Listen to these important words from our friend Ellen White. She says, *"The Spirit of God is manifested in different ways upon different men"* (Review and Herald, *May 5, 1896*). Just as we loved and cared for each of our ducks individually, God loves and cares for us individually. No matter what type of person you are, Jesus has a special, one-of-a-kind love waiting just for you.

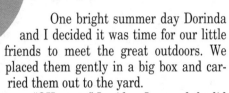

One bright summer day Dorinda and I decided it was time for our little friends to meet the great outdoors. We placed them gently in a big box and carried them out to the yard.

"OK, guys," I said as I opened the lid and tilted the box slightly so they could jump out. "Don't wander off too far."

If I could understand duckling talk, I'm sure they were saying stuff such as "Hey, what's this long, green stuff? Smells nice. And check out these little yellow flowers. And these weird rocks." When they'd pause and gaze skyward, I could imagine they were saying, "Will you look at those big fluffy things up there? Where'd they come from? This is great. I wonder how bugs taste."

They were waddling around exploring the soft earth when, far away, a hawk called out. All 10 ducklings suddenly froze in their tracks. In the next split second they were racing across the lawn to where my wife was sitting. Without a sound they dove under her legs and completely disappeared from view.

Dorinda smiled up at me. "Looks like God cares for ducks the same way He cares for us. He put in their minds an escape plan even before they were hatched."

Something tells me that the shepherd boy David understood this amazing fact, too. He wrote, *"You are my hiding place; you will protect me from trouble and surround me with songs of deliverance"* (Psalm 32:7, NIV).

When temptations and dangers come, follow your instincts. Run to God.

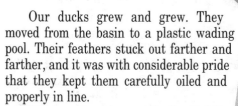

Our ducks grew and grew. They moved from the basin to a plastic wading pool. Their feathers stuck out farther and farther, and it was with considerable pride that they kept them carefully oiled and properly in line.

When we'd go for a walk, they'd fall in behind us like well-trained soldiers, following us around the yard.

A more curious bunch you'd never find. They had to explore every nook and cranny of the yard, every fallen log, every sweet-smelling flower.

As their wing feathers continued to develop, they'd stand in one spot and flap like crazy, sometimes lifting themselves off the ground a few inches. They looked like clumsy ballerinas scurrying across the grass, half walking, half flying, mostly stumbling.

One day one of them quacked. It surprised the duck as much as it surprised us. It looked around as if to say, "What was *that?*"

Often Dorinda and I would sit on our favorite bench under the hickory tree and the ducklings would gather at our feet, tuck their heads under their wings, and snooze. We thought of the verse *"I will lie down and sleep in peace, for you alone, O Lord, make me dwell in safety" (Psalm 4:8, NIV).*

There was still one place we hadn't taken our brood. As yet, they hadn't seen the pond. I wanted to make sure they could fly away from danger before I introduced them to their final home. After all, once they laid eyes on that peaceful body of water, they'd never come to the yard again. Right?

"It's time," I announced one afternoon. The ducks had been with us for almost six weeks. They could fly short distances, although their landings left a lot to be desired. They'd sort of flutter and crash around the big yard in front of the house.

"All right, you guys," I called. "It's time you started living at the pond." They looked up at me and nodded—at least, it seemed like they were nodding.

Dorinda and I made our way along the forest path, our ducks following obediently at our heels. We walked them right down to the shoreline. I felt kind of sad, knowing that they'd never want to leave their beautiful new home.

When they saw the water, they stopped dead in their tracks. They strained their necks, studied the sparkling waves, listened to all the mysterious new sounds drifting about, then sat down on the ground and refused to budge. No way were they going any farther.

My mouth dropped open. "It's a pond," I said. "Not molten lava. You're ducks. You're supposed to love ponds."

They stayed right where they were. I pleaded, begged, beseeched, threatened, and even tried to bribe them with a juicy lettuce leaf, but they wouldn't move one inch.

I wonder if God ever gets frustrated with us. He knows what would make us happy, but we refuse to accept His loving invitation because we fear things we don't understand.

Here were 10 ducks who were afraid of a pond. What was I supposed to do now?

Ten ducks who were afraid of a little old pond. How embarrassing!

Down the country road from our house lives an 11-year-old girl named Dusty. She's very wise, as are all juniors. When I explained my predicament to her, she shrugged. "I know why they won't go in."

"You do?" I gasped.

"Yup. No one's ever taught them how to swim in a pond."

I blinked. "Wait a minute. You're not suggesting that I . . ."

Dusty smiled.

"There's a snake in that pond!" I protested.

My young friend lifted her hands. "You're all the daddy they've got."

That's why, if you'd walked past the little pond at the edge of our property on a certain summer day two years ago, you would've seen a curious sight. How many times have you ever witnessed 10 half-grown ducks sitting on dry land watching a human swim?

Once, long ago, God came to a dark place where a serpent lived, to teach us how to survive in a world of sin. He did that because He loves us, and knew we couldn't learn any other way.

A few days later, when we returned from an overnight business trip, our 10 ducks weren't waiting for us at the house. We found them swimming in the pond, happy as could be.

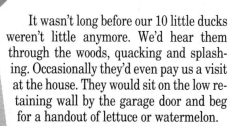

It wasn't long before our 10 little ducks weren't little anymore. We'd hear them through the woods, quacking and splashing. Occasionally they'd even pay us a visit at the house. They would sit on the low retaining wall by the garage door and beg for a handout of lettuce or watermelon.

As their feathers filled in, we discovered we had three males and seven females. How beautiful they were, waddling around, looking plump and happy, dressed in their colorful coats.

We even developed a daily ritual. Each morning I'd get up and go to the back window. I'd quack out a greeting that sounded more like Donald Duck than a mallard duck. I'd hear them respond from the pond. A couple minutes later, here they'd come, all in a line, waddling through the woods to their favorite perch on the retaining wall.

Dorinda and I would hurry down to feed them handfuls of cracked corn and sunflower seeds. What a happy bunch they were. When they'd had their fill, they'd take off with a windy fluttering of wings, circle the house a couple times, then head for the pond. We'd hear their splashy touchdowns.

Occasionally, while I was sitting in my second-floor office, I'd see 10 fast-flying ducks streak by my window. They seemed to be checking to make sure I was all right. Each time they did this, I'd think of David's words. *"Oh that I had wings like a dove! for then would I fly away, and be at rest" (Psalm 55:6).* I'd watch them sweep out across the valley, wondering what it's like to fly, and what it's like to be at rest.

"Something's wrong," I told my wife as we watched our ducks swimming across the pond one warm afternoon. "See that female over there? She's having trouble keeping up with the rest."

Sure enough, one of our feathered friends seemed to be struggling, as if she couldn't get her legs to work properly. "We'd better keep an eye on her," Dorinda said.

The next morning I stood waiting to greet the mallards as they emerged from the woods. One by one they waddled down the path, quacking softly to themselves. Four, five, six, seven, I counted. Eight, nine . . .

I waited. And waited. Then the tenth duck appeared. My breath caught in my throat. She was stumbling, falling, one wing dragging helplessly on the ground. She was trying her best to join the others, who were already waiting on the top of the retaining wall.

Tears stung my eyes. One of our friends was sick and dying.

As I stood there watching the horrible scene, my heart breaking, the Lord placed in my mind a Bible verse I will never forget. Let me share it with you: *"If a man have an hundred sheep, and one of them be gone astray, doth he not leave the ninety and nine, and goeth into the mountains, and seeketh that which is gone astray?" (Matthew 18:12).*

I had nine healthy ducks waiting to love me, but my whole attention was focused on the one duck who was suffering. I suddenly understood how Jesus could die for one sinner. At that moment I realized how much He cares for me. We must never feel alone in this world. Jesus sees our pain and cries with us.

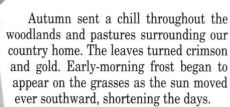

Autumn sent a chill throughout the woodlands and pastures surrounding our country home. The leaves turned crimson and gold. Early-morning frost began to appear on the grasses as the sun moved ever southward, shortening the days.

The nine ducks at the pond seemed to grow restless, glancing more often at the sky, watching winged V's of geese and other waterfowl pass high overhead.

Then one morning they were gone, leaving behind two people whose lives they'd touched in so many wonderful and profound ways.

The pond seemed lonely after that. Oh, we still had the frogs and turtles and the little water snake to keep us company, but even they were getting ready to disappear into hiding places far from the reach of the winter storms to come.

Would our ducks come back in the spring? Or would they follow new friends to distant waters, beginning again the cycle of hatching, growth, and migration?

It's been a year now. Several pairs of mallards have visited our pond. Were they ours? We don't know. They didn't stay. Perhaps our little body of water isn't big enough for raising a family. Maybe they found lakes and rivers more to their liking. But we'll continue to look and listen, just in case others stop by for a visit.

Whenever we see a group of ducks passing overhead, Dorinda and I always stop and watch them go. And without fail, one of us will say, with a catch in our voice, "Hi, guys."

Do you think I'll go to heaven if I wear pants? I know it's a sin and I don't want to sin.

—*Ashley, 11, New York*

Ashley, some parents are very concerned about what their children wear, and they should be. It's easy for teenagers to go overboard about fashion, always wanting the latest style.

Many moms and dads have definite ideas of what boys and girls should wear. Pants often fall into the "boy" category. The Bible itself suggests that men should always dress like men and women like women.

Clothes can become a sin in three ways. First, when you spend excessive amounts of money on them and have nothing left to help the poor and less fortunate. Job said, *"If I have seen any perish for want of clothing, or any poor without covering . . . then let mine arm fall from my shoulder blade" (Job 31:19-22).*

Second, fashion can become like a god to us, taking up all our time and attention. *"Thou shalt have no other gods before me,"* Jesus says in Exodus 20:3.

Third, clothes can cause us to want to disobey those in authority above us, such as parents. *"Honour thy father and thy mother,"* God says in verse 12 of Exodus 20. When we fail to honor parents who are trying their best to raise us by Bible principles and Christian love, we break one of the Ten Commandments.

Someday you'll have to choose for yourself what you wear. Then, and now, don't allow clothes to make you selfish, turn you from God, or entice you to disobey your parents.

AUGUST 12

When did dinosaurs rule the earth?

—*Roy, 11, Washington*

To have a dinosaur, or any other creature, "rule" the earth would mean that it was the most powerful, most intelligent animal alive.

Think back, Roy. The Bible says God created the heavens and the earth, and on the sixth day He formed humans from the dust. They were brought to life during Creation week. Since they are the most intelligent and powerful beings alive, no other creature has ever "ruled" except them.

So dinosaurs have never been in charge. Only humans.

"People aren't as powerful as lions," you say. "They don't have the strength of a rhinoceros." True. But humans have intelligence. They can plan and dream. They can remember far more than any animal. And they can communicate complex ideas to others. That makes them very, very powerful.

There was a time in history when dinosaurs roamed the earth. Then they mysteriously vanished, leaving only their bones to remind us of their passing. What event in the Bible would explain such a sudden and complete termination of an entire family of mammals? Here's a hint: think of water.

King David stated, *"It was you [God] who split open the sea by your power; you broke the heads of the monster in the waters. It was you who crushed the heads of Leviathan and gave him as food to the creatures of the desert" (Psalm 74:13, 14, NIV).* Dinosaurs vanished in the Flood less than 10,000 years ago.

What should you do if a friend is doing drugs?
—*Joel, 12, Florida*

First, pray. There's power in asking God to help someone overcome such a destructive habit.

Listen how our friend Ellen White advises us to deal with acquaintances who've gotten themselves into trouble: "Give the erring one no occasion for discouragement. . . . Let no bitter sneer rise in mind or heart. Let no tinge of scorn be manifest in the voice. . . . Let him feel the strong clasp of a sympathizing hand, and hear the whisper, Let us pray" (*Christ's Object Lessons,* p. 250).

People do drugs for a lot of different reasons. Some just think they're being cool. Others don't want to be considered weird if everyone else is into them. Still others have emotional problems they can't handle, so they escape into the mind-altered world that these chemicals create. Trouble is, all of these people pay a terrible price for their choice. Drugs kill more than the body. They also destroy brain and talent potential and quickly spin lives out of control.

Prayer is the first step to finding a way out. Mrs. White adds, "Prayer brings Jesus to our side, and gives to the fainting, perplexed soul new strength to overcome the world, the flesh, and the devil" (*ibid.*).

Joel, I'm so glad you want to help your friend. But you can't do it alone. Begin by asking God to join your team. He'll give you the power you need to meet the challenge, and the strength your friend needs to overcome this horrible habit.

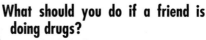

What should you do if a friend is doing drugs?

—Joel, 12, Florida

The battle to overcome drugs begins with prayer and sympathy. Next comes action! I believe the same method Jesus suggested for dealing with all sinners works here, too. Listen:

"If your brother sins against you, go and show him his fault, just between the two of you" (Matthew 18:15, NIV).

You might say to your friend, "I know you're doing drugs, and that's not healthy. You're going to mess yourself up bad and maybe do some serious damage. If you'd like, I'll help you figure out a way to kick the habit. Whadda ya say?"

The Bible says, *"If he listens to you, you have won your brother over. But if he will not listen, take one or two others along"* (verses 15, 16, NIV).

These "one or two others" should be people trained in helping teens get off drugs. It might be a health professional from school, a pastor who's qualified to deal with drug abuse, or a parent who understands this particular problem.

"If he refuses to listen to them, tell it to the church" (verse 17, NIV).

To the church? That's right. Teen problems sometimes get swept under the rug because members don't know about them. When a church filled with dedicated Christians takes on a challenge, good things result. Perhaps the members will vote to start a drug prevention program, bring in professional help, create a library of resources aimed at the problem. God will lead.

What should you do if a friend is doing drugs?
—Joel, 12, Florida

Prayer, sympathy, action. These three steps must come before this last part.

If every effort fails, if your friend chooses to remain locked in his or her habit, there's only one thing left to do. *"If he refuses to listen even to the church, treat him as you would a pagan or a tax collector" (Matthew 18:17, NIV).*

Now, before you think Jesus is suggesting that you write your drug-doing friend off completely, remember how Christ treated pagans and tax collectors. Pagans He worked tirelessly for, offering them healing, hope, and love, teaching them a better way to live and ultimately dying for their sins. He shared meals with tax collectors. Remember Zacchaeus?

Joel, drug abusers need help. They can't overcome their habit alone. They've allowed powerful, destructive changes to take place in their bodies and minds. These drugs alter their senses and reasoning abilities, making them prisoners to habit.

Your friend may choose to accept your kind offering of help or he or she may laugh and turn his or her back on you. Either way, you can know you've done your best. All that's left is to love this friend, pray for him or her, and most important of all, forgive.

Remember: *"The Lord delights in a man's way, he makes his steps firm; though he stumble, he will not fall, for the Lord upholds him with his hand" (Psalm 37:23, 24, NIV).* When your friend rejects your helpful hand, leave him or her in the Lord's.

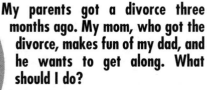

My parents got a divorce three months ago. My mom, who got the divorce, makes fun of my dad, and he wants to get along. What should I do?
—*Boy, 12*

I hate divorce. I really, really hate it. Juniors like you suffer so needlessly when homes break up, and it's not even your fault. Life just isn't very fair, is it?

Parents divorce for a lot of reasons. The process leaves hearts hurting and minds searching for ways to cope. One way of coping is to make fun. Other ways include violence toward self or family, anger at God, becoming a hermit, getting married a whole bunch of times right in a row, or even stalking the ex-husband or wife just to make life miserable for him or her. All of these actions spring from a deep sense of loss or failure.

Your mother is probably hurting. To cover her true feelings, she makes fun of your father. And here you are, trying to be a kind, loving son to both parents. Tough assignment.

Consider this suggestion. When your mom makes fun, don't join in. Just gently say, "He's still my dad and I love him, just like I love you." And if your dad speaks unkindly of your mom, remind him how much you love them both. What you're demonstrating with your thoughtful words is that you accept their faults and still care for them in spite of their mistakes.

Ask God to give you wisdom to meet this challenge. Like David, say in your heart, *"From birth I have relied on you; you brought me forth from my mother's womb. I will ever praise you"* (Psalm 71:6, NIV). Then show your parents the proper way to love.

AUGUST

17

Why do people not believe in Black and White going together or getting married?
—Angela, 16, Oklahoma

The subject of interracial marriages has been argued for centuries. While it's becoming more common nowadays, many people still have a problem dealing with the matter.

Some bring up 2 Corinthians 6:14, which states, *"Be ye not unequally yoked together."* They leave out the next two words: *"with unbelievers."* Paul was suggesting that men and women of different *religious* beliefs shouldn't marry.

Black-and-White relationships present a cultural, not moral, dilemma. There's nothing wrong with falling in love and marrying someone not of your color. Love is not only blind, it's color-blind as well. But in today's society, mixing races in marriage still raises eyebrows, still makes heads wag. This is sad, and can be devastating to newlyweds trying to fit in.

A married couple must live in society, as ignorant and ungiving as that society may be. Making any relationship work is hard enough. Adding cultural friction to a marriage only makes the job more difficult.

Angela, two people who are falling in love must take into account all known potential pitfalls to their relationship, both religious and social. Black-and-White marriages still face a thorny wall of prejudice. You can say "We won't let it affect us!" But it will.

Love requires fertile soil for growth. Plant your affections where they have the greatest potential for happiness.

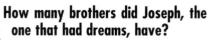

How many brothers did Joseph, the one that had dreams, have?

—*Jessica, 11, California*

Jacob, Joseph's father, had 12 sons by four women. Joseph and his younger brother, Benjamin, came into this world via Rachel, the young lady Jacob had worked so hard for but ended up married to her sister Leah instead. This exciting story is found in Genesis.

Joseph not only dreamed really weird dreams, he was his father's favorite son. Have you ever met a junior who was a favorite son or daughter, or a teacher's pet? Yes, I see you rolling your eyes and nodding your head. Sometimes teacher's pets and mommy's favorites can be a royal pain.

When I taught school, there were a couple kids whom I considered my favorites, although I made sure I treated them the same as all my other terrific students. When a child is kind to others, thoughtful, does his or her duties without whining and moaning, and completes homework on time, a teacher's heart can't help swelling with pride.

When a son or daughter is affectionate, considerate, and respectful, a parent's heart does the same. Even God has favorites. Listen to how He describes one of the characters from the Old Testament: *"I have found David the son of Jesse, a man after mine own heart, which shall fulfil all my will"* (Acts 13:22).

Want to be your teacher's, parent's, or God's favorite? Think of others first. Find out how to bring joy into lives, and smiles onto faces. Then try not to be a pain.

When is it a sin to be jealous?
—Emily, 11, New York

Here's how my *Merriam-Webster's Dictionary* describes the word "jealous": (1) intolerant of rivalry or unfaithfulness; (2) maliciously grudging another's advantages; and (3) given or prone to suspicion.

Not a very nice way to be, wouldn't you say? But before we condemn all who have feelings of jealousy, consider this startling verse from the Bible: *"For thou shalt worship no other god: for the Lord, whose name is Jealous, is a jealous God" (Exodus 34:14).*

A number of times the Old Testament labels God as "jealous." If we're supposed to be Godlike, then it's OK for us to be jealous, too. Right?

Not exactly. God's jealousy was aimed directly at those who were following Satan and his evil angels. He wanted them back safely in His fold of love and was willing to do anything to accomplish the task, including allowing His only Son to die.

If our jealousy drives us to harm others, to lift ourselves up at other people's expense, then it's definitely a sin. But if we, like God, feel jealous of the good things heaven offers, such as freedom from Satan's grasp, forgiveness from sin, and hope for eternal life, then it's OK.

David says, *"Depart from evil, and do good; seek peace, and pursue it" (Psalm 34:14).* This we can do with a determined mind and a jealous heart.

Will a person who commits suicide be in heaven?

—Lindsey, 12, Washington

Keep in mind this simple truth: God is more interested in *why* we act than *how* we act. The Bible states, *"The Lord does not look at the things man looks at. Man looks at the outward appearance, but the Lord looks at the heart"* (1 Samuel 16:7, NIV).

People take their own lives for many reasons. Some kill themselves because life has become more than they can handle. I only wish someone had introduced those people to their friend Jesus, who could help them face their challenges.

Some commit suicide because they're ashamed of something terrible they did. Jesus could help here, too, by offering forgiveness and teaching them how to live with the results of their mistakes—even if that means prison.

Still others end their lives because they're afraid of dying of a painful illness they've contracted, such as AIDS or cancer. They'd rather die peacefully than in agony.

We can't judge whether a suicide is sin because we can't read thoughts and understand motives. But God can, and does. Lindsey, rest assured that our heavenly Father takes into account every aspect of this human tragedy and reserves a place for that person in heaven if at all possible.

If you're tempted to commit suicide, give God a chance to bring you hope and courage. Allow Jesus to place answers in your mind. Be patient and listen for that still small voice that can turn despair into joy, and death into life eternal.

AUGUST 21

Why am I always bored at school?

—*Kendra, 13, Alabama*

Two things serve to make a perfectly wonderful activity boring. First, it's not challenging enough. Second, you see no value in what you're doing.

I'm going to tell you something right now that will help you until the day you breathe your last, if you allow it to. Are you ready? Here goes: *Life is what you make it.*

Boredom is a sure sign that you've decided to let someone else take charge of your life. You're no longer in control. You're making your life miserable by allowing yourself to just drift along with the tide.

Kendra, it's time to shake loose those feelings and take charge again! Is school boring you? Then ask your teacher to assign you something really challenging instead of, or in addition to, what everyone else is doing. Studying the Civil War? Instead of writing about the Battle of Gettysburg, research what type of weapons were used, how far they could shoot, what the battle must have sounded like.

Try to uncover those areas in your studies that match your personal interests. This creates value in your mind. Like music? art? science? In French class, study French music. Trace art styles while reviewing history. Keep a list of the scientific advancements made in the countries highlighted during geography class. See what I mean?

Boredom is a choice. Stop making that choice.

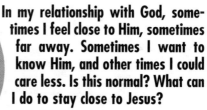

In my relationship with God, sometimes I feel close to Him, sometimes far away. Sometimes I want to know Him, and other times I could care less. Is this normal? What can I do to stay close to Jesus?
—*Kacie, 14, Montana*

When you have a few moments, read the book of Psalms. It'll be a real eye-opener!

Every Christian who has ever lived has experienced the very same conditions you're facing. Even Jesus Himself had moments of doubt and feelings of uncertainty while He walked the dusty paths of our sinful world.

Is it normal? Yes. Is it something we should just ignore? No way! We must fight to stay connected to our heavenly Father at every moment. Why? Because any feeling that draws us away from God has been placed in our mind by the devil himself.

A working relationship with God isn't supposed to be a constant high. Jesus cried, experienced deep concern, felt inadequate, weathered loneliness—all of the emotions we cope with. But His foundation faith was strong.

You see, Kacie, faith isn't a feeling. It's a piece of knowledge we hold firmly in our minds. Faith says, "No matter how I feel, I *know* Jesus loves me. I *know* I'm valuable to Him. I *know* He will save me." Then, when we feel far away, or find ourselves not caring, we step up on that foundation faith and say, "These are only feelings. I do care. I'm not far away."

Second Corinthians 5:7 says, *"For we walk by faith, not by sight."* We mustn't walk by feelings, either.

Where in the Bible does it say you should not wear jewelry and not adorn yourself?
—*Travis, 16, Oklahoma*

AUGUST 24

You're probably thinking of 1 Timothy 2:9, 10, where Paul says, *"I also want women to dress modestly, with decency and propriety, not with braided hair or gold or pearls or expensive clothes, but with good deeds, appropriate for women who profess to worship God"* (NIV).

Like everywhere else in the Bible, there's a deeper meaning hiding behind these verses.

When I was a junior, a rock group from England took America by storm. They were called the Beatles, and I, like millions of other teenagers, thought they were the next-best thing to sliced bread (which only *sounds* like the name of a rock group). The stores soon started to carry tons of Beatles merchandise—Beatles wigs, Beatles coats, and most attractive to me, Beatles shoes. I wanted a pair of Beatles shoes so I could look like John Lennon.

You see, Travis, I wanted to adorn myself with something that had no *real* value. Beatles shoes weren't good for climbing mountains or playing football or even walking to school. They were good only for looking like a Beatle.

Any article of clothing, any piece of jewelry, that we as Christians wear should be more than something that just draws attention our way. When fashion ignores modesty, good taste, and usefulness, it's time for us to ignore fashion. *"A wicked man puts up a bold front, but an upright man gives thought to his ways"* (Proverbs 21:29, NIV). That includes how we adorn ourselves.

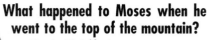

What happened to Moses when he went to the top of the mountain?
—Victoria, 11, California

Moses had two "mountaintop" experiences. The first was when God gave the children of Israel the Ten Commandments; the other was when Moses died.

The first was filled with thunder and lightning. God made the earth shake and the rocks crunch together; fire and smoke were everywhere.

The second was quiet, peaceful, serene. Moses simply talked with God for a little while, then lay down and died.

Did you notice that the same two people were at both mountaintops? But what a difference there was between the experiences!

Occasionally storms rumble across our part of West Virginia. The winds blow, the sky crackles with lightning, and thunder roars up the valleys. But I know God is with me.

Other times, soft clouds hug the ridges, a wood thrush sings from the hickory tree, and the wind is but a whisper. God is there then, too.

No matter what happens in your life, Victoria, no matter how noisy and mixed up and scary it may become, you can be sure that your Saviour is right beside you, loving you in spite of the commotion. When the thunder rolls, trust Him. In the quiet times, whisper your praise. You, like Moses, will find Jesus waiting in every valley, and on every mountaintop.

How do you know you're doing the right thing?
—*Girl, 13, Maine*

There's a text in the Bible that used to make me nervous. Listen: *"There is a way which seemeth right unto a man, but the end thereof are the ways of death"* (*Proverbs 14:12*).

Excuse me? You mean I can go through life thinking I'm doing the right thing when I'm really not?

Solomon, who wrote Proverbs, wasn't exactly Mr. Sinless. He lived his life the way he saw fit, disregarding God most of the time. He firmly believed he was doing the right thing, but it was *his* thing, not God's.

Later in life Solomon wrote, *"I denied myself nothing my eyes desired; I refused my heart no pleasure. My heart took delight in all my work. . . . Yet when I surveyed all that my hands had done and what I had toiled to achieve, everything was meaningless, a chasing after the wind; nothing was gained under the sun"* (*Ecclesiastes 2:10, 11, NIV*).

Poor King Solomon. He hadn't learned the lesson you can learn right now. Doing the right thing begins by discovering what God considers to be the right thing. That's why He handed down the Ten Commandments and His many ideals and formulas for living a satisfying life. Solomon thought he knew better than God. He didn't.

You're doing the right thing when you're living by God's laws as clearly outlined in the Bible. Everything else is meaningless.

Are you close to God? What religion are you?

—Amber, 11, Washington

Sometimes I feel very close to God. Other times I get so busy with work and stuff that I don't think about Him as much as I should. That's why I always remember to pray at each meal, and also when I get up in the morning, and when I go to bed at night. Praying brings me back to God's side and reminds me how much He loves me.

My mom and dad live in Tennessee, a long way from West Virginia. Each week, on Sunday, I phone them or they phone me. We talk for about 20 minutes. Why? Because it brings us close together, even though many miles of interstate highway separate us. I listen closely to their voices and can quickly tell if one is sick, tired, sad, or worried. I'm sure they're listening to my voice, searching for clues on how I'm doing. Letter writing is fine. E-mail works great. But it's the sound of a voice that reveals the most.

We must daily talk to God for the same reason. He wants to hear our voice. He wants to know how we're feeling inside. That way He can know what type of help we need.

When we listen to His still small voice in our ear, we'll find courage, hope, and endless love waiting in His words.

"Evening, morning and noon I cry out in distress, and he hears my voice" reports David in Psalm 55:17, NIV. I'm closest to God when I'm talking to Him and He's talking to me.

AUGUST

27

249

Are you close to God? What religion are you?

—Amber, 11, Washington

One summer, when I was younger than junior age, I visited my grandparents in North Carolina. A nearby church was holding a Vacation Bible School and invited me to attend.

We had loads of fun making crafts, listening to stories, and doing all the neat stuff kids do at VBS.

At the end of the week the pastor came in and asked us if we wanted to join his church. Everyone had been so kind, and I'd had such a great time, that I said, "Sure." He gave me a paper to fill out and suggested that I check with my parents before making a final decision.

When I showed the paper to my dad and told him what I wanted to do, he took me aside and sat me down for a man-to-man talk. "I'm glad you want to join," he said, "but don't you want to be a member of a church that obeys *all* the Ten Commandments?"

"Of course," I nodded.

"Did you know that this church doesn't keep the Bible Sabbath holy? Are you aware they teach that God is going to burn sinners forever and ever? And how about the fact that they say when you die, you go straight to heaven or hell? That's not what the Bible says."

I was shocked. How could I join a church that doesn't preach Bible truth? So I waited a few more years and found the perfect church. It was the same one I'd been attending all my life. I became, and still am, a Seventh-day Adventist.

AUGUST
28

How do you tell your friend that he or she is doing something wrong?
—*Veronica, 13, Florida*

Pointing out a friend's error is a touchy situation. Done incorrectly, it can turn a person off religiously for years. Done right, it can change a life for the better.

Let's see how Jesus handled His friends. Acts 10:38 says, *"[He] went about doing good, and healing all that were oppressed of the devil; for God was with him."*

First, we have to make sure we're not committing the same sin as our friend. If this person is abusing his or her body with drugs, we can't come to him or her with a can of pop in one hand and a chocolate bar in the other. If a companion is using God's name in vain, we must always speak the words "Jesus" and "God" with reverence. See what I mean?

For human beings like us, going about "doing good" doesn't mean we're perfect. It means our friends see us trying seriously to live up to the biblical truths we teach.

How do we "heal all that are oppressed"? By forgiving and loving them. Jesus said, *"[The Father] hath sent me to heal the broken-hearted" (Luke 4:18)*. He wasn't talking about a physical broken heart. He was talking about people who were broken by guilt and shame. Forgiveness and love have great healing powers.

Finally, introduce your friend to Jesus by demonstrating His character in your life. What you're aiming to do takes commitment, Veronica. But if you follow these steps, your friend may choose to listen to your advice, and change.

Why do some Christians believe that it's wrong to dance?

—Heather, 13, Montana

There was a lot of dancing in the Bible. King David said, *"Thou hast turned for me my mourning into dancing"* (Psalm 30:11). Solomon suggested there is *"a time to weep, and a time to laugh; a time to mourn, and a time to dance"* (Ecclesiastes 3:4).

The text that has the best answer for your question is found in Psalm 149:3. It urges, *"Let them praise his name in the dance."*

Combine this with the verse that says, *"Whether therefore ye eat, or drink, or whatsoever ye do, do all to the glory of God"* (1 Corinthians 10:31), and you've found the answer to your question.

Many Christians, and I include myself in this group, feel that most types of dancing do anything but glorify God. As a matter of fact, they turn minds away from Him and generate impure thoughts and spark immoral imaginings. Many dances are nothing more than thinly veiled sex acts. I think you know what I mean.

I hasten to add that many cultures, ours included, have dances that do glorify God, or nature, or love in its purer forms. Watch a Native American dance his or her respect for the earth, peek at a child jumping for joy, witness a young married couple holding each other close and moving slowly to the beat of their future dreams, and you see dancing as God intended.

Heather, do you want to dance? Then make your dance an expression of love and respect for God and His creation.

Why are people in the church so critical?

—Student, 15, Oklahoma

Because they don't have Jesus in their hearts. Critical people need our love and prayers because they're holding on to a character flaw that will keep them out of heaven.

Through the years I've had to deal with many critical people. What I found was that most had perfectly valid concerns and ideas, but didn't know how to express themselves properly. Perhaps no one had ever listened to them or taken them seriously before. So they began loading their words with anger.

More important than why the church contains critical people is what you and I are going to do about it. Solomon has some great suggestions. He says, *"A soft answer turneth away wrath: but grievous words stir up anger" (Proverbs 15:1).* Whenever you give your opinion about something, use soft words, not angry ones. That's the correct way to respond to criticism, too.

Solomon also states, *"Pleasant words are as an honeycomb, sweet to the soul, and health to the bones" (Proverbs 16:24).* When someone is critical of you, don't turn around and be critical of him or her. Go to that person and ask for advice. This does two things: It snuffs out their anger like water on a fire, and also gives you an opportunity to learn something. Remember, critical people aren't stupid. They're just not very good communicators.

Solomon says, *"The words of a man's mouth are as deep waters" (Proverbs 18:4).* Critical people may want to drown you. But now you know how to swim!

AUGUST

31

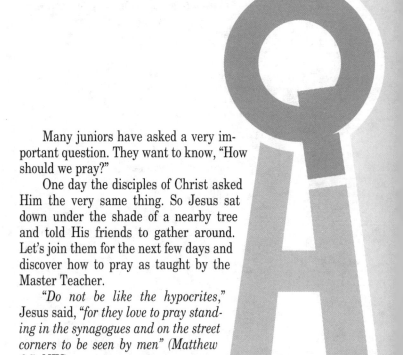

Many juniors have asked a very important question. They want to know, "How should we pray?"

One day the disciples of Christ asked Him the very same thing. So Jesus sat down under the shade of a nearby tree and told His friends to gather around. Let's join them for the next few days and discover how to pray as taught by the Master Teacher.

"*Do not be like the hypocrites,*" Jesus said, "*for they love to pray standing in the synagogues and on the street corners to be seen by men*" *(Matthew 6:5, NIV).*

SEPTEMBER 1

The disciples nodded their agreement. They'd seen people stand up in church and give prayers that went on and on forever. It seemed like they wanted to make sure everyone knew how smart and righteous they were.

"*When you pray,*" Jesus continued, "*go into your room, close the door and pray to your Father. . . . And when you pray, do not keep on babbling like pagans, for they think they will be heard because of their many words*" *(verses 6, 7, NIV).*

Prayer is a private communication between the speaker and God. When we pray aloud in public, like at church or school, our words should glorify Christ, not draw attention to ourselves. Simple requests and heartfelt praises are always best.

But in the privacy of our own rooms we can take our time and talk as long as we want to our heavenly Friend.

What Jesus said next may surprise you!

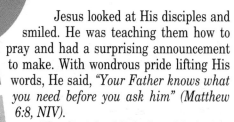

Jesus looked at His disciples and smiled. He was teaching them how to pray and had a surprising announcement to make. With wondrous pride lifting His words, He said, *"Your Father knows what you need before you ask him" (Matthew 6:8, NIV).*

The disciples blinked and looked at one another. "Wait a minute," I can hear them say. "We thought we had to bring God up-to-date on our troubles; you know, tell Him how a friend said unkind words to us, or how the tax collector cheated our business, or how we're afraid of this or afraid of that."

Jesus listened to His disciples speak, then He raised His hand. "Your Father knows what you need before you ask Him," He kindly repeated, letting His words sink in slowly.

One by one His hearers began to nod. "Of course, God knows," they whispered among themselves. "He knows everything. God sees the sparrow fall. He hears the cry of children from beds of sickness. He knows when hearts are breaking and when hands shake for fear. Our Father doesn't have to be told what He already knows. That's not what prayer is for."

Jesus gazed down at His disciples. *"This, then, is how you should pray [verse 9, NIV],"* He said, getting ready to begin.

Now He had everyone's attention. They wanted to know exactly what they were supposed to say to a God who knows everything.

Jesus closed His eyes. "Our Father in heaven," He stated.

The disciples may have snickered. Why would anybody have to say that? Didn't the God who knew everything know where He lived?

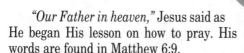

"*Our Father in heaven,*" Jesus said as He began His lesson on how to pray. His words are found in Matthew 6:9.

Juniors, I've visited many countries in this world. I've seen some pretty incredible things. But nothing prepared me for a sight I saw in the Philippines years and years ago. A certain religious sect in that country believes that if they hurt themselves, the god they worship will forgive their sins.

So they gather together once a year for a great festival. They eat, drink, and then do something horrible. One by one men have metal fishhooks pressed into the flesh of their chests and backs. On these hooks they hang heavy weights or attach themselves to wooden carts by long wires. Then they pull the carts and carry the weights as the hooks tear into their skin.

Others beat their own backs with whips embedded with razor-sharp pieces of glass. I think you get the picture.

By beginning our prayers with "Our Father in *heaven,*" we're reminding ourselves of exactly which God we worship. He doesn't live in a mountain, as some people in Peru insist. He doesn't work out of a tree or rock, as others in the Amazon Basin will tell you. He lives in heaven. The way we communicate with Him is not in bloody ritual or painful sacrifices. We bow and pray. He hears every word, and forgives simply because we ask.

"*Our Father in heaven, hallowed be your name,*" Jesus said softly (verse 9, NIV). The disciples frowned. Not everyone spoke the name of God with reverence. Is it important that we hallow even the *name* of God?

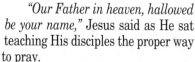

"Our Father in heaven, hallowed be your name," Jesus said as He sat teaching His disciples the proper way to pray.

This statement in Matthew 6:9 carries a lot of importance for us today. If you spend 10 minutes watching a sitcom on television or a movie rented from the local video store, you're more than likely going to hear someone speak God's name in a very *un*hallowed way. Why? Because those actors and scriptwriters don't recognize the power and majesty wrapped around the beautiful name of God. To them, it's only a curse word, or a way of getting a laugh. Christians shouldn't laugh at such language.

Your name is important to you, isn't it? You want people to be respectful when they include it in conversation. How a person says your name is an indication of their feelings for you.

When you say the name "Jesus," or "God," picture in your mind the Ones those words represent, and what They've done and are doing for you. Jesus died for your sins. God is preparing a glorious new home for you in heaven.

"Hallowed be your name," Jesus repeated, His face radiant with love and respect for the power behind the name.

The disciples nodded in agreement. In the back of their minds they were remembering the command their nation had heard generations ago at Mount Sinai. From the billowing smoke and flashing fires at the summit, God's voice had called out, *"You shall not misuse the name of the Lord your God, for the Lord will not hold anyone guiltless who misuses his name" (Exodus 20:7, NIV).*

It was important then. It's important now. God's name is holy.

SEPTEMBER

4

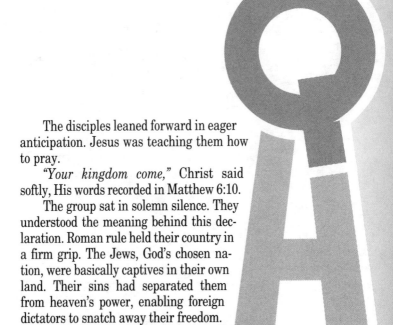

The disciples leaned forward in eager anticipation. Jesus was teaching them how to pray.

"Your kingdom come," Christ said softly, His words recorded in Matthew 6:10.

The group sat in solemn silence. They understood the meaning behind this declaration. Roman rule held their country in a firm grip. The Jews, God's chosen nation, were basically captives in their own land. Their sins had separated them from heaven's power, enabling foreign dictators to snatch away their freedom.

The disciples, their friends, and neighbors had longed for the promised Messiah to come. Jesus was that Messiah, but few recognized the fact. They figured the coming king would overthrow their enemies, not say we should love them. They hoped their promised leader would live in a palace, not sleep under the stars. In their minds, the new kingdom would rule the earth, not preach humbleness and forgiveness.

Juniors, what do you expect God's kingdom to be like when it sets itself up in your heart? Perhaps you're looking for sudden relief from sin and temptation. Maybe you're hoping for a grand life filled with miracles, where everything works out in your favor. If this is what you're hoping for, your disappointment will be as great as that felt by the Jews of Christ's time.

But when you say "Your kingdom come," and you understand that you're inviting God to help you fight sin and discover ways to survive this life, then you're praying as Jesus prayed.

Jesus continued His lesson on how to pray. He told His disciples to say, *"Your will be done on earth as it is in heaven"* *(Matthew 6:10, NIV).*

Ever heard people say "That was God's will"? What they're really saying is, "I'm not sure why that happened, but God must've been behind it."

God's will gets blamed for a lot of stuff, from airplane accidents and hurricanes to new jobs and even marriages. People say "It was God's will that I do this or go there." But Jesus was inviting His Father's will to be done on earth as it is in heaven, where there are no airplanes, hurricanes, jobs, and marriages. What did He mean?

The disciples asked the same question. Here was Christ's answer: *"For my Father's will is that everyone who looks to the Son and believes in him shall have eternal life" (John 6:40, NIV).* We can sum up God's will in four words: He wants us saved.

Many times while I was growing up, my father would say, "Charles, the most important thing in life is getting to heaven." That was his will for me. That's God's will for all of us, too.

By including this little phrase in your next prayer, you're asking God to place in your heart a desire to be saved.

Having a hard time at home or school? Do you get discouraged or frightened? Say to God, "Your will be done on earth as it is in heaven." Then start enjoying a new excitement for the future, and a deeper determination to be saved. Make God's will and your will the same.

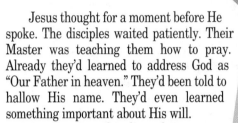

Jesus thought for a moment before He spoke. The disciples waited patiently. Their Master was teaching them how to pray. Already they'd learned to address God as "Our Father in heaven." They'd been told to hallow His name. They'd even learned something important about His will.

Jesus continued with another suggestion. He told them to say, *"Give us today our daily bread" (Matthew 6:11, NIV).*

Wait a minute. Our daily bread? The disciples gasped. Hadn't they read Psalm 50:10 just a week ago, which stated, *"For every animal of the forest is mine, and the cattle on a thousand hills" (NIV)?* How about some feasts thrown in for good measure? What would a few parties hurt? Was Jesus suggesting that all we could expect from our heavenly Father was daily bread? Big deal!

My dad has probably saved me thousands of dollars by giving me a really good piece of advice. He said, "When you're standing in a store looking at something you want to buy, don't ask, 'Do I want this?' Don't even say 'Do I need this?' Just ask yourself, 'Can I possibly get along without this?'" It's amazing how much in life I've discovered I can get along without.

I believe Jesus understood this fact. When He told His disciples to ask God for their daily bread, He was saying that when we ask God for stuff, it should be for those things we absolutely must have to survive. Anything beyond that, we're free to work hard and earn for ourselves.

Ask for daily bread, and God will deliver every time.

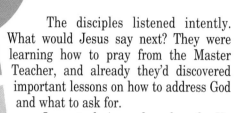

The disciples listened intently. What would Jesus say next? They were learning how to pray from the Master Teacher, and already they'd discovered important lessons on how to address God and what to ask for.

Jesus took in a deep breath. He knew this next part would be difficult for some to accept. *"Forgive us our debts,"* He said in Matthew 6:12, *"as we also have forgiven our debtors"* (NIV).

Some of the disciples squirmed. Forgiving those who did unkind or even mean things to them was hard. They had their pride. But here was their Master telling them that unless they forgave others, God wouldn't forgive them for their wrong doings.

Have you ever had someone do something thoughtless to you? Perhaps a classmate told a lie that got you into trouble. Maybe a friend didn't stick up for you when you needed him or her most, or said harsh words that turned others against you. According to Jesus, you have to truly—from the heart—forgive that person before God can forgive you your sins.

One of the disciples in the group must have learned a valuable lesson from hearing what Jesus had to say about prayer. He later wrote, *"Be merciful, just as your Father is merciful. . . . Forgive, and you will be forgiven"* (Luke 6:36, 37, NIV).

When we pray as Jesus taught, there can be no room in our hearts for vengeance and anger. God knows that only when we forgive others will we appreciate the powerful love He's demonstrating when He forgives us.

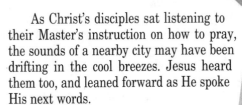

As Christ's disciples sat listening to their Master's instruction on how to pray, the sounds of a nearby city may have been drifting in the cool breezes. Jesus heard them too, and leaned forward as He spoke His next words.

"And lead us not into temptation," He said as recorded in Matthew 6:13, NIV.

What did He mean by this surprising statement? Can God actually keep us from being tempted?

When I was a boy, my dad was our family's TV policeman. Whenever a program became too violent, whenever a musical selection became too "jazzy" or wild, whenever a love scene got too steamy, Dad would get up from his chair, walk across the room, and turn off the set with a determined *click*. "That's not something we should be looking at," he'd say. I accepted my father's word on this. After all, he was older and wiser. His judgment was more mature. If he said it was bad, it was bad.

My father was keeping temptation at bay. He was not allowing me to be influenced by the evil flickering on the television screen. Even today, if a program or video I'm watching strays from the high standard my father set for me, I reach for the remote control and zap the images off the screen.

When we pray the Lord's Prayer, we're asking God to lead us away from temptation by teaching us right from wrong. For the disciples, it was the lure of the city whose distant sounds echoed in the cool breezes. For us it can be something as innocent as a television screen.

What Jesus said next in His how-to-pray lesson made everyone's head nod in total agreement. With seven simple words, our Saviour highlighted the greatest need of every human heart.

Just after He said, *"And lead us not into temptation,"* Jesus added, *"but deliver us from the evil one" (Matthew 6:13, NIV).*

Boy, do we need this sentence in our prayers!

I once had a friend named Greg. He was hilariously funny, smart as a scholar, could cook like the best chefs anywhere, a hard worker, and honest. He was also a homosexual.

Several years ago Greg died of AIDS. I was told that his family was right there by his side, speaking words of love and comfort as he slipped away. What a tragedy. But when my friend made a choice to live as a homosexual, he placed himself at a greater risk of contracting AIDS. He didn't allow God to deliver him from an evil that all of us can easily avoid. Greg paid for his choice with his life.

When we pray "Deliver us from evil," and then faithfully follow God's leading, we're protecting ourselves from the *results* of that evil, too. With God at our side, we can bypass many of the problems that plague society. Think about it. If we as individuals and as nations allowed the power of God to reign in our lives, there'd be no wars, no innocent children shot in the streets, no car bombings or hijackings. Wouldn't our world be a much better place to live?

God longs to deliver us from evil. But first we must ask for help, then allow Him to keep His word by our choices.

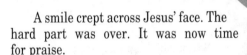

A smile crept across Jesus' face. The hard part was over. It was now time for praise.

He was teaching His disciples how to pray. They'd learned how to address their heavenly Father, what to ask for, and what their responsibilities were.

Now I can imagine Jesus lifting His hands as He said, *"For thine is the kingdom, and the power, and the glory, for ever. Amen" (Matthew 6:13).*

"Amen!" the disciples repeated as in one voice.

Do you know how to praise God? You might be surprised at how easy it is. The songs you sing in Sabbath school and church—that's praise. Whenever you marvel at the beauty of nature and recognize by whose hand everything was made, that's praise. Each time you say "I love you" to a family member or special friend, that's praise. And whenever you speak God's name with reverence and affection, that's praise, too.

As the disciples sat thinking about what Jesus had told them, I imagine that slowly, one by one, they closed their eyes and bowed their heads. There, with the world and its temptations all around them, with minds that had known fear and anger, with the uncertainty familiar to all human hearts, they prayed. But now they knew the words to speak that would help lift their concerns to a God who was eager to hear and respond.

The next time you pray, use Matthew 6:9-13 as your guide. Tell your heavenly Father what's on your heart. The more time you spend with Him, the easier the words will come.

Is God like a bright light?

—*Michael, 10, California*

How many times have you been told "Don't look at the sun"? Allow me to add my voice to that chorus. "Michael, don't look at the sun." Why? Because it's so bright it can do permanent damage to your eyes if you sit there like an idiot and gaze at it. Not a good idea, but a terrific lesson about God.

There are some things our feeble human eyes simply can't look at because they've been weakened by generations of disease and harmed by endless exposure to pollutants.

It didn't used to be this way. God the Creator and Adam were once close friends. *"Now the Lord God had formed out of the ground all the beasts of the field and all the birds of the air. He brought them to the man to see what he would name them" (Genesis 2:19, NIV).* No bright light here. Just friends.

Some time later, Adam and Eve *"heard the sound of the Lord God as he was walking in the garden in the cool of the day. . . . God called to the man, 'Where are you?'" (Genesis 3:8, 9, NIV).* Seems Jesus used to walk and talk with His newly formed friends. No lightning or ground rumblings going on here, either.

You see, Michael, sin did more than separate us from God. It weakened our eyes to the point where we can't even look at His kind, loving face without being destroyed by His perfect power. But this will change. Paul says, *"now we see through a glass, darkly; but then [when Jesus comes] face to face" (1 Corinthians 13:12).* I can hardly wait to see God's loving, life-giving smile!

SEPTEMBER 12

Why did God choose Mary to be the mother of Jesus?

—Ashley, 11, New York

The answer to your question is hidden in a little verse recorded in the New Testament.

The Bible says, *"God sent the angel Gabriel to Nazareth, a town in Galilee, to a virgin pledged to be married to a man named Joseph"* *(Luke 1:26, 27, NIV).* Mary, the engaged virgin, looked up one day, and there stood an angel in her doorway—not exactly a common sight. "Greetings," said Gabriel. "You're highly favored."

Mary was also highly scared. After Gabriel had calmed her down a bit, he launched into his message. *"You will be with child and give birth to a son, and you are to give him the name Jesus. He will be great and will be called the Son of the Most High"* *(verses 31, 32, NIV).*

The woman blinked. *"'How will this be,' Mary asked the angel, 'since I am a virgin?'"* *(verse 34, NIV).*

Good point. Virgins engaged to be married aren't supposed to suddenly show up pregnant.

After explaining how the Holy Ghost would make it happen, the angel stood waiting for her response. Now, here comes the answer to your question: *"'I am the Lord's servant,' Mary answered. 'May it be to me as you have said'"* *(verse 38, NIV).*

Why did God choose Mary? Because she was willing to put personal feelings and the fear of tongue-wagging neighbors aside, and allow Him to work a miracle in her.

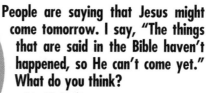

People are saying that Jesus might come tomorrow. I say, "The things that are said in the Bible haven't happened, so He can't come yet." What do you think?

—*Erin, 12, Washington*

Whenever someone tries to tell me that God's hands are tied by prophecies, I remind them of Nineveh.

After Jonah's run-in with the great fish (we assume it was some sort of whale), he continued on to the evil city of Nineveh, the place God had directed him to go originally. There he delivered these stern, prophetic words: *"Forty more days and Nineveh will be overturned" (Jonah 3:4, NIV).*

The Bible records that *"the Ninevites believed God. They declared a fast, and all of them, from the greatest to the least, put on sackcloth"* (verse 5, NIV). Even the king himself sent out a decree calling for everyone to repent.

Listen carefully to what happened next. *"When God saw what they did and how they turned from their evil ways, he had compassion and did not bring upon them the destruction he had threatened" (verse 10, NIV).*

We know God's promises are conditional. So, it seems, are His prophecies. If this is true, the things that are said in the Bible concerning Christ's second coming will come to pass if—*if*—we as a people remain in our sins and refuse to surrender our lives to God.

Could Jesus come tomorrow? I believe He could, in spite of fulfilled or unfulfilled prophecies. What could change His mind? The same thing that changed it at Nineveh—repentance of His people and a worldwide turning from sin.

What happens to us when we die?
—*Vanosdale, 11, Florida*

Years ago I worked at Faith for Today, our church's longest-running television ministry. We were filming a documentary on the subject of suicide, and we paid a visit to a very unsettling place—the Los Angeles coroner's office.

Several portions of the show were shot in the morgue (the place where dead people are brought for processing before being handed over to funeral homes or other agencies for burial). I probably saw more than 100 corpses that day, some waiting to be identified by relatives, some undergoing autopsies to find out how they died, and others lined up on gurneys along the hallways waiting to be studied.

After seeing all those bodies lying around like abandoned shells on a seashore, I began to see how useless we are without God's breath of life in us. We're just a collection of tissue and bone. Nothing more.

But when God breathes into our nostrils the breath of life as He did for Adam (see Genesis 2:7), we become alive. Our arms move, legs kick, heart beats, lips smile, voice speaks, lungs expand, eyes blink, toes wiggle—everything that makes us who we are comes with that glorious rush of air.

The moment we die, that breath (or ability to live) returns to God, who gave it. Our bodies eventually crumble into useless piles of dust. But don't worry. On that wonderful day God will breathe again. And so will we.

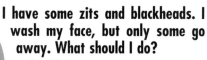

I have some zits and blackheads. I wash my face, but only some go away. What should I do?
—*Boy, 12, Montana*

Skin problems seem to be a way of life for most teenagers. It's not enough that you have to deal with parents, school, relationships, and religion. Now you must fight blemishes.

Let me say, without going into a lot of detail about acne, what's worked for many teens over the years. Don't think you can do just one or two of these things and solve your problem. You have to do *all* of them continually for the rest of your life.

1. Drink lots of water. Water flushes your system of impurities, many of which try to escape through your face.

2. Cut *way* back on sweets. While being processed in your body, refined sugar uses up the same vitamins and minerals that your skin needs to stay healthy.

3. Keep your skin clean by scrubbing it daily. Pores need to breathe. If they get clogged, blackheads develop. A flexible, rough cloth helps get the job done.

4. Eat mostly foods your body can digest and eliminate easily. Raw fruits, vegetables, along with legumes (beans) and nuts keep things moving in your bowels, holding back the development of toxins that may seek escape through your skin.

Remember, there is absolutely no cream, pill, or medicated makeup that beats consistent health practices. And if you think it's uncool to munch a salad occasionally while everyone else is scarfing down french fries, glance in the mirror. Enough said.

SEPTEMBER 16

What's wrong with going to the movies?
—*Melissa, 15, Oklahoma*

Let's take a close look at moviegoing.

Is it the building that's evil? Hardly. Movie houses are made of cement, mortar, steel, glass, and wood. Your house is made of the very same materials.

How about the seats, big screen, projector, or popcorn? Afraid not. Nothing evil here.

Perhaps it's the movie itself? Wait a minute. You're going to tell me that *Lassie, Come Home* or *The Sound of Music* is going to make me lose my eternal soul? Get real!

So what is wrong with going to the movies? Absolutely nothing. The same can be said about playing hide-and-seek with a rattlesnake or putting together a homemade bomb. Neither one of these activities is a sin. They're just potentially destructive.

To me, the greatest problem with most movies is that they glorify sin and rebellion. Through colorful, exciting images, Satan finds a direct path to our minds. We hear words we shouldn't hear, see sights we shouldn't see, feel emotions that don't generate pure, unselfish love.

The apostle Paul suggests, *"Whatsoever things are true, . . . honest, . . . just, . . . pure, . . . lovely, . . . of good report; if there be any virtue, and if there be any praise, think on these things" (Philippians 4:8).*

A movie can turn an innocent room into the devil's playground. It can do the same thing to your mind.

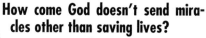

How come God doesn't send miracles other than saving lives?
—*Danny, 11, California*

Good news, Danny. God does send miracles! Most people simply don't recognize them.

Listen to this rather frightening Bible verse: *"Your enemy the devil prowls around like a roaring lion looking for someone to devour"* (1 Peter 5:8, NIV). Romans 6:23 warns that *"the wages of sin is death."*

Devour? Death? Not a pleasant thought. Haven't you ever sinned, Danny? I know I have. The Bible says, *"For all have sinned, and come short of the glory of God"* (Romans 3:23). But you're not dead. I'm not dead. Why? Because of a miracle.

You see, the devil would have us in constant pain, constant turmoil, and constantly dead. Anything, ANYTHING other than dead is a miracle from God.

The fact that you can learn interesting stuff at school is a miracle. When your mom or dad does something that makes you laugh and laugh, that's a miracle. When you feel love for an animal or person, when you enjoy your favorite food, when you feel the cool breezes of summer or soak in the warmth of a crackling winter fire, those are miracles, too.

Paul says, *"I pray that you may be active in sharing your faith, so that you will have a full understanding of every good thing we have in Christ"* (Philemon 6, NIV).

Danny, the next time you take in a breath or experience joy, remember that you've received yet another miracle from God.

Why do people fall out of love?
—*Girl, 13, Maine*

Because they choose to. Love isn't something that runs on automatic like a dishwasher or heat pump. It takes constant, prayerful, serious attention in order to survive.

I'm sure you've had feelings of love. You've probably lost some of those feelings over time because of circumstances, many beyond your control. Things change. You change.

However, there comes a time when love is supposed to last, no matter what changes take place in life. It's called marriage. When you say "I do," you're saying a mouthful. Before God and witnesses, you're promising to keep love alive no matter what— sickness, health, adversity, poverty, wealth, good and bad times.

Couples fall out of love before marriage for many reasons. They find they're not compatible, realize that circumstances won't allow their love to grow and mature, discover they weren't in love in the first place, or become strongly attracted to someone new. They choose to move on.

Couples fall out of love after marriage because one or both have allowed their weaknesses or fears to interfere with the love-growing, love-protecting process. This time, a sacred promise is broken as well. They've stopped choosing to love.

"For where you have envy and selfish ambition, there you find disorder and every evil practice," says Paul in James 3:16, NIV. And there, we might add, you also find love on the rocks.

When you decide to love, allow it to grow. When you *promise* to love, refuse to let it die!

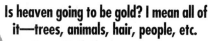

Is heaven going to be gold? I mean all of it—trees, animals, hair, people, etc.

—*Danny, 13, Florida*

Here's how John the revelator describes the heaven he saw in vision. We're looking in Revelation 21.

The walls around the New Jerusalem were jasper and *"the city was pure gold, like unto clear glass" (verse 18)*. Its foundation was *"garnished with all manner of precious stones" (verse 19)*. Pearls formed the 12 gates and *"the street of the city was pure gold, as it were transparent glass" (verse 21)*.

Sounds beautiful, doesn't it? And to think we'll someday live there. *Wow!*

In chapter 22 John describes other scenes. He speaks of *"the river of the water of life, as clear as crystal" (verse 1, NIV)*. Arching over this waterway he saw *"the tree of life, bearing twelve crops of fruit, yielding its fruit every month" (verse 2, NIV)*.

Isaiah was allowed to peek into the future, too. He discovered that *"the wolf also shall dwell with the lamb, and the leopard shall lie down with the kid; and the calf and the young lion and the fatling together; and a little child shall lead them" (Isaiah 11:6)*.

We won't be living in an all-gold country, Danny. But there'll be plenty of it around for us to enjoy. Like here on earth, we'll have colors and textures and sights to bring us happiness. One difference—in heaven they'll never fade.

Why are parents so strict?
—*Jason, 13, Montana*

My first reaction is to say "Because they love you." But strictness may not always come from love alone. It can also grow out of fear, or uncertainty, or even anger.

Most parents haven't a clue how to raise a child. I know I wouldn't. There's no instruction manual attached to our big toes at birth. We're just plopped into our parents' lives, red-faced and hollering, leaving them to raise us as best they can.

So they ask around for advice, read a few books, pray a lot, and cross their fingers. You'll find parents to be strictest in those areas that cause them the most fear or uncertainty. Like the old saying goes: "A sweater is something a child wears when its mom is cold." Parents often raise their offspring the way they feel *they themselves* needed to be raised. And herein lies a potential problem. They end up raising the wrong kid.

The best way for you, or any son or daughter, to ease the "strictness" of your home environment is to be totally open and honest with your parents. Show them who you are inside. Share your feelings. The less mystery that surrounds you, the more trust you'll generate with good old Mom and Pop.

Solomon, who was a dad more times than he cared to admit, says, *"My son, if your heart is wise, then my heart will be glad; my inmost being will rejoice when your lips speak what is right" (Proverbs 23:15, NIV).*

The more your parents understand you, the less fear, uncertainty, and anger will exist. Try it.

How can all bad things that happen work out to good?
—*Paula, 15, Oklahoma*

I believe you're referring to this much discussed but little understood Bible verse. The King James Version reads: *"And we know that all things work together for good to them that love God, to them who are the called according to his purpose" (Romans 8:28).* The New International Version translates it this way: *"And we know that in all things God works for the good of those who love him, who have been called according to his purpose."*

There's something you need to understand, Paula. God does not *cause* bad things to happen. He *allows* them. If you jump out of an airplane at 30,000 feet without a parachute, you're going to die because God allows the laws of physics to operate even when you do something foolish.

Also notice that according to the verse we have just read, good-from-bad happens only to certain types of people—those who love and obey God.

So how can all bad things that happen work out to be good? They can't, unless you trust the God who allows them, and choose daily to love and obey Him. Then, and only then, can bad things become lessons of survival or even stepping-stones to a better life. Bad events can serve to draw you closer to Jesus, making you more and more dependent on Him. Under these conditions, He can guide you, encourage you, save you.

David said, *"Yea, though I walk through the valley of the shadow of death, I will fear no evil: for thou art with me" (Psalm 23:4).* Good can come from bad only when we walk with God.

Is there life in space?
—*Ruben, 11, California*

You mean other than God, the angels, the perfect beings on other planets, the animals waiting in heaven, and the numberless worlds filled with beautiful forests, mountain lakes, rivers, and meadows? Probably not.

We humans have a very narrow view of the universe. We look through our telescopes and see exploding suns, stars going nova, rings of poisonous gases, boiling oceans of fire, and huge dry, dusty moons circling dead-looking heavenly bodies. Yuck!

But beyond our feeble gaze, farther than our most powerful lenses can see, wait solar systems filled with life, filled with intelligence, filled with excitement.

We mustn't get the idea that we're all there is out there. Although we're nothing but an oxygen-and-water-saturated speck floating in space, we're God's speck, and that makes all the difference.

Ruben, someday you're going to travel beyond the horizons of even your wildest dreams. After we reach heaven, you'll be free to wander for eternity throughout God's limitless space. What you'll find won't scare you or cause you one moment of pain. Instead you'll be dazzled by sights unimagined, make new friends on worlds not even thought about on Earth, and get to know the universe like you know your own bedroom.

For a change of scenery, head on back to the new earth. We'll sit under a shade tree, and you can tell me all about your journeys, and about the life you found beyond your dreams.

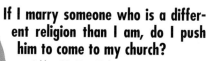

If I marry someone who is a different religion than I am, do I push him to come to my church?

—*Ashley, 11, New York*

Ashley, I'm going to make a suggestion. If you follow it, you'll save yourself much grief, frustration, guilt, and anger. I'm serious here. Don't take what I'm about to say lightly. I've got too much proof to back me up.

Here goes, and please hear me out. Don't even *think* about marrying someone whose religion is different from yours.

When a Methodist marries a Baptist, or a Catholic marries someone who belongs to the Church of Christ, the differences in beliefs aren't terribly great. There are a few methods of worship, a few ideas about God that don't quite mesh, but the situation is usually workable.

However, when a Seventh-day Adventist marries a non-Adventist, the differences are huge! Most non-SDA spouses will quickly start insisting, "It doesn't matter on which day you worship. God isn't concerned about doctrine. He just wants us to love Him. Right?"

Wrong! God does want us to love Him. He also asks that we *obey* Him, as well. That means keeping all the commandments and taking seriously Bible doctrines.

When you watch your husband or wife willfully breaking several of God's beautiful commandments week after week, one of two things happens: You try to push your spouse into your church, which never works, or you find yourself losing your faith and starting to believe that it really doesn't matter. It does.

If I marry someone who is a different religion than I am, do I push him to come to my church?"

—Ashley, 11, New York

Yesterday we discovered the dangers hiding in interreligion marriages. Now let's consider a different slant.

Ashley, what if you were already married, and one fine day you decide to *become* a Seventh-day Adventist? You've learned about God's plan of salvation, how He wants His people to be different from the rest of the world by keeping *all* His commandments. You've discovered God's desire that we obey Him as well as love Him (actually, to love Him is to obey Him). How do you convince your husband that he too should start living with the Bible as his guide?

Do you stomp your foot and say "Come to church or I'll leave you for good"? Do you stand on the kitchen table and preach the Word day after day? Do you buy him videos and tons of cassette tapes that proclaim Bible truth?

Of course not. You do what Jesus did. Simply put, He made religion *attractive*. While everyone else was worried and frightened, He kept saying, *"Peace be unto you" (Luke 24:36)*. While everyone else spoke unkindly of their neighbors, Jesus showed respect, even for sinners. *"Love one another,"* He said in John 13:34. *"As I have loved you, so you must love one another" (NIV)*. While everyone else cheated in business and disobeyed the laws of the land, Jesus insisted, *"Give to Caesar what is Caesar's, and to God what is God's" (Matthew 22:21, NIV)*.

Jesus lived His religion. He made it attractive and satisfying. This has always been the most effective witness.

Will I be in heaven?

—John, 11, Florida

I once had a dream. I was standing on a mountaintop watching the Second Coming. There was Jesus, and the angels, lots of clouds, and even someone blowing a trumpet.

Everyone around me started rising up into the air, happy smiles on their faces. I waited . . . and waited . . . and nothing happened. I kind of gave a little jump, you know, to get my journey to heaven started, but it didn't work. Suddenly I realized that I wasn't going to go.

With terrible sadness I sat down on a rock and began to cry. I woke up and found warm tears on my cheeks. Boy, was I glad that was just a dream!

Since then I've discovered something wonderful about God, and something terrible about Satan. God wants us to look forward to our new home with eager anticipation. Satan wants us to keep asking the question "Will I be in heaven?" *He's* the one who makes us doubt. *He's* the one who planted that horrible thought in my mind that turned into a frightening dream.

John, you and I must fight such fearful ideas. We've got to say to ourselves, "I've given my life to Jesus, and He's building a mansion for me. The decision has *already been made*. I'll be in heaven because Jesus paid for my ticket with His own blood. As long as I allow God to teach me new things from my mistakes, as long as I recognize that Jesus' perfect life makes up for my imperfect one, heaven is my future home." Forget doubts. Forget dreams. Remember Jesus.

I like girls. But if I like one, I can't talk straight to her face. I'm always so shy. What do I do?
—*Todd, 12, Montana*

Hey, Todd, how many times have you fallen in love, gotten married, had children, and grown old with a girl?

Never done any of that, huh? Then don't be surprised that the feelings that launch all of the above tend to leave you speechless. You're beginning to outgrow childhood.

Love is the most powerful emotion on earth. Nothing else even comes close. You're simply being overwhelmed by new and mysterious feelings you've never experienced. That girl, who for years was just a friend, suddenly looks different. Strange emotions tickle your gut. Same girl. New you.

Don't be concerned. Shyness isn't a character flaw. My wife is shy. I'm not. We get along great!

Maybe you can do what my wife did before we got married. Because she was so shy and made me do most of the talking when we were together, she wrote beautiful letters and notes to me. Almost every week I'd get a colorful card from her saying, in picture and rhyme, what she couldn't say in words. I still have those letters. I dig them out and read them occasionally, much to her embarrassment. She's still shy.

Speaking isn't the only way to communicate. Put your artistic talents to work. Draw pictures, write a letter, create a card, or (the perennial favorite) buy her something. Who knows, you just may leave *her* speechless!

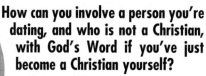

How can you involve a person you're dating, and who is not a Christian, with God's Word if you've just become a Christian yourself?
—*Elsie, 16, Oklahoma*

Recently I wrote a story about this very situation. It involved two young people, one in Tennessee, the other in Saudi Arabia.

The Gulf War was about to begin. Steve Schultz, a safety technician in the Air Force, found a letter from Kim Manning lying among many such notes and cards in the "friends from home" barrel. He responded. Soon they were writing regularly.

Steve had little interest in religion. Kim was a Seventh-day Adventist who was trying to find her way back to God.

Several times Kim mentioned something about her faith. Steve began asking questions, which made Kim study harder in order to answer them. As she grew closer to her heavenly Father, she couldn't help sharing her newfound happiness and confidence. The more excited she became, the more Steve wanted to know what was causing it.

To make a long story short, after the war they met face-to-face and confirmed that they were head over heels in love with each other. Steve joined the Adventist Church through baptism, they got married, and are now facing the future together, strong in love, strong in Christian faith.

Elsie, dig in and get to know Jesus better. Let God's love so fill your life that your friend will want to know Him too. Whatever you do, don't lose your grip on faith. Romance is nice. But don't trade eternal life for it.

SEPTEMBER

28

Why did Cain kill his brother Abel?
—*Lillian, 10, California*

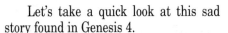

Let's take a quick look at this sad story found in Genesis 4.

We discover that Abel was a shepherd, while Cain was a gardener—both noble occupations. God blessed one with healthy animals, the other with rich soil.

In order to remind earth's inhabitants that someday Jesus would die for their sins, God asked everyone to offer a lamb for a sacrifice. Everyone did, except Cain. He figured a sacrifice is a sacrifice. Why slaughter a perfectly healthy lamb when he had tons of fruit hanging from the trees in his orchard?

The Bible says, *"The Lord looked with favor on Abel and his offering, but on Cain and his offering he did not look with favor" (verses 4, 5, NIV).* Cain got really depressed, so God said, *"Why are you angry? . . . If you do what is right, will you not be accepted? But if you do not do what is right, sin is crouching at your door; it desires to have you, but you must master it" (verses 6, 7, NIV).*

Cain didn't take God's advice. He felt so angry that he led his brother out into a field and killed him.

Cain murdered Abel because he felt guilty, embarrassed, and mad. Lillian, if you ever experience these emotions, watch out! People do terrible things under their influence. Instead of doing something you'll later regret, find a quiet corner and calm down. Think things through. Ask God for help.

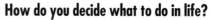

How do you decide what to do in life?
—*Girl, 13, Maine*

I can tell you how I made that decision. Maybe it'll generate some ideas for you.

When I was in ninth grade, Elder Taylor, the pastor of our church in Syracuse, New York, came to our little school and taught a photography class. Photography fascinated me.

John Milton, who worked in the Public Relations Department of the New York Conference, helped me pick out my first camera and taught me how to use it. My excitement grew.

Later, while I was attending college in Beirut, Lebanon, my English teacher, Mrs. Hepker, praised me for something I'd written. She said I could be an author someday.

While attending Southern College in Tennessee, the manager of the college radio station offered me a job talking on the air. I added broadcasting to my "what to do" list.

Skillful teachers at college showed me how to make motion pictures and videos. I was hooked after the first class.

People, especially my parents, have always provided me with lots of encouragement, helping me decide what to do with my life. Look around you. What catches your eye? What makes you excited? In what direction do your natural, God-given talents point?

Seriously consider the *positive* comments others offer. They may see something in you that you didn't even recognize. Then make your decision based on what will bring you joy and help further God's work on earth. Learn, practice, and do. Have fun!

What church do you attend? asks a friend.

"I'm a Seventh-day Adventist," you say.

"And what does a Seventh-day Adventist believe?" the speaker wants to know.

Could you answer that last question? Do you know what you believe?

While most of you juniors attend church because your parents tell you to, the time is coming when you'll be out on your own. You'll have to decide whether or not to remain a church goer or, in some cases, a Seventh-day Adventist. To help you make that decision, you've got to have some cold, hard facts. For the next few days let's discover what it is we Adventists believe, and how it can help us and our friends live a better, more productive life.

First, we believe in God's Word, the Bible. We look at it as a love letter from the Creator to His people.

My wife writes great love letters to me. She tells me how much she loves me. With carefully chosen words she lets me know that she thinks I'm the best possible husband for her and how much she enjoys being my friend. After reading them, I want to work hard to be worthy of such sweet and unselfish praise.

The Bible is a love letter too. *"All scripture is given by inspiration of God, and is profitable for doctrine, for reproof, for correction, for instruction in righteousness"* (2 Timothy 3:16).

We believe in the Bible because we know it's God's love for us written down in beautiful words.

OCTOBER 1

Seventh-day Adventist juniors believe in not just one God, but three: the Father, the Son, and the Holy Spirit—the Godhead.

While They are three separate beings, with personalities of Their own, They think exactly the same way. There are no arguments going on between these spiritual powers. They agree 100 percent on everything. But They do different jobs.

My father worked for the Adventist Church for 43 years. I saw him sitting behind many desks, laboring in the treasury departments of conferences, institutions, and world divisions, making sure tithes, offerings, and other income ended up in the right place. Down the hall, the conference president sat at his desk. Nearby, the secretary was busily doing his thing.

Here were three men doing different jobs, but working for the same goal—the salvation of souls.

That's also the goal of the Godhead. They want you and me to live with Them in heaven, not lost with Satan and his hordes.

God the Son, Jesus, created this world, died for our sins, and represents us to the universe, covering our sins with His perfect life. God the Father acts as judge, discovering who does and doesn't want to live in heaven with Him. God the Holy Spirit works as the voice of our conscience, pointing out our sins and helping us overcome temptation. Three Gods, one goal—salvation.

We believe in the Godhead because without Them we'd be lost. With Them working by our sides we can have eternal life.

OCTOBER 2

Seventh-day Adventist juniors believe in Creation. "Doesn't everyone?" you ask.

What would you say if I told you that there are millions of people who truly believe we evolved from the same ancestors as monkeys? Yup. Monkeys.

They think that a few billion years ago a little sea creature crawled up on the shore of some prehistoric land. Over the centuries its descendants grew legs. More descendants developed fingers and a tail. Then this animal, after thousands of centuries, evolved into a human being.

Where was God during all this? Nowhere.

When faced with such a fantastic saga, we need only open our Bibles to find the true answer to the question "Where did I come from?" *"In the beginning, God created the heaven and the earth" (Genesis 1:1).* Yes, He made sea creatures and monkeys, too. But they didn't evolve one to another. They, like human beings, were spoken into existence by God.

Years ago my wife and I bought a new car—a Honda Civic wagon. It came with a radio, air-conditioning, and something very important—a manufacturer's warranty. You see, the people at Honda had such faith in their product that they promised to fix anything that went wrong with it within three whole years.

I like to think the Bible is the warranty issued to us when we were born. Only our manufacturer, God, can grant such an important document. In it He promises to fix whatever's wrong in our lives if we'll just bring ourselves in for service. The Bible presents, and then supports, Creation.

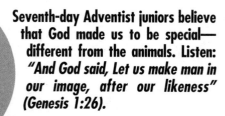

Seventh-day Adventist juniors believe that God made us to be special—different from the animals. Listen: "And God said, Let us make man in our image, after our likeness" (Genesis 1:26).

All week long, Jesus had been busy creating stuff such as winds, oceans, mountains, and aardvarks. Then He paused and said, "Now I'm going to do something unique. I'm going to create humans in My own image. They'll look, talk, and even think like Me."

Why is this important to know?

Every once in a while I'll glance at a mirror and scare myself. Instead of my mouth smiling back, I'll see what looks like my mom's mouth. Instead of my chin, there's my father's chin. My eyes become my grandmother's. Those ears look like those on my grandfather. And my nose? Definitely Dad's. I look like them because I came from them. I have the same genes, the same chromosomes, the same family history.

If God made me in His image, I should be able to see Him in that mirror, too. Sure, sin has affected every generation since Eden, wreaking havoc on the perfect faces and bodies humankind used to possess, but there should be traces still remaining.

Sure enough, if I'm persistent, I begin to see a little of Jesus in me. When I speak kindly to someone, I hear His voice. When I forgive, it's His heart beating in my chest. As my hands work in His service, I feel Him making my muscles strong.

I believe God made me special because I sometimes see Him in me, caring for others and loving unconditionally.

OCTOBER 4

Seventh-day Adventist juniors believe there's a war raging, and they're right in the middle of it!

I've been in wars. The first happened when I was just a baby. Communist forces from North Korea swept down into the city of Seoul, where my folks were missionaries. My dad took movies of airplanes strafing the roads as we hurried to the boat docks for evacuation. Those planes bombed our house into oblivion.

Years later we were living in Beirut, Lebanon, when another war broke out. We had to leave there quickly, too.

War is always frightening, heartless, and deadly.

The war between Christ and Satan isn't a battle over land, or mineral reserves, or seaports. It's fought with one prize in mind—*you*.

Satan says, "That junior is mine because he's chosen me as his general. See how he sins so often? Notice how she makes mistakes when she should know better. Yup. She's all mine."

"Not so," counters Christ, positioning Himself between the devil and the prize. "They're mine. I've forgiven them. I died for every junior in every land. Hands off, Satan!"

On and on and on the battle rages. Evil forces throw up endless temptations. God's still small voice pleads in every ear. Satan gains an inch, then loses it. God fights to victory, only to be rejected by the prize.

We believe in this war because we feel it happening in our hearts and minds. Which side will win? That's up to you.

Seventh-day Adventist juniors believe that Jesus lived on this earth, was murdered on a Roman cross, and rose again.

Why is this important? Millions of people have lived on this earth. Thousands have died on crosses. The Bible even records many instances of resurrection: Moses, Lazarus, the widow's son, to name a few. But when *Jesus* rose from the dead, something amazing happened. For the first time Satan knew he was fighting a lost cause. Before Christ's death the devil thought he was winning the war between good and evil.

You see, the most destructive thing Satan can do to you as a human being is kill you. Sure, he can make your life miserable with sin and disease, but from these you can usually recover. Death, on the other hand, seems so permanent, so final. In his twisted and sick mind, he figured death was the ultimate separation between a human being and God.

When Jesus died on the cross, Satan was beside himself with glee. He'd done it. He'd destroyed the very source of life for all humankind. "The war is over!" he shouted. "And I've won!"

Satan may have forgotten for the time that, to God, death is only a sleep. And on that Sunday morning, when God the Father "woke up" His sleeping Son, the devil knew he was doomed. God had triumphed over the worst Satan can do.

"He himself bore our sins in his body on the tree, so that we might die to sins and live for righteousness; by his wounds you have been healed" (1 Peter 2:24, NIV).

Christ's death and resurrection paved our pathway to heaven.

OCTOBER 6

Seventh-day Adventist juniors believe in partnership.

I recently went for a trip across the Atlantic Ocean. Took eight hours of flying time. When I landed and was getting off the airplane, I caught a glimpse of our pilot. He was sitting in the cockpit flipping switches, reading through checklists, and making sure everything was ready for the next flight.

For the past eight hours I had placed my life in the hands of that gentleman. I wouldn't know how to fly a plane that big on such a long journey. I wouldn't be able to get it off the ground in one piece. But he knew how. He had the skills and the knowledge necessary to take me where I wanted to go.

Suddenly I realized something about God. I don't know how to get to heaven, but God knows the way. I don't have the knowledge and the power necessary to overcome Satan, but God does. Without my heavenly Father, I'm doomed.

So what am I supposed to do? Jesus says, *"Come unto me, all ye that labour and are heavy laden, and I will give you rest" (Matthew 11:28).* Notice we both do something. I come. He gives.

Partners work together. Partners depend on each other. Partners accomplish great things when they work side by side.

Do you want to go to heaven, juniors? You can't get there on your own. You can't be good enough, faithful enough, perfect enough. But God, your pilot and your partner, knows the way. His goodness, His faithfulness, His perfection makes up for your flaws and changes you into a citizen of heaven.

We work. God saves. What a beautiful partnership!

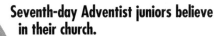

Seventh-day Adventist juniors believe in their church.

I once visited a rather unusual church. It was deep in the heart of a South American jungle.

To get to this highly irregular sanctuary, I had to travel for hours and hours in the back of a bouncing Jeep. When I arrived I was covered with dust and grime, but I didn't care. The smiles and joy radiating from the faces of those I met made up for the long journey.

"Where's your church?" I asked a young person through an interpreter. He waved his hand over his head. "It's everywhere," the boy said.

"Everywhere?" I gasped.

Then he explained. Since the village was very poor, they hadn't been able to build a building in which to hold their Sabbath services. So they gather at a different spot each week. Sometimes they worship in a grove of trees. Other times they sit at the river's edge. If it's raining, they pack themselves tightly into someone's hut and praise God while the thunder rolls overhead.

I learned that a church isn't made of bricks or stone. It doesn't have to have wooden rafters, or glass in its windows. A church is people gathering to worship God, to fellowship, to get instruction from the Bible, and to learn how to be of service.

God says, *"For where two or three are gathered together in my name, there am I in the midst of them" (Matthew 18:20).* We truly belong to an *everywhere* church.

OCTOBER 8

Seventh-day Adventist juniors believe they have an extremely important job to do.

There are millions and millions of people who believe in God. But in order to live in heaven with Jesus, simply believing without choosing to obey God's commandments isn't enough. It takes both belief and obedience.

From this great throng of believers will come in the last days a small group who will announce the arrival of the judgment hour. They'll tell everyone they meet, "It's time we start obeying *all* of God's commandments. It's time we keep the seventh day of the week as God's holy Sabbath. We must stop stealing, killing, and coveting other people's possessions. We must look to Jesus as our only path to salvation."

OCTOBER 9

The Bible has a name for this little group. Paul, looking to the Old Testament book of Isaiah for guidance, reports, *"Though the number of the Israelites be like the sand by the sea, only the remnant will be saved" (Romans 9:27, NIV).*

Did you catch that name? It's "remnant." This means a small portion of a larger amount.

In describing those who will be taken to heaven at the Second Coming, John the revelator states, *"Here are they that keep the commandments of God, and the faith of Jesus" (Revelation 14:12).* Look around you. How many keep all of the commandments? How many depend on Jesus as their only source of salvation?

The number will be small. But it's large enough to contain every junior who loves and obeys God.

Seventh-day Adventist juniors believe that some of them are arms and some are legs. Several are certain they are ears.

No, I'm not talking about a physical body. They know they're part of a *spiritual* body, with Jesus as the head.

Let's say you're sitting down to enjoy a big slice of hot, cheesy pizza. As you're reaching for this delicious meal, your hand suddenly changes course and begins scratching your chin. At the same time, your other hand starts pounding the table.

Embarrassed, you get up to walk away, and your feet and legs begin dancing. While everyone watches, you jump and hop across the floor until you stumble out of the restaurant.

That's what happens when the different parts of a human body refuse to follow directions from the head. The same thing takes place when God's spiritual body, made up of everyone who loves and trusts Him, turns its back on His leading. Our church becomes disorganized. We have a hard time going anywhere, accomplishing anything, doing the work God has asked us to do.

But when we arms and legs and stomachs and lips and toes work together in unity, what a difference!

Paul says, *"The body is a unit, though it is made up of many parts. . . . So it is with Christ. For we were all baptized by one Spirit into one body—whether Jews or Greeks, slave or free. . . . You are the body of Christ, and each one of you is a part of it"* (1 Corinthians 12:12-27, NIV).

Without unity, a body is useless. With unity, it can march to the kingdom.

OCTOBER
10

Seventh-day Adventist juniors believe in baptism.

While attending camp meeting as a young boy, I listened breathlessly to countless stories told around the big bonfire down by the ball field. Glowing embers and flickering flames warmed our faces as exciting adventures warmed our hearts.

Many times the stories centered around a man or woman, boy or girl who, after attending evangelistic meetings in their village, decided to be baptized. When their family heard about their decision, they suddenly found themselves being threatened with knives, axes, whips, and worse. Did that stop them? No! They went through with their plans and often paid a terrible price.

What is it about baptism that motivates people to willingly take such courageous steps? The answer is love. They've fallen in love with Jesus, and they want the whole world to know about it. Baptism is an outward demonstration of an inward determination to follow the Saviour, even if it means death.

Jesus showed us the correct method of baptism that day in the Jordan River when John the Baptist lowered Him gently under the waves. When we choose to join God's church through baptism, we're telling friends, family, and those around us that we are burying our old life of sin and are being resurrected into a new life of victory.

"Repent, and be baptized every one of you in the name of Jesus Christ for the remission [forgiveness] of sins" (Acts 2:38). Every junior who loves God should be baptized.

OCTOBER 11

Seventh-day Adventist juniors believe in the Lord's Supper.

Anyone who's read this book knows something about me: I love and respect my earthly father greatly. No, he's not perfect. He'll be the first to tell you that. But a more dedicated Christian I've never met. And nothing demonstrates his undying admiration for God more than when I see him take part in the ceremonies called the Lord's Supper.

I see it in the way he holds that little cup of grape juice, which represents Christ's spilled blood. I see it in the way he reverently takes the tiny piece of bread and holds it while the minister speaks. And most of all, I see it when he kneels before me—me, his son—and washes my feet in the cool water.

What would make a father bow before his grown son and wash his feet? The answer lies, not in the ceremony, but in the God who created it. My father, and every adult and young person who reverently takes part in the Lord's Supper, are following an incredible example of humbleness set forth by Jesus.

One fisherman-turned-disciple says, *"God resisteth the proud, and giveth grace to the humble. Humble yourselves therefore under the mighty hand of God, that he may exalt you in due time"* (1 Peter 5:5, 6).

The Lord's Supper reminds us all of a great sacrifice made by a Son who loved a Father, and a Father who, seeing our sinfulness, bowed low and washed us clean in the blood of His Son. That's humbleness born of unspeakable love.

OCTOBER 12

295

I like a boy in my church. He's asked me out but isn't serious about it. How do I let him know I'm serious about it?
—*Elisa, 11, Florida*

Becoming serious about another person is usually one of those things that takes time. You certainly wouldn't want two people to rush into a relationship. They might miss a warning sign along the way.

Time is also a pretty good test of someone's commitment. While I understand that you don't want to get married to this guy right now, you do want him to make a short commitment to you; to consider you special, to treat you different from all your female friends. There's nothing wrong with this.

Here's a suggestion. The next time he asks you for a date, tell him how much you're looking forward to your time together. Don't get all gushy or anything. Just say, "I know we're going to have a great time. It'll be fun. Thanks for asking."

And, whatever you do, don't go around bragging about your upcoming date to all your friends. Let the guy know that you consider his invitation as private and important, not simply fuel for your ego.

Also, don't take your dates *too* seriously. You're just beginning to learn about girl-boy relationships. Enjoy the journey. If your heart gets battered once in a while, it'll survive. And ask God to come along on your dates. He wants you to experience the happiness of true love, too! After all, He invented it.

Why are boys so rowdy? How can they be helped?
—*Girl, 12, Montana*

That's a question women have been asking for centuries.

Members of the male species tend to be more aggressive and "rowdy" across the entire animal kingdom. Physically men are usually stronger, taller, and louder.

As I've mentioned before, the reason for this must be somehow tied into the original plan God had for men as protectors and providers for their female partners. In Eden, these differences didn't cause concern. Man's characteristics were designed by the Creator to interlock perfectly with woman's special characteristics.

How can boys be helped? I believe, more than anything, they have to be *tolerated*. They're not about to change—at least, not quickly.

I'd like to add something *very* important here. You must never allow a guy's rowdiness to violate your personal space. Boys can be aggressive with footballs, bicycles, musical instruments, and each other. But they cannot be aggressive with you unless you grant permission. You have rights. You are of great value and must be treated with respect at all times. Anyone who crosses the line and allows his rowdiness to damage you or your self-respect is sinning in the eyes of God. You don't have to take it.

"Be devoted to one another in brotherly love," says Paul in Romans 12:10. *"Honor one another above yourselves"* (NIV). Rowdy, you have to live with. But there are limits. Enforce them.

OCTOBER 14

Why can't we go to the movies on Sabbath?
—*Lance, 15, Oklahoma*

I'm not quite sure how best to answer your question, Lance. Most movies I've seen advertised on television wouldn't be worth going to on Tuesday, Thursday, or any other day of the week, much less on God's holy Sabbath day. They're trash, glorifying hatred, revenge, violence, and immorality.

Your question also raises a concern of mine. Why can't we Adventists make Sabbath special? Many of our young people spend those precious hours complaining about what they *can't* do instead of creating activities that would bring more joy and excitement into their lives than any Hollywood production ever could.

We look at Sabbath as a list of do's and don'ts instead of viewing it as 24 hours of opportunity to better ourselves and others. I have seen young people who've made the switch. They spend their Sabbaths on the streets, at the beach, going door-to-door, holding evangelistic meetings, spreading the good news of God's love. Sabbath is, for them, a day of extreme activity, extreme challenge, extreme rewards. To these frontline warriors, moviegoing is a waste of time. They've got better things to do.

Here's my advice, Lance. For every "don't" you find on Sabbath, create a "do." God has blessed you with a mind. Don't let some movie producer do your thinking for you. Make your own adventures. Gather your own cast of characters. And spend your Sabbaths touching lives for God. Ask your pastor to help.

When we go to heaven, are we going to see all the people who were here on earth before us, like Adam, Eve, or Noah?
—Karina, 11, California

We'll not only see them, we'll talk with them, live next door to them, truck around the universe with them, and praise God by their sides.

Our friend Ellen White reminds us of something we may have overlooked as we contemplate meeting the famous characters of the Bible. She says, "When the Life-giver shall come to bring the captives from the great prison house of death, father, mother, and children may meet, and the broken links of the family chain be reunited, no more to be severed" *(Testimonies,* vol. 1, p. 654).

As awesome as it will be to run into Adam, Eve, and Noah on the streets of gold, my greatest joy will be in meeting some people called Aunt Helen, Cousin Johnny, Grandmother Mills, and Uncle Rudy. I won't have to introduce myself to them. Their smiles will broaden even further when they see me. We've met before—before sickness, before death, before all those tears.

Mrs. White reports, "Our eyes will be fixed upon Jesus, and we shall learn from him to dwell in love and harmony with one another here, and shall finally be permitted to dwell with Christ and the angels and all the redeemed throughout the ceaseless ages of eternity" *(Historical Sketches,* p. 126).

I'm going to add another name to the list of people I'm looking forward to meeting in heaven. That's Karina with a K, right?

OCTOBER

16

Why do little babies have to suffer for the mistakes of others?
—*Girl, 13, Maine*

Because sin isn't fair. It never has been.

I've seen newborns suffering through terrible withdrawal pains because their mothers took drugs while they were in their wombs.

Many tiny children are victims of abuse. The very moms and dads who were supposed to be their guardians and source of love turn against them, sometimes crushing out their very lives.

There's no better illustration of the unfairness of sin than innocent babies suffering. They can't defend themselves. They're totally dependent on others.

Our friend Ellen White adds, "Many infants are poisoned beyond remedy by sleeping in beds with their tobacco-using fathers. By inhaling the poisonous tobacco effluvia [that which flows out], which is thrown from the lungs and pores of the skin, the system of the infant is filled with poison" *(Selected Messages,* book 2, p. 467).

Sin makes people selfish, unthinking, unkind. Sin buries our God-given gifts of mercy and love under dirty piles of pride and anger. Because of sin, babies suffer.

What can we do about it? We can determine to break the chain of abuse. We can choose to be parents who love, protect, and cherish children. We can refuse to allow Satan to rule our homes. With Jesus by our side, we can keep our babies safe and secure, wrapped gently in caring arms.

That's how God loves us.

OCTOBER 17

Will I meet Satan before I go to heaven?

—*Crystal, 13, Florida*

I'm assuming you mean face-to-face, for we meet Satan every day through the sinful acts we witness and sometimes take part in.

Our friend Ellen White mentions a terrible temptation that will come to God's people prior to Christ's second coming. Listen: "In the last days he [Satan] will appear in such a manner as to make men believe him to be Christ come the second time into the world. He will indeed transform himself into an angel of light" *(Last Day Events,* p. 163).

We're longing for Christ's return. We're homesick for heaven. Then suddenly someone shouts, "He's here! He's finally come back! Glory, glory!"

The Bible warns, *"If any man shall say to you, Lo, here is Christ; or, lo, he is there; believe him not: For false Christs and false prophets shall rise, and shall show signs and wonders, to seduce, if it were possible, even the elect"* (Mark 13:21, 22).

Will we fall for such an awful trick? Will we drop to our knees before the very being who has caused so much suffering and death in this world? "But while he will bear the appearance of Christ in every particular, so far as mere appearance goes," says Mrs. White, "it will deceive none but those who . . . are seeking to resist the truth" *(ibid.).*

We will not be taken in because we've gotten to know the real Jesus, the real Saviour, the real coming King.

OCTOBER 18

301

I'm afraid of dying. How can you help me?

—Girl, 12, Montana

Death has two parts—the act of dying, and the act of being dead.

Do you remember back in 1969 when Neil Armstrong walked on the moon? You don't? Why? Oh, you weren't alive yet. In a sense, you were dead in 1969. How was it? Did you have a lot of pain? Were you afraid? No. You experienced none of these things because you were . . . well, not alive. So you already know what it's like to be dead. The Bible calls it a "sleep." Not a bad description, huh?

Dying is another matter, although many people who've clinically "died" and then been brought back to life by skilled doctors and modern medical equipment say it's no big deal. They report it's like going to sleep, which makes sense.

Believe me, there are worse things than dying—much worse. Living in constant pain isn't very pleasant. Many terminally ill people say they look forward to death because it will stop their agony.

Don't be afraid of death, because it's not the end. Think of it as a very short nap between this life and Christ's second coming. Like Paul, proclaim, *"O death, where is thy sting? O grave, where is thy victory?" (1 Corinthians 15:55).* Put thoughts of dying out of your mind. It's time to live your life for Jesus and look forward to the glorious eternal life to come. You can sleep later.

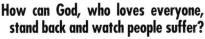

How can God, who loves everyone, stand back and watch people suffer?
—Joseph, 15, Oklahoma

Joseph, listen to me. Listen very carefully to what I'm about to say. God is NOT standing back and watching people suffer. He's doing something about it every minute of every day.

First, most suffering on this earth is the result of the choices men and women make. They damage their bodies through unhealthful habits such as smoking, drinking, and eating foods that do more harm than good. The Bible and Ellen White's books are brimming with sound health advice and life-enriching ideas provided by God to ease suffering and pain.

Second, the Holy Spirit is *constantly* at work trying to direct minds heavenward. You won't find too many active criminals who have a loving relationship with God. Painful violence happens when people reject the gentle voice of conscience, choosing rather to live by Satan's rules.

Third, even death itself has been overcome by the sacrifice of God's own Son. At this very moment, He's preparing a home for us far from this house of horrors we call Planet Earth.

Standing back and watching? Hardly! Heaven is buzzing with activity designed to end our suffering as quickly as possible.

I like the way *The Living Bible* paraphrases 2 Corinthians 4:17: *"These troubles and sufferings of ours are, after all, quite small and won't last very long. Yet this short time of distress will result in God's richest blessing upon us forever and ever."* He's working hard for you, Joseph. Trust Him.

OCTOBER
20

303

How did David die?
—*Andy, 13, California*

The Bible doesn't say, Andy. It just reports, *"So David slept with his fathers, and was buried in the city of David"* *(1 Kings 2:10)*. No, he didn't crawl into bed with anyone. That's Bible talk for "like his fathers before him, he died."

Modern archaeology has shed a lot of light on the past. By studying the dusty bones of kings and princes who ruled thousands of years ago, we can get a pretty good idea of how people lived. And how they died.

Wonder of wonders, they succumbed to many of the same problems as we have today. High cholesterol, cancer, heart disease, crippling arthritis, and liver failure because of excessive drinking top the list. The devil has made sure that every generation since Adam has experienced their share of maladies.

David probably died of some common illness or simply of old age. Our friend Ellen White says, "David died a natural death like other men" *(Spirit of Prophecy,* vol. 3, p. 270). At least, he didn't leave the land of the living violently, as did so many other rulers of that time.

David led an exciting life, filled with giants, harps, swords, and glory. But there was a darker side, too. He had very real, very tragic failings. But God never abandoned him.

When you think of David, remember him standing firm against Goliath, sling in hand, ready to battle with anyone who made fun of God's holy name. Don't you think we could use a few more Davids today?

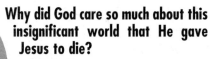

Why did God care so much about this insignificant world that He gave Jesus to die?

—*Girl, 13, Maine*

Books have been written trying to answer your question. Truth is, sinful human minds can't understand why He did it.

Our friend Ellen White says it best. "Oh, the mystery of redemption! the love of God for a world that did not love Him! Who can know the depths of that love which 'passeth knowledge'? Through endless ages immortal minds, seeking to comprehend the mystery of that incomprehensible love, will wonder and adore" (*Patriarchs and Prophets*, p. 63).

A Bible writer puts it this way: *"Behold, what manner of love the Father hath bestowed upon us, that we should be called the sons of God" (1 John 3:1).*

When I was a little boy, my father and I would spend hours trudging through the fields and forests of upstate New York, bird-watching. Sometimes we'd happen upon a tragic scene. We'd find a beautiful songbird lying on the ground dead, victim of a predator, disease, or age.

My young heart would ache as tears trickled down my cheeks. Dad would kneel beside the stricken creature and shake his head slowly. "God knows," he'd say. "He knows even when a sparrow falls. That's how much He loves this world, Charlie. That's how much He loves us."

Throughout all eternity I'll marvel at a heavenly Father whose heart is touched when a sparrow falls, and when a child cries.

OCTOBER 22

Why do friends fight over the smallest things?

—*Jessica, 11, Florida*

Because friends spend more time together than nonfriends. They share each other's joys and sorrow. They're all too familiar with each other's weird ways as well.

Everything affects a meaningful friendship—I mean everything from how a person feels to the type of day they're having, even what they ate for breakfast. Good friends get so close that when one is bothered or fearful, the other tends to get that way, too.

Under times of stress, such as when an important exam is coming up or things aren't going too hot at home, one of the friends may get a little grouchy. The other person in the relationship begins to feel the strain. Suddenly unimportant things take on new meanings. "You did that to bug me," one will yell.

"I did not," the other might counter. "Besides, you do this and this, and I never complain. So lighten up!" And off they go fighting with each other over stuff that didn't used to faze them.

Some friends test each other without even thinking about it. They want to make sure the other person really cares about them, so they set little traps in the relationship, saying, "If he really likes me, he'll do so-and-so." When the other person innocently doesn't respond a certain way, *bang!* Fight time.

As Solomon says: *"A man that hath friends must shew himself friendly" (Proverbs 18:24).* When the smallest things tear two people apart, perhaps it's time they take that text to heart.

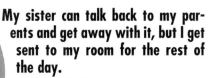

My sister can talk back to my parents and get away with it, but I get sent to my room for the rest of the day.

—Heather, 13, Montana

Having a brother or sister can be a real pain sometimes, huh? Growing up, I had two older brothers and one younger sister. Although I loved them all dearly, there were times when I got seriously frustrated.

My question for you is, Why on earth would you want to talk back to your parents? I mean, just because sister does something she shouldn't and gets away with it doesn't mean you should try to do likewise. Hey, Heather. Maybe you should rethink this situation.

How your sister and parents interact with each other is between them. It has nothing to do with you. Likewise, how you and your mom and dad communicate is none of your sister's business. I can only assume that your parents treat your sister the way they do because they've found what works and what doesn't. Given the chance, your sister would probably say, "Heather gets away with this and this, and I don't." Trust me, she has her own list.

Here's a suggestion. Don't try to pattern yourself after sister. Be yourself. Figure out what works for you. And when you hear your sister talking back to the people she's supposed to be honoring, ask Jesus to come into her heart. Then love her the way God loves us. *"I will . . . love them freely, for my anger has turned away from them"* (Hosea 14:4, NIV).

OCTOBER

24

Why does God let people hate each other?

—*Ryan, 15, Oklahoma*

Don't forget, Ryan, He also lets people love each other. In other words, He gives all of us the choice of whether to love or hate. It's up to us.

God allows us this freedom because, a long time ago, Satan accused our heavenly Father of being a dictator, of trying to manipulate people into worshiping and serving Him by taking away all their choices. In essence the devil said, "People obey You because they *have* to. Given a choice, they'd run from You like scared rabbits."

Here's how our friend Ellen White puts it. "God might have created man without the power to transgress His law; He might have withheld the hand of Adam from touching the forbidden fruit; but in that case man would have been, not a free moral agent, but a mere automaton. Without freedom of choice, his obedience would not have been voluntary, but forced" *(Patriarchs and Prophets,* p. 49).

There've been many kings and dictators in history who've ruled by using fear, violence, and even the law to keep their subjects in check: Hitler, Caesar, Saddam Hussein, to name a few.

That's *not* how God operates. He rules by choice. Our choice. To do otherwise would prove Satan correct.

Ryan, I choose not to hate. I choose to obey God out of respect and love. People who hate each other haven't accepted Christ as their king. They serve another dictator, whose domain is death, whose law leads to destruction.

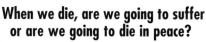

**When we die, are we going to suffer
or are we going to die in peace?**
—*Erin, 11, California*

First of all, Erin, remember that it's a very real possibility that we're not going to die at all. That's right. If Jesus comes during our lifetime, which I certainly hope, death won't touch us.

When our Saviour appears, there'll be two groups of people waiting to go to heaven with Him. Listen: *"For the Lord himself will come down from heaven, with a loud command, with the voice of the archangel and with the trumpet call of God, and the dead in Christ will rise first. After that, we who are still alive and are left will be caught up together with them in the clouds to meet the Lord in the air. And so we will be with the Lord forever"* (*1 Thessalonians 4:16, 17, NIV*). I like what Paul says in the very next verse: *"Therefore encourage each other with these words."*

As to whether we'll suffer when (and if) we die, all I can tell you is there are ways to reduce the risk. A smoker runs a greater chance of dying in agony from lung cancer than a nonsmoker. Healthful eating habits assist the body in fighting diseases that can end life painfully. Living a moral, temperate existence improves the odds of falling asleep in Jesus peacefully.

No matter how we die, Jesus waits just beyond our sleep. Someday soon He'll awaken us to a new life with Him, a life where suffering doesn't exist, where peace will reign forever.

How do you get two friends back together?
—*Frank, 11, Florida*

Now, there's a challenge! I'm glad you're concerned, Frank. It shows you care about those around you. Good for you!

Almost every day on the evening news, I see pictures of a man who must live on airplanes. Whenever two countries get to squabbling with each other, this much-traveled gentleman shows up immediately. He's called the secretary of state.

The president of our nation assigns this man the task of doing exactly what you want to do, except he's attempting to bring two *countries* back together. Sometimes he even tries to stop two enemies from killing each other!

This is how he does it. He goes to the head of the first country and says, "What's the problem here? What do you want to happen?" Then he jets to the other country and asks them the same thing. Once he knows all the facts, he does his best to create solutions, suggesting ways the two nations can work out their differences. Soon he has leaders from both sides sitting around a big conference table, hashing out their grievances face-to-face. If he's lucky, we get to see pictures of presidents and dictators shaking hands and signing agreements.

Maybe you could try the same process with your two friends. Get them talking. Come up with some compromises. Find ways to end the stand-off. God says, *"Blessed are the peacemakers: for they shall be called the children of God"* (Matthew 5:9). Good luck, Frank. I'll be praying for you.

My best friend belongs to a church some consider a cult. Everyone's rejected her. But she's the kindest person I've ever met and firmly believes in her religion. She's always asking me what I think of her church, and I don't know what to say.
—Girl, 13, Montana

George Vandeman, who for many years was speaker on the *It Is Written* television program, wrote an interesting book entitled *What I Like About . . .* In it, he lists all the things he admires about the different religions he's come in contact with through the years.

What Elder Vandeman has done is to close the gap between, say, Adventists and Catholics by finding common ground between the two churches. We both love Jesus. We both believe in God. We both think worship is an important part of any Christian's life. And we both value family and fidelity.

Why don't you try the same thing with your friend? Find areas in her religion that match yours. Concentrate on the "common ground" between your beliefs. If you find differences, explain your side of the story, listen to hers, then go on your way praising God.

Here's a Bible text to keep in mind. Jesus said, *"I have other sheep that are not of this sheep pen. I must bring them also. They too will listen to my voice, and there shall be one flock and one shepherd"* (John 10:16, NIV).

Always use the Bible as the basis for your beliefs. You'll find it teaches tolerance and acceptance, something we all need.

OCTOBER

28

Why is Satan so ugly?
—*Tim, 14, Oklahoma*

Our friend Ellen White gives us a fascinating description of the devil. Check this out!

"I was shown Satan as he once was, a happy, exalted angel. Then I was shown him as he now is. He still bears a kingly form. His features are still noble, for he is an angel fallen. But the expression of his countenance is full of anxiety, care, unhappiness, malice, hate, mischief, deceit, and every evil. That brow which was once so noble, I particularly noticed. His forehead commenced from his eyes to recede. I saw that he had so long bent himself to evil that every good quality was debased, and every evil trait was developed. His eyes were cunning, sly, and showed great penetration. His frame was large, but the flesh hung loosely about his hands and face. As I beheld him, his chin was resting upon his left hand. He appeared to be in deep thought. A smile was upon his countenance, which made me tremble, it was so full of evil and satanic slyness. This smile is the one he wears just before he makes sure of his victim, and as he fastens the victim in his snare, this smile grows horrible" (*Early Writings*, pp. 152, 153).

Wow! What a pitiful, pitiful creature. And to think he was once a bright, glorious angel.

Tim, now you know. Satan is ugly because he's doing to himself what he tries to do to us. Without the love of God in our hearts and on our faces, we eventually lose all beauty and take on the hideous countenance of sin.

OCTOBER 29

Why do people kill their best friends for no reason at all?

I once knew a girl who was quiet, had a pretty smile, liked to listen to music, and carried a terrible hurt in her heart. When she was young, her father picked up a hitchhiker along a California back road. The stranger returned the courtesy by murdering the kind man who'd given him a lift.

Questions like the one you're asking echo through my thoughts many times. My friend's father wasn't rich. He was just being thoughtful. The stranger had nothing to gain by killing him.

Whenever I hear an interview on television with a murderer, I listen closely, trying to find an answer. Here's what I've discovered.

Many murderers report that rage made them lose all sense of reason. They acted without thinking. Others insist they don't even remember doing the terrible deed. In these cases they usually admit to having been high on drugs or filled with alcohol.

I believe people kill because they've allowed sin to flood their minds with feelings of anger and revenge, thus effectively shutting out God's words of warning.

The Bible says, *"In his pride the wicked does not seek him; in all his thoughts there is no room for God. . . . He lies in wait near the villages; from ambush he murders the innocent"* (Psalm 10:4-8, NIV).

Keep close to God, Michael. Allow Him full access to your mind. And pray for those who wait in ambush.

OCTOBER
30

313

How can you really get into the Bible?
—Kendra, 13, Alabama

I like the way Kendra phrased her question. She doesn't just want to read and contemplate God's Word. This girl wants to *get into* it!

Here's something I do that helps me time after time. Before I sit down with the Bible, I think about my life. What are my needs right now? Do I long for encouragement? Am I afraid? Do I have doubts? Am I having problems with someone at that moment?

Then I ask God to whisper to me through the texts I'm about to read. I'm always *amazed* at what happens next. Bible passages that didn't mean a thing to me before suddenly speak directly to my problems. Old memory verses, long ago learned and forgotten, jump out at me with new and exciting messages.

You see, Kendra, it's not so much that I'm getting into the Bible; the Bible is getting into me! The God I worship has been waiting for this moment. He's primed and ready to fill my thoughts with unique revelations, with workable plans, with forgiveness.

I've also found that a Bible "promise book" helps a lot. You can buy them at Christian bookstores. They list texts covering any number of subjects.

Paul says, *"The word of God is living and active . . . it judges the thoughts and attitudes of the heart. Nothing in all creation is hidden from God's sight"* (Hebrews 4:12, 13, NIV).

Dig in, Kendra. Let God's Word amaze you, too!

OCTOBER 31

Knowing what you believe is part of knowing who you are. It's not enough to say "I'm a Seventh-day Adventist." You've got to understand what that means.

Seventh-day Adventist juniors believe that God gives every member of His earthly church at least one gift to use in loving ministry. This gift may be as simple as a smile or as lofty as an incredibly complex talent.

The apostle Paul says our heavenly Father *"gave some to be apostles, some to be prophets, some to be evangelists, and some to be pastors and teachers, to prepare God's people for works of service, so that the body of Christ [the church] may be built up"* (Ephesians 4:11, 12, NIV).

What is your talent? Can you sing? Are you a good speaker or writer? Do you have the ability to cheer someone up, offer useful advice, or give encouragement? Do you find you enjoy doing things with your hands such as painting pictures, building with hammer and nail, working in the earth to make a garden? More than likely, you're already using the "spiritual gift" God gave you. Your number one job is to find ways to put your talent to work for Jesus.

When I was a boy, I loved taking pictures with my camera. Now, whenever an image I've created shows up in one of our beautiful Christian magazines, I'm thrilled that my talent is being used for Jesus. Even this book is an attempt to share whatever writing ability God has given me with my spiritual family.

Find your talent and prepare it for a life of service.

NOVEMBER 1

Seventh-day Adventist juniors believe that Ellen White possessed the gift of prophecy.

God's church on earth has always had prophets among its members. Moses' brother Aaron, Samuel, Jeremiah, Daniel, John the revelator—all these men had this wonderful gift.

Why does God need prophets? Amos 3:7 reports, *"Surely the Lord God does nothing, unless He reveals His secret to His servants the prophets"* (NKJV).

Men and women who have the gift of prophecy serve as messengers, broadcasting God's words to any who'll listen.

That's exactly what our friend Ellen White did. Her books are filled with important information sent by God to His remnant church. When you read her words, you're actually discovering what God wanted to say to *you*.

Yes, her books reflect the time in which she lived. But the principles are changeless. If she suggested, "You shouldn't go to dance halls," we can easily apply that to today and say, "We shouldn't go to bars." See what I mean?

Do your best to discover how her words apply to you. God will stand by your side, helping you make the connection.

Prophets present sound advice, warn of future problems, and offer faith-building encouragement to anyone smart enough to take note. Include the writings of our friend Ellen White in your personal library. Her words are God's words. She was His prophet.

Seventh-day Adventist juniors believe in the Ten Commandments.

Some people don't like God's law of love. They say, "Keeping the commandments isn't fun. It takes away my freedom."

I even heard one person refer to them as God's 10 *suggestions* for life, like it didn't matter whether you actually kept them or not. We know differently, don't we?

The Ten Commandments act as warning signals. If we find ourselves breaking one of these beautiful laws, it's a pretty good indication that we need more God and less Satan in our lives. Anytime kids happen to sneeze near their parents, they find themselves being whisked off to bed to fight the terrible cold Mom or Dad just knows is trying to overtake their precious offspring. Sneezing is often a symptom of something worse. Same with breaking a commandment. It's a sign that evil is eating away at the soul.

Working hard to *obey* the commandments strengthens the character. Like preventive medicine, obeying every commandment keeps Satan on the run and allows God full access to the mind where He can offer quiet guidance and encouragement.

No, commandment keeping doesn't earn you a ticket to heaven. It just makes the journey on this earth more bearable. Think about it. How many lawbreakers do you know who are happy and satisfied with their lives?

Juniors keep God's laws because they highlight the safest, healthiest, most fulfilling way to live.

NOVEMBER 3

Seventh-day Adventist juniors believe in the Sabbath.

Behind my house, in the cool shade of a hickory tree, sits a little wooden bench. The forest hovers overhead like a mother hen shielding her chicks from the sun.

Here my wife and I often spend Sabbath hours. Resting on that bench, surrounded by birds and squirrels, I can easily understand why God created such a wonderful day.

But rest is only one of the reasons Jesus set aside Saturday as the Sabbath. It's also a sign between us and Him.

When we keep His day holy, we're sending a signal to the entire universe that we believe in the saving power of God. We're proclaiming, "This day is holy. God said so, and we believe His every word."

We're also sending a signal to the Creator. "We know You made us. We appreciate Your sacrifice for us on the cross. So we're obeying Your commandments, respecting Your laws, doing exactly what You asked us to do."

No matter how you keep the Sabbath—whether it's a busy day doing church activities, having friends over for a simple lunch, walking along the beach, or sitting quietly on a forest bench—you're honoring the Creator as you remember what makes those hours so important to Him, and to you.

Jesus said, *"The Sabbath was made for man, not man for the Sabbath" (Mark 2:27, NIV).* Juniors keep this day holy because they understand the message it sends and the rewards it brings.

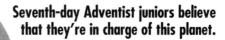

**Seventh-day Adventist juniors believe
that they're in charge of this planet.**

One Christmas morning long ago I got a wonderful surprise. There, waiting for me by the tree, was the fastest, shiniest, coolest, most awesome bicycle I'd ever seen.

I rode that critter from sunup to sundown. This was no easy task, since we were living in Syracuse, New York, at the time and the highways and byways were covered with piles of snow. Not to worry. I just plowed through 'em.

Did I pay for the bike? No, my dad did. He picked it out, and everything. But he knew what I wanted.

Did I take care of that bike? You bet! I polished, scrubbed, oiled, and waxed that puppy within an inch of its life. Why? Because someone I loved had given it to me. By taking good care of it, I was showing my dad how much I appreciated his gift.

God has given us this world to enjoy. It's our job to care for, protect, and nurture it. He's also provided time to spend, talents to share, work to accomplish, money to manage, and love to spread. We're stewards (or caretakers) of every one of these bountiful blessings.

When we return our tithes, recycle our trash, keep litter in its place, share our talents, provide honest labor, and respond to the needs of others, we're saying to God, "We know You own this world and everything in it, and we're showing our appreciation by being faithful stewards of all You've created. Thank You for letting us be a part of Your universe."

NOVEMBER ✝

5

Seventh-day Adventist juniors believe that they're a little different.

While most everyone else is breaking God's commandments, they're keeping them. While friends are getting into smoking, alcohol, and drugs, they're choosing to exercise, eat healthful foods, and keep their minds clear.

Even though a vast majority of their neighbors trudge off to church on Sunday, Adventist juniors put on their best clothes and head for church on Saturday.

While others spend great sums of money on the latest fashions, juniors continue to value modesty and quality.

That's why some of their friends snicker behind their backs. "You're weird," they say. "Don't you want to have any fun?"

"Sure," Adventist juniors respond with a smile. "But we want our fun to benefit us and others, not ruin our health or bring grief to those around us."

Listen to what the Bible says about God's people. *"But ye [Bible-following Christians] are a chosen generation, a royal priesthood, an holy nation, a peculiar people; that ye should shew forth the praises of him who hath called you out of darkness into his marvellous light"* (1 Peter 2:9).

Let's face it, my friends. We're different. We're unique. We're peculiar. That's because most people have chosen to turn their backs on God and His laws of love. But we haven't. If the Bible says it, we do it, no matter what others may say.

Someday we *will* be like everyone else. Where? In heaven.

Seventh-day Adventist juniors believe in marriage and the family.

"Doesn't everyone?" you ask. Yes, sort of. But most people look at marriage and family as a *social* system—you know, people-to-people. But we believe that marriage and family have a much greater importance. To us, they are spiritual and moral systems as well. We include God in the mix.

Adventist juniors understand that marriage was created for an important purpose—to form a bond between heaven and earth. God assigned husbands and wives the task of providing their family with a safe, positive atmosphere in which to grow. Our friend Ellen White says, "In every home there is missionary work to be done; for the children in every family are to be brought up in the nurture and admonition of the Lord" *(Review and Herald,* Oct. 25, 1892).

Marriage is also the place where love and commitment between two people can flourish without fear of separation or rejection. When two dedicated Christians join their lives together, divorce is not an option. They've promised to love each other until death parts them.

Some juniors don't enjoy a happy homelife. Many live in homes in which one parent isn't even around anymore. Here's a Bible text especially for those who live in broken homes! Jesus says, *"He that loveth me shall be loved of my Father, and I will love him, and will manifest myself to him"* (John 14:21).

Juniors believe in home because God created it.

NOVEMBER 7

Seventh-day Adventist juniors believe that Jesus is hard at work forgiving their sins.

It must have been an awesome sight. Solemn priests carrying bowls of blood collected from sacrificed animals into the sanctuary, prayers echoing in the desert air, sweet incense hanging like a cloud over the encampment. The ceremony took place every year and had a name. It was called the Day of Atonement.

In that long-ago service the sanctuary was "cleansed" with the blood of animals. All the sins of the children of Israel had been transferred to spotless animals. On this day their sacrifices pointed symbolically to the spilled blood of another spotless Lamb to come—Jesus Christ.

The Bible reports there's a new sanctuary in which a priest is performing the work of cleansing the earth of sin. This temple isn't in a desert. It's in heaven. Christ is both high priest and sacrifice. His blood on the cross is purifying the life of any man, woman, boy, or girl who asks forgiveness for his or her sins. This heavenly "judgment" allows Jesus to tell the universe, "The sins of those who've chosen to love and obey Me are cleansed. They are forgiven!"

Juniors believe in the heavenly sanctuary because they know that's where Jesus is right now, forgiving sins, making lives clean again, preparing souls for His kingdom. Paul says, "*Since we have a great high priest who has gone through the heavens, Jesus the Son of God, let us hold firmly to the faith we profess*" (Hebrews 4:14, NIV). I say, "Thank You, Jesus, for Your love."

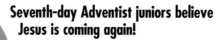

Seventh-day Adventist juniors believe Jesus is coming again!

He promised He would. And Jesus always keeps His promises.

A few weeks ago my mom and dad were expected to come to West Virginia to pay us a visit. Dorinda and I looked forward to the day with eager anticipation. While she busied herself with preparing tasty meals, hurrying about the house cleaning and scrubbing, and fixing up the guest room just so, I turned my attention to the lawns and trees outside. I gave the grass a good clipping, trimmed out dead or broken limbs, cut down the weeds along the driveway, and put everything in order.

Why did we go to such trouble? Because some people we loved were coming. We wanted them to feel welcome.

That's the same reason juniors keep their lives clean, hearts filled with forgiveness, and minds focused on God's Word. Jesus is coming soon. He's going to appear suddenly and without warning in the sky. But they're ready. Their spiritual house is in order. They've been busily scrubbing sin from their lives, cutting down temptations, fixing up their hearts for heaven.

We know Christ's return won't be a secret, for *"every eye shall see him" (Revelation 1:7)*. We know we won't be afraid, either, because the Bible says we'll shout, *"Lo, this is our God; we have waited for him, and he will save us: this is the Lord; we have waited for him, we will be glad and rejoice in his salvation" (Isaiah 25:9)*.

I know juniors believe in the Second Coming because I see them preparing to meet Jesus. What a happy day that will be!

Seventh-day Adventist juniors believe that death is only a sleep.

Near my house is a little country church. It sits atop a hill, with big trees all around. Sometimes on Sunday mornings I hear its bell ringing. It's such a lovely sound.

Beside the church rests an old cemetery with crooked tombstones and a carpet of summer grass covering the ground. As I walk along the pathways leading between the gravesites, I can't help wondering whether these people loved and obeyed Jesus. Were they students of the Bible? If they were, they died knowing something wonderful would happen someday in the future.

As disease, violence, war, or old age threatened them, they understood that death wasn't the end. In their hearts they knew that someday they'd open their eyes and see the kind face of Jesus looking down at them.

The Bible says, *"The wages of sin is death; but the gift of God is eternal life through Jesus Christ our Lord" (Romans 6:23).* Do you realize what a wonderful promise that is? I believe juniors should commit that verse to memory, so the next time they stand in the shade of an oak tree gazing down at an old or new tombstone, they'll know how to feel, and how to grieve.

Juniors believe in death. Everyone does. But Christian juniors believe in resurrection, too. And that makes death a whole lot less sad.

By a little church, at the end of a country road, there are people waiting to hear God's voice and see His gentle smile.

Seventh-day Adventist juniors believe that someday sin and Satan will have vanished from the universe.

After Jesus returns and takes those who've chosen to love and obey Him to heaven, Satan will have a long time to think about what he's done to this old world. For a thousand years he'll be alone down here, wandering aimlessly through the destruction his actions brought about.

Here's how the Bible describes it. *"And he [God] laid hold on the dragon, that old serpent, which is the Devil, and Satan, and bound him a thousand years, and cast him into the bottomless pit, and shut him up, and set a seal upon him, that he should deceive the nations no more, till the thousand years should be fulfilled"* (Revelation 20:2, 3).

After this time, Christ will bring the New Jerusalem, and us, back to this earth. His appearing will raise the evil dead to life. Satan, who doesn't seem to ever give up, tries to get all his cohorts organized in one last attempt to overthrow God's kingdom. That's when it will happen. What will happen?

"Then death and Hades [the place of death, or 'grave'] were thrown into the lake of fire. . . . If anyone's name was not found written in the book of life, he was thrown into the lake of fire" (Revelation 20:14, 15, NIV).

Ever see a house burn down? It's terrible! When the flames subside, there's nothing left. Nothing.

When God's final fire cools, sin, sinners, and Satan will be no more. What will remain is God, us, and eternity.

NOVEMBER 11

325

Seventh-day Adventist juniors believe that someday they'll live on a new earth.

I'm not talking science fiction here. I'm talking Bible.

"I [John] saw the Holy City, the new Jerusalem, coming down out of heaven from God, prepared as a bride beautifully dressed for her husband. And I heard a loud voice from the throne saying, 'Now the dwelling of God is with men, and he will live with them. They will be his people, and God himself will be with them and be their God. He will wipe every tear from their eyes. There will be no more death or mourning or crying or pain, for the old order of things has passed away'" (Revelation 21:2-4, NIV).

Oh, juniors, sometimes my heart aches for heaven, doesn't yours? Sometimes I get so tired of sin and sickness, tears and trouble, that I can hardly stand it.

But I know, and *you* know, that we've got a brand-new home waiting for us in the near future. Do you realize that we won't even have to pray in heaven? That's right. We can just walk down those golden streets and talk with Jesus face-to-face if we want to.

Of all the doctrines we as Seventh-day Adventists believe, this one is my favorite. Knowing there's a new heaven and a new earth in my future brings me such hope and encouragement! No matter how tough life gets, no matter how many tears I cry, I find comfort in knowing that eternity will be different; it will be joyous. Why not spend today thinking about that world to come? Share your enthusiasm with someone who needs a lift, or a reason to live. Tell them, "Your future is bright. Hold on. Hold on!"

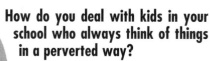

How do you deal with kids in your school who always think of things in a perverted way?

—*Travis, 13, Montana*

The word "perverted" means "weird, corrupt, debased, and warped." Sounds like you have some real characters sitting around you in class.

Some kids find reality boring, so they try to change it. They go to extremes emotionally, physically, and mentally. In other words, they distort life, usually through their words and actions. They're not happy with things as they are.

Perhaps you've even been guilty of doing some harmless "perverting" of your own. How many times have you said, "Elizabeth snitched on me; I'm gonna knock her block off"? Or "What's for supper? I'm starving"?

There are more dangerous forms. Thinking about death all the time and insisting on wearing black, homosexual activity, and militant behavior are all forms of perversion.

How can you deal with it? First, guard yourself. Make sure that your mind is firmly grounded in what's real and what's right. Second, stick to your beliefs and values, no matter what someone else may suggest. Third, keep close to your heavenly Father.

The prophet Jeremiah wrote, *"A voice was heard upon the high places, weeping and supplications of the children of Israel: for they have perverted their way, and they have forgotten the Lord their God"* (Jeremiah 3:21). Some perversion is harmless. Some isn't. Learn the difference by studying God's Word.

NOVEMBER

13

Where did the water go after the Flood?
—Judy, 12, Oklahoma

The Bible presents a very simple explanation.

When the Flood broke upon the earth, we read that *"the fountains of the great deep [were] broken up, and the windows of heaven were opened. And the rain was upon the earth forty days and forty nights"* *(Genesis 7:11, 12)*. The water came from two sources—from the sky as rain ("windows of heaven") and from below the surface of the earth ("fountains of the great deep").

After everything had been covered with water and every living creature had died (except Noah and the occupants of the ark), the Bible records *"God made a wind to pass over the earth. . . . And the waters returned from off the earth continually: and after the end of the hundred and fifty days the waters were abated"* *(Genesis 8:1-3)*.

What happens to water when a wind passes over it? That's right—it evaporates, forming clouds and humidity. Where would "the waters returned from off the earth" go? Yes, back underground, into the great fountains of the deep.

Of course, this Bible writer (Moses) is trying to explain the unexplainable. Any attempt to account scientifically for an act of God is usually frustratingly useless. God does what God does whether or not we can figure out how He accomplished it. It should be enough for us to say "He covered the world with water, then made it go away." Period. End of story.

"Great and marvellous are thy works, Lord God Almighty," shouts John in Revelation 15:3. Let's add our voices to his.

Is it true that scientists found a hole where they think God lives?
—Ana, 11, California

This is an old story that gets updated every decade or so. When I was a kid, I remember hearing of a telescope that allowed scientists to gaze into a particular area of the universe where bright, colorful lights danced in the night sky. "Are we looking at the very front door of heaven?" some asked.

Many times I sit watching the stars, wondering if I'm looking in the direction of heaven. I want so much to catch a glimpse of my future home.

Ana, I don't think it's possible to see heaven from earth. Why? Our eyes and modern instruments probably wouldn't understand what they were looking at. Man didn't build heaven. God did. And His ways are mysterious and glorious. Our ways are imperfect and sinful.

But someday God's going to adjust our eyesight. He's going to do some serious brain surgery on us, enabling us not only to see the glories waiting beyond the night sky but also to understand them as well.

Until then, keep watching the stars. Continue wondering what it will be like to live eternally with Jesus. And when someone says they think they can see heaven with this new, powerful telescope, just smile and say, "My friend, you ain't seen nothin' yet."

Why, when friends fight, does everyone turn against each other?
—*Frank, 11, Florida*

Usually because everyone tends to take sides. Some believe Joe is correct in whatever he's fighting for, while others insist Jessica is in the right. Then these people start arguing among themselves, and away you go.

Would you like for me to share with you one of the most valuable lessons I've learned in my life? It's so simple. Applying this truth to your day-to-day living can save you endless frustration and anger. Here it is: In almost every case, there's more than one "right."

Writers face this continually. As I sit here typing on my computer, I know that someone at the Review and Herald Publishing Association is going to edit my manuscript. This person will probably make some changes in my words. No, he or she won't alter the meaning of what I'm saying. This person will just make some adjustments here and there so that, in his or her opinion, it reads better. Who's right? Truth is, sometimes we both are. We just do things differently, that's all.

When you find two friends fighting, stay out of it, because they both may be right. Instead of taking sides, suggest a compromise. Get them talking with each other and not screaming at each other. And if someone asks you which side you're on, just say "I'm on the side of getting these two guys back together again."

"The meek will he guide in judgment: and the meek will he teach his way" (Psalm 25:9). God's way is the way of peace.

NOVEMBER
16

My parents "favor" my big and little sisters. Sometimes I get jealous and side with my brother and become really mean. How can I be nicer?
—Michelle, 12, Montana

Here are a couple thoughts to consider. Busy parents sometimes take the easiest road possible in a situation. This could be interpreted as "favoring" one child over another, but it's really not the case. For instance, if there's something you want to happen, and a sibling wants another thing to happen, tired, worn-out moms and dads will choose whichever takes the least amount of explaining and planning. Understand?

Perhaps your sisters are better salespersons than you. They may have learned how to get their way by being more skillful in explaining what they want. Perhaps you need to stop and think about *how* you ask for stuff. Do you use nonthreatening words? Are you looking at your requests from an adult perspective?

You side with your brother and get mean out of frustration and anger over the situation. As you've learned, I'm sure, this doesn't help your cause any.

Being nice is a choice. Sometimes you can't wait for feelings of tolerance to flow naturally. You have to say to yourself, "I'm not going to let this seemingly unfair predicament ruin my day. I'm going to be nice even if I don't feel like it." You'll find that when you force your mouth to smile and speak cheery words, the rest of your body soon joins the fun. *"A happy heart makes the face cheerful, but heartache crushes the spirit"* says Solomon in Proverbs 15:13, (NIV). Decide to be nice.

NOVEMBER 17

Could you find some new texts in the Bible? All people do is preach the same stuff over and over.
—*Freddy, 14, Oklahoma*

Well, Freddy, the Bible isn't a work in progress. It was completed a couple thousand years ago.

However, I'll bet there are tons of texts you didn't even know were in there, texts that could teach you important stuff. Let's see if I can dig up a couple in just one book.

Did you know that loving God helps fight sickness? *"Fear the Lord and shun evil. This will bring health to your body and nourishment to your bones"* (Proverbs 3:7, 8, NIV).

I'll bet you weren't aware that the Bible contains a sure formula for getting rich. Here it is: *"Lazy hands make a man poor, but diligent hands bring wealth"* (Proverbs 10:4, NIV).

Want to know how to keep other people's words from hurting you? *"With his mouth the godless destroys his neighbor, but through knowledge the righteous escape"* (Proverbs 11:9, NIV).

Worrying about someone cheating you? *"He who puts up security for another will surely suffer, but whoever refuses to strike [shake] hands in a pledge is safe"* (verse 15, NIV).

Tempted by get-rich-quick opportunities? *"He who works his land will have abundant food, but he who chases fantasies lacks judgment"* (Proverbs 12:11, NIV).

Want to accomplish something great? *"Plans fail for lack of counsel, but with many advisers they succeed"* (Proverbs 15:22, NIV).

Freddy, why not discover some treasures of your own?

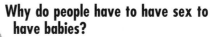

Why do people have to have sex to have babies?
—Xenia, 10, California

Well, actually, they don't. Not in this modern age. It's possible for a man and a woman to produce a child and never meet face-to-face. Happens often.

A woman who wants a child simply has to go to a place (usually a hospital) that specializes in sexless reproduction. She chooses a "father" from a list of sperm donors (men who've provided some of their sperm for such purposes), and has one of her eggs removed from her body. The doctors place the egg and sperm in a test tube under ideal conditions. When the sperm fertilizes (enters) the egg, the egg is put back into the woman's body and, nine months later, it's baby time.

Sometimes husbands and wives who can't produce a child on their own use this method with good results.

But most married couples create babies the old-fashioned way by using sex to set the miracle in motion. Why did God create sex? To make launching a family a happy, pleasurable experience. *"Be fruitful, and multiply, and replenish the earth,"* God told Adam and Eve in Genesis 1:28. Homes were designed to be little heavens on earth for God's people. Within their walls He wanted joy and peace, smiles and laughter. Sex was, and is, the Creator's way for getting things off to a happy start.

Why do some people think having an attitude is cool?
—*Kendra, 13, Alabama*

I know what you mean, Kendra. These people walk around like they're better than everyone else, or they shout putdowns and give certain gestures with their hands. We see it a lot on music videos.

People develop "attitudes" usually as a cover for their insecurities. They don't know how to be natural, so they become unnatural. Those who are afraid of the dark will go around saying, "Nothing scares me, man. I'm brave and heroic." What they're doing is trying to convince themselves of that fact. This even works sometimes!

We all should develop an attitude. Every one of us must decide who we are and how we're going to let life affect us. The best place to look for an example to follow isn't MTV or Hollywood. It's in the footsteps of the One who had the greatest attitude of all, Jesus Christ. *"For I have given you an example, that ye should do as I have done to you,"* He says in John 13:15.

What does Jesus do to us? He loves us unconditionally, on our bad days, sad days, fearful days, and sinful days. He forgives us when we do stupid, mindless things. He never leaves us, even when we try to push Him away.

When a person has this type of attitude, his or her gestures, words, and even the way he or she walks will reveal it for all to see. No longer will this person be saying "Look at me. Pay attention to me." Instead, the message will be, "May I show you Jesus?"

NOVEMBER
20

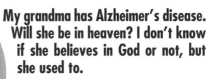

My grandma has Alzheimer's disease. Will she be in heaven? I don't know if she believes in God or not, but she used to.
—*Girl, 12, Montana*

First, let me tell you a secret. There's Someone who loves your grandma even more than you do. God is bound and determined to bring as many people as possible into the beautiful new home He's creating. Leave your grandma in His loving care. She couldn't be in better hands.

Alzheimer's is a sad disease. It robs the very thing from people that make them who they are—their memory.

My aunt Helen, before she went to sleep in Jesus, didn't even know who I was. When I'd go to visit her, she'd smile at me. I'd ask, "Do you remember when we used to sit at the piano and play happy tunes? Do you remember when you visited us for Thanksgiving and we sang songs and sat in church together?" She'd continue to smile, shaking her head slowly.

"Do you know who I am?" I'd say, hoping for a hint of recognition. "No" would always be her response.

People with Alzheimer's may have loved God. They just don't remember. But God does. He sees them as they were before sin took their thoughts away. He hears the prayers they used to utter. In God's mind, their voices still praise Him, still sing His love, still speak of His sacrifice. That's because our heavenly Father isn't affected by sin the way we are. His mind remembers even when ours forgets. He knows, He cares, He saves.

How is a Ouija board satanic?
—*Dana, 13, Oklahoma*

For those who may not know what a Ouija is, it's a board that has letters and symbols printed on it. When used with a pointing device called a planchette, it can successfully aid someone in communicating directly with the devil.

As I've said before, what makes something satanic isn't the material used to make it, or even the words printed across its face. Something becomes satanic when Satan uses it to reach us. Television can be satanic, as can music, art, journalism, photography, even words. Most horrifying of all, people can become satanic when they allow the devil complete control over their lives and actions.

The Ouija board doesn't pretend to be anything noble or righteous. It has been designed with one purpose in mind: to communicate with evil forces. Because of this, it's extremely dangerous and should be avoided at all costs. If someone came up to me with a Ouija board tucked under his or her arm I'd run away. No, I'm not afraid of wood or paint, but I'm very afraid of anyone who's given the devil such open access to his or her heart.

James admonishes us to *"submit yourselves therefore to God. Resist the devil, and he will flee from you" (James 4:7)*. Objects known to be used by Satan to touch human lives must be avoided. The Ouija board is one such object.

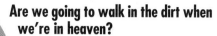

Are we going to walk in the dirt when we're in heaven?

—*Daisy, 10, California*

My wife hates dirt. Well, she doesn't hate *all* dirt. As long as dirt stays out on the lawn or in the forest where it belongs, she actually enjoys it. But when someone we all know (me) tracks that beautiful substance onto her kitchen floor, watch out! She's down on her hands and knees scrubbing away faster than you can say "disinfectant."

Dirt definitely has its place here on earth. And it will definitely have a place in heaven. I see no reason that it can't be enjoyed in both places. Take a bunch of dirt, add some water or rain, throw in a kid or two, and what do you have? *Mud!* And mud means *fun!*

If wiggling your toes in a pile of dirt makes you happy, then get ready to make the mother of all mud pies in heaven. And don't be surprised to find the One who created sand and soil in the first place standing knee-deep beside you, asking if He can join in your fun.

There is one major difference between earth dirt and heaven dirt. In a sinful world soil can contain microorganisms that may do us harm if we're not careful. Much of our dirt includes pesticides, pollutants, and other unhealthy substances.

In heaven even the dirt will be clean. No dangers hiding there! Just loads and loads of fun for all of us who, on occasion, like to mix with the mud. Oh, and when you come to visit me at my very own palace, don't forget to wipe your feet!

There's a girl at school who has emotional problems. She calls me her best friend, but we were never good friends. I just brush her off. I can't stand the way she acts. What should I do?

—*Girl, 13, Alabama*

One of the most challenging things a Christian must learn is how to love the unlovely.

One day Jesus and His disciples were traveling in the region of Galilee. A large crowd was following them because they loved to hear Christ speak.

Suddenly everyone fell silent and backed away, their faces strained with terror. There, in their midst was the most unlovely human being imaginable. *"A man with leprosy came and knelt before [Jesus] and said, 'Lord, if you are willing, you can make me clean'" (Matthew 8:2, NIV).*

Leprosy turns pleasant men and women into horrible-looking creatures. Their ears and noses may be eaten away, their entire faces and bodies disfigured. Thick, white liquid oozes from open sores. Dried blood cakes their pitiful frames. In the days before the disease was medically understood, no doctor would treat them. No relatives would invite them home for dinner. They were outcasts, some living in graveyards and dark, damp caves.

The Bible records that *"Jesus reached out his hand and touched the man,"* healing him instantly (verse 3, NIV). He touched him. Jesus *touched* this horrible mess. Why? Because the Saviour looked beyond the disease, beyond the unloveliness, and saw a person who needed the healing touch of love.

There's a girl at school who has emotional problems. She calls me her best friend, but we were never good friends. I just brush her off. I can't stand the way she acts. What should I do?

—Girl, 13, Alabama

The first step in loving the unlovely is recognizing their true value. We're all brothers and sisters in the family of God. Our love must not be based on appearances, or even on actions. We cherish people simply because they're family.

"A new commandment I give unto you, That ye love one another; as I have loved you, that ye also love one another" *(John 13:34).*

Although our love for the unlovely is unconditional, it must have limits. You don't invite a homeless person into your home if it puts your family at risk. Instead, you arrange for him or her to enjoy a warm meal and a safe night's sleep at an established shelter. You don't join the harmful or perverted activities of someone who has a mental or emotional problem. Instead, you ask a teacher or professional trained in those areas for help.

The problems you mentioned in your original question are serious. Your classmate needs more help than you can give. But there are ways you can love her. Tell her you'll set aside 10 minutes each day to spend just with her. Send an encouraging note from time to time. Always speak of her with kindness and sympathy. Share a little of your time and energy with this unlovely and, I'm sure, lonely child of God.

Jesus says, *"Whatever you did for one of the least of these brothers of mine, you did for me"* *(Matthew 25:40, NIV).*

NOVEMBER

25

I have trouble talking to my parents about personal things. Do you have any advice?

—Girl, 12, Montana

Juniors face many, many questions. They're growing, changing, being given new and bigger responsibilities. Sometimes life can be a little overwhelming. (By the way, it doesn't get any better.)

Personal things are the toughest subject to handle. You wonder, "Am I supposed to know how to deal with this? Am I dumb or something?"

No, you're not dumb. You're just learning. And that's the secret to talking to parents about personal stuff. Don't go to them with the attitude "I should be able to figure this out on my own." Instead, say to yourself, "I'd better learn what I need to know so I won't make big mistakes down the road." Use your parents as a library of experience. They've been where you are. They've probably gone through the very same challenges you're going through. Think of them as guides, not police officers. Use what they've learned to help you succeed.

Solomon says, *"Instruct a wise man and he will be wiser still; teach a righteous man and he will add to his learning"* (Proverbs 9:9, NIV). Smart people learn from other people's mistakes. They don't try to go it alone. Talk to your parents about personal things, not because you're dumb, but because you're smart, and want to be smarter. Soon you'll be able to say with pride, *"Counsel and sound judgment are mine; I have understanding and power"* (Proverbs 8:14, NIV.)

I have trouble talking to my parents about personal things. Do you have any advice?
—*Girl, 12, Montana*

Many young people are shy when it comes to talking to their parents about personal topics. Perhaps they feel embarrassed by the subject, or don't want to be considered uncool by not knowing certain stuff.

Whatever you do, don't keep your questions inside or try to find all the answers among your friends. While your buddies may be whizzes at math or geniuses at science, they may not be your best choice for some of the tough "adult" matters you're facing.

I suggest you make a private appointment with a pastor, teacher, or some other grown-up you've come to trust. Remember, the only thing worse than having no information is having the *wrong* information. Save yourself some embarrassment down the road by getting your facts from a reliable, experienced source.

Juniors have a lot of personal questions that need to be addressed right away. That's why Adventist publishing houses such as the Review and Herald and Pacific Press print books and magazines especially for young people. This devotional book that you are reading sprang from a desire to answer some of the most pressing problems facing boys and girls in today's world.

And never forget your number one source of guidance—the Bible. It contains timeless principles that can be applied to any situation. Also, check out *Messages to Young People*, by our friend Ellen White. You deserve answers. Find them now.

NOVEMBER 27

What will my name be in heaven?

—Neal, 13, Oklahoma

Sounds like you've been reading the book of Revelation, Neal. Good for you. I like to see juniors digging into the richest treasure chest of all, the Bible.

You're also trying to trick me, aren't you? For those who might not know what Neal is up to, let's read Revelation 2:17. Here we find God's angel addressing people who have the same characteristics of the church members at Pergamum. The angel says, *"He who has an ear, let him hear what the Spirit says to the churches. To him who overcomes, I will give some of the hidden manna. I will also give him a white stone with a new name written on it, known only to him who receives it"* (NIV).

In the next chapter God's angel addresses those who are similar to the members in Sardis. The angel says, *"I will write upon him the name of my God, and the name of the city of my God, which is new Jerusalem, which cometh down out of heaven from my God: and I will write upon him my new name"* (Revelation 3:12).

Now, Neal, as you know, the new name God is going to give us is "known only by him who receives it" and is written by an angel. Personally, it won't matter to me if I have to keep my old, worn-out earthly name as long as I can live forever with Jesus. Like the television commercial says: "You can call me Slim, or you can call me Jim." The most important thing is that when Christ returns, He calls me.

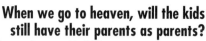

When we go to heaven, will the kids still have their parents as parents?
—*Antoinee, 11, California*

While no one will be getting married and having babies in heaven, there will certainly be families. As a matter of fact, our friend Ellen White reveals an amazing secret. She insists we can begin preparing for heaven right now in our own homes.

Here's what she says: "God would have our families symbols of the family in heaven" *(The Adventist Home,* p. 17). In another place she reveals, "It is God's design that there shall be perfect order in the families on earth, preparatory to their union with the family in heaven" *(Signs of the Times,* Sept. 25, 1901).

What this means, Antoinee, is that all families on earth who love and obey God will someday join together in one big, happy, joyous, heavenly family. While your mom will still be your mom, and your dad your dad, you'll suddenly have more cousins, aunts, uncles, grandparents, brothers, sisters, nephews, and nieces than you'll know what to do with. And they'll *all* be kind, loving, unselfish, giving, thoughtful, and tons of fun.

Anyone who thinks heaven is going to be a boring place where nothing interesting happens hasn't been to one of my family reunions. When my relatives get together, there's music and laughing, funny stories, and lots of hugs. That's the way it will be in the earth made new. And for my junior friends who haven't experienced the joy of a happy family here on earth, just wait! You're going to love your new family in heaven. It'll be big, noisy, joyful, and overflowing with love.

NOVEMBER

29

My parents won't let me get a BB gun. How can I convince them?

—Jonathan, 14, Montana

First, let me ask you a few questions. Do your folks see you enjoying shoot-'em-up shows on television? How do you treat the animals you meet? Do you lose your temper a lot? When you get angry, do you become violent? Think about it.

Jonathan, to your mom and dad, that BB gun represents a door to more deadly weapons. Next year you might want an air rifle, then a .22, then something more powerful. They won't be able to say "We don't believe in guns" when that little ol' BB pistol is resting on your dresser.

Make no mistake. Guns are deadly. They kill and maim people, often by accident. "But I'll be careful," you plead. That's what I said when my brother bought me a BB gun one Christmas when I was young. Mom and Dad gave in and let me keep it. A few days later I was shooting it at a little target I'd set up in the living room. Just for fun, I shot a round into the fireplace to see what would happen. The BB ricocheted off a burning log, streaked in my direction, and hit me in the face. I hurried to a mirror to survey the damage. The BB had left a little circle of ash between my eyelid and my eyebrow. That's how close I came to losing the sight in one eye. And I was being careful!

I choose not to have a gun in my house for the same reason I don't have a pet water moccasin. It's a risk not worth taking. Jonathan, select a hobby that saves lives, not endangers them.

Did the Bible in any way predict the fate of America?

—*Jorge, 11, California*

God had shown the prophet John symbolic images of nations to come. A terrible beast rose out of the sea, a creature that looked like a leopard. It had horns on its heads, the feet of a bear, and the mouth of a lion.

Then a new image appeared. *"I beheld another beast coming up out of the earth; and he had two horns like a lamb"* (Revelation 13:11). The great kingdoms ruling the world prior to this new lamblike creature had been shown as beasts of prey, creating awful scenes of conflict and destruction. They'd also come from the sea, which, in prophetic language, meant they'd risen to power from among "peoples, multitudes, nations, and tongues" (Revelation 17:15, NKJV). The continent of Europe fits that description perfectly.

But the lamblike beast rose out of the earth—a place in which there were few people and no major governments. And it was a peaceful creature, nonthreatening, nonviolent.

What nation rose to power promising peace and freedom to all? Where did it establish itself? That's right. The United States of America rose from a new land that at one time wasn't even on anyone's map. And its message to the world was (and is): "All men are created equal."

America is mentioned in the Bible in powerful, prophetic terms. But God's Word contains a warning that we'd better hear. All isn't well with the lamblike beast. Tomorrow we'll discover what fate awaits this country and its inhabitants.

DECEMBER

1

Did the Bible in any way predict the fate of America?
—*Jorge, 11, California*

Yesterday we learned that the United States of America is represented in Revelation 13 as a "lamblike" beast that seems to be peaceful. But there's more to the prophecy.

"And I beheld another beast coming up out of the earth; and he had two horns like a lamb, and he spake as a dragon. And he . . . causeth the earth and them which dwell therein to worship the first beast, whose deadly wound was healed. And he doeth great wonders, so that he maketh fire come down from heaven on the earth in the sight of men, and deceiveth them that dwell on the earth by the means of those miracles which he had power to do . . . ; saying to them that dwell on the earth, that they should make an image to the beast" (Revelation 13:11-14).

The "first beast" mentioned here is papal Rome, the religious power that ruled Europe for centuries. It almost lost authority when its leader, the pope, was taken prisoner. But it survived and later flourished.

These startling verses show the lamblike beast doing two things: making "fire come down from heaven" and telling everyone to "make an image to the beast."

What fire has the United States created that "comes down from heaven"? Yes, the atomic bomb first used on Hiroshima and Nagasaki, Japan, at the end of World War II. But this is nothing compared to what it's about to do. We'll talk more about this incredible prophecy tomorrow!

Did the Bible in any way predict the fate of America?
—*Jorge, 11, California*

The lamblike beast mentioned in Revelation 13 is about to do something very unlamblike.

The Bible says that this seemingly peaceful creature *"spake as a dragon. . . . And he causeth all, both small and great, rich and poor, free and bond, to receive a mark in their right hand, or in their foreheads: and that no man might buy or sell, save he that had the mark, or the name of the beast" (verses 11-17).*

We noted earlier that this other "beast" is the power and teachings of papal Rome. What the Bible is saying is that the mark (or authority) of this power will change the actions (mark in right hand) and beliefs (mark in foreheads) of the people who make up the lamblike nation. Unless you believe and act a certain way, you won't be able to buy or sell. In other words, your life will be directly affected by the first beast that the lamblike beast has come to worship. Intense stuff, huh?

Jorge, papal Rome has always taught two dangerous errors: (1) that Sunday is the Sabbath, and (2) that the pope and his priests can forgive sins. We know that Saturday is God's holy day, and that only Jesus can forgive us when we break one of His commandments.

Juniors, someday the lamblike beast will roar like a dragon, telling us to worship a power that teaches error. But we'll know better. Even if we lose our freedom, we'll stand by Jesus' side, obeying the beautiful truths of the Bible. Our future lies not with the lamblike beast, but with the Lamb of God.

Did the Bible in any way predict the fate of America?

—*Jorge, 11, California*

As we've seen, Jorge's question is an important one. The events found in the answer spotlight the closing scenes of this earth's history.

The lamblike beast of Revelation 13 represents the United States of America. It will someday speak as a dragon in its attempt to get everyone to worship "the first beast," a power that teaches, among other things, that Sunday is the Sabbath and that man can forgive sins. These issues will split the Christian world into two great classes—those who keep God's commandments and those who don't.

Allow me to show you one other scene. It's also found in Revelation. Listen closely: *"And I [John] saw as it were a sea of glass mingled with fire: and them that had gotten the victory over the beast, and over his image, and over his mark . . . stand on the sea of glass, having the harps of God. And they sing the song of Moses . . . and the song of the Lamb, saying, Great and marvellous are thy works, Lord God Almighty; just and true are thy ways, thou King of saints. Who shall not fear thee, O Lord, and glorify thy name? for thou only art holy: for all nations shall come and worship before thee"* (Revelation 15:2-4).

Juniors, stick close to Jesus from this day forward. Learn as much as you can about that Book you carry under your arm each week as you head off for church. I want to find *you* standing on that sea of glass someday, singing out your love for God.

How great is God?

—Benjamin, 11, Oklahoma

Benjamin, your question really gets me thinking. I mean, here's this divine being called "God" telling me to worship Him, obey Him, trust Him, and basically turn my whole life over to His leading.

I don't do this for just anybody, you understand. No, sir. For me to worship, obey, trust, and follow someone, that person has to be really, really, really great!

To find the answer and discover just how great God is, I have to gather some serious information. So I open my Bible, which contains the most complete description of God available. And what do I find? Lots of stories *about* Him. Tons of testimonies *concerning* Him. Rules and regulations created *by* Him. And a bunch of moaning and groaning people who insisted on turning their backs *on* Him.

Then, like a jewel in the sand, I find Jesus. He's walking through the countryside healing the sick, raising the dead, loving the unlovely. I hear Him speaking words of comfort and hope. With wondering eyes I watch Him die for me.

The answer to your question springs into my thoughts. How great is God? He's so great that He can love a sinner like me. He's so great that He gave His only Son to pay a terrible price for my mistakes. He's so great that He's willing to forgive and forget my stupid actions and thoughtless deeds.

"He that hath seen me," says Jesus, *"hath seen the Father"* (John 14:9). Look to Jesus, Benjamin, to discover the greatness of God.

DECEMBER

5

I argue with my parents, and every time I do I feel awful. Is there any way I can prevent arguments?
—*Girl, 12, Montana*

Arguments spring from a very simple source. Whenever two people think or believe in different ways, there's the potential for discord, even if those people love each other.

No one wants to give in. No one wants to abandon his or her ideas. No one wants to be proven wrong. So it looks like arguing is here to stay.

There are ways to change an argument with your folks from a bad experience to a learning or even sharing experience.

First, listen. It's very possible that your parents have a valid reason for thinking the way they do. Try to see the issue from their perspective. Say to yourself, "If I had the responsibilities they have, would I look at things differently?"

Second, learn. An argument is a great time to discover some of the hidden fears your folks may have. The more you know about them, the better you'll be able to get your point across.

Third, compromise. Give a little. Take a little. Try to find that all-important common ground between their ideas and yours. You'll discover you agree more than disagree.

Finally, ask God for help. He's been settling arguments ever since Adam blamed Eve and Eve blamed the serpent. *"Let us then approach the throne of grace with confidence, so that we may . . . find grace to help us in our time of need" (Hebrews 4:16, NIV).* Transform arguments into open, honest times of sharing.

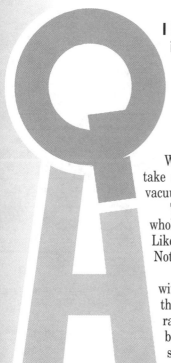

I like watching TV more than cleaning. What should I do?

—*Tasha, 11, California*

Well, of course, you do. So do I. I'll take an exciting adventure story over a vacuum cleaner any day!

Trouble is, life isn't all play. There's a whole lot of work thrown in there, too. Like it or not, work makes play possible. Not the other way around.

When what I *have* to do interferes with what I *want* to do I simply look out the back window of our house for inspiration. In the forest, high among the branches of the oaks, lives a family of squirrels. I see them scurrying about, ceaselessly gathering nuts and seeds, scampering from limb to limb searching for food. This is serious business for them. Without a large store of rations, they'd not survive the coming winter months.

All of a sudden, they stop their work and launch into what appears to be a high-flying game of tag. With blinding speed and breathtaking agility, they streak across the leaves, leaping great distances between branches, sometimes bringing their fun to the forest floor, where they tumble and roll in the dirt. After a few moments of this seemingly blissful play, they pause to catch their breath, then continue with their nut gathering.

You like watching TV, Tasha? Take a lesson from the squirrels. Work hard, clean hard, then reward yourself with a little break and enjoy your favorite show. Then get back to the important jobs at hand. *"Let us labour therefore to enter into that rest" (Hebrews 4:11).* Find time for both work and play.

DECEMBER 7

351

Why is it that all my friends can talk about me unkindly, but if I say something about them they slug me?
—*Girl, 13, Montana*

Ouch! Sounds like you could use some new friends.

Jesus had the very same problem. The spiritual leaders in Jerusalem said all kinds of mean and nasty things about Him. They spread lies, got crowds all worked up, even paid men and women to testify falsely concerning Him.

But let Jesus try to correct their errors, let Him address their problems with words of kindness, and watch out! Have you ever stopped to realize that Christ was crucified, not because of what He did, but because of what people *said* He did? And they weren't telling the truth. So it looks like you're in good company.

Most people say mean things about another person because they don't like themselves. Knocking you down makes them feel better, smarter, more popular. Isn't that sad?

What did Jesus do under these circumstances? Listen to this astonishing verse: *"He was oppressed, and he was afflicted, yet he opened not his mouth: he is brought as a lamb to the slaughter, and as a sheep before her shearers is dumb, so he openeth not his mouth"* (Isaiah 53:7).

When your so-called friends talk mean about you, stand and take it like Jesus did. And when you do speak, consider the words your Saviour uttered while hanging on the cross: *"Father, forgive them; for they know not what they do"* (Luke 23:34).

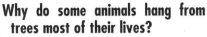

Why do some animals hang from trees most of their lives?
—*Ruben, 11, California*

There are several animals who like to view the world upside down. The opossum and bat spring to mind. I've seen squirrels hanging by their hind feet while munching on a sunflower seed. And don't forget the tree-climbing nuthatch and brown creeper, as well as those marvelous acrobats of the jungle, monkeys. They all spend a lot of time head-down, tail-up.

Why they like to hang around like this is anybody's guess. Personally, I prefer sitting to dangling. Of course, I'm not into eating bugs or swinging from limb to limb, either.

Somehow I think that the actions of animals, as weird as they may be, serve a purpose only they and their Creator fully understand. Your question is a good one to ask Jesus someday while you two are sitting under the tree of life, discussing important stuff. He'll have a ready answer, I'm sure.

You know, Ruben, people sometimes act in strange ways too. While the rest of us are happy to live normally, they're out climbing mountains, jumping out of airplanes, swimming around the bottom of the ocean, and finding adventure wherever they can. Even juniors get into the act by mastering the piano before their voices change, reading every book in the library, or becoming smarter than their teachers. Cool!

We normal people could learn a lot from those in our midst who live life a little differently. God loves us all, whether we like to climb trees, sit on limbs, or hang from them.

9

There's a guy in my classroom who has bad body odor and a zit-covered face. He flirts with all the girls or tries to, but they won't talk to him or sit by him in worship because he stinks. Is it OK for them to act like that?
—*Girl, 13*

Our human bodies are quite capable of being really—how shall I say—odoriferous, which is a polite way of saying we can stink to high heaven! Stomach ulcers, bad teeth, disease, cancers, tumors, and persistent infections can send the smell scale into orbit.

After reading your complete description of this unfortunate chap, I'd say here's a guy whose body is under attack from many fronts.

Now comes the challenge. God expects you and your friends to love that young man as much as you love yourselves. Why? Because every person, even those with zits and body odor, is a child of heaven and worthy of Christ's great sacrifice.

How did Jesus react to those who stank? I'm sure His stomach churned a few times as He walked among the lepers, bent low over the sick and dying, put His arms around the crippled and infected. But the sweetness of His love overpowered the stench of their lives. He looked beyond their vileness and saw their soul-stirring desire for salvation.

On a practical level, your classmate probably could use a radical change of diet and a few tips on personal hygiene. On a spiritual level, he needs someone to show him Jesus. How about you being that someone?

If I go to heaven when I'm still a little girl, will I stay that way?

—Karina, 11, California

God made all things to grow. Nothing remains young, not even people. Just as puppies become dogs, kittens turn into cats, so all little girls will become beautiful women in heaven.

But growing up in the new earth won't be filled with fear or even the hint of pain. All children will have loving parents. Every boy and girl will feel safe and secure in that land.

There is one kind of growing that won't affect the citizens of God's kingdom. In heaven, no one will ever grow old.

"All the treasures of the universe will be open to the study of God's redeemed. Unfettered by mortality, they wing their tireless flight to worlds afar. . . . With unutterable delight the children of earth enter into the joy and the wisdom of unfallen beings. . . . With undimmed vision they gaze upon the glory of creation" *(The Great Controversy,* p. 677).

Do you know what I think will be the very best part about growing up in heaven? In that new home beyond the stars, there will be not one, *not one*, broken home. Daddies will never leave. Moms won't abandon their children. The family will be as strong and lasting as eternity itself.

Although we will grow up, we'll always enjoy the loving intimacy of belonging to a family. But this time there will be no goodbyes. In heaven, grandparents and cousins and aunts will always be there to smile at us, play with us, walk by our sides. Growing up in heaven will be a joyful, satisfying experience.

DECEMBER 11

355

Why do the Mormons say there are three heavens? I feel like they are kind of treating themselves unfairly.
—*Girl, 14, Montana*

When I was a kid, I had a friend who lived several houses down from us. One day he looked kind of sad.

"What's the matter?" I asked.

"My cat died," he said with a sigh. "I miss him."

Shaking my head slowly, I said, "I'm sorry."

My friend sat down beside me and pointed skyward. "He's in heaven, you know, probably chasing birds like he always did."

My neighbor was one of millions who firmly believe that when people or animals die, their soul goes to heaven —or hell, depending on how they lived.

People hold to a certain idea because it helps them understand the dark mysteries of life. If a group of well-meaning individuals insist there are three heavens, that belief must be important to their concept of God. Trouble is, many people form ideas from traditions or the imaginations of human beings who've struggled with the same questions they're facing.

We Seventh-day Adventists look to only one source for truth. We depend on the words of just one Person as we construct our beliefs. The Bible and Jesus Christ form the foundation of everything we hold as truth.

As you grow up, you'll find many religions and many beliefs trying to attract your attention. But keep your eyes on Jesus, and your mind firmly anchored in God's holy Word.

When we go to heaven, are we going to see the people we knew who are already in heaven?

—*Erin, 11, California*

When we reach that beautiful place, we'll joyfully find many friends and family members whom we haven't seen for a long, long time. For a brief moment, we'll recall the sad days on this earth when we said goodbye to them, laying them gently in their graves. But those tearful images will quickly fade, replaced by the unspeakable happiness that we'll never have to say goodbye again.

So, yes, we are going to see people we knew. But they won't already be in heaven. They'll be getting there at the same time we do. We make the trip together!

Listen to these thrilling Bible words: *"For the Lord himself shall descend from heaven with a shout, with the voice of the archangel, and with the trump of God: and the dead in Christ shall rise first: Then we which are alive and remain shall be caught up together with them in the clouds, to meet the Lord in the air: and so shall we ever be with the Lord"* (1 Thessalonians 4:16, 17).

Isn't that exciting! Right this minute, as you read these words, Jesus and the angels are preparing heaven for us. They're building mansions, planting gardens, forming nature trails, setting up science projects, collecting fascinating creatures from around the universe, and shining up those streets of gold for all, alive or dead, who have made God the very center of their lives. And that includes you, Erin, if you choose.

DECEMBER

13

Are your parents divorced? If yes, why does it cause a problem to the family?
—*Michael, 11, California*

No, Michael, my mom and dad are still married to each other. But the rest of my family hasn't fared so well.

Divorce causes a problem in a family for the same reason cancer causes a problem in a body. Both destroy what's needed to maintain health and strength.

God intended that families be made up of three parts: a loving father, a loving mother, and loving children. He placed in the Bible many suggestions and words of guidance to help the family survive in a sinful world. He told moms and dads not to commit adultery or lust after someone else's partner. He taught them how to forgive mistakes, overcome temptations, and even how to love, just in case no one else took the time to teach them.

God's instruction to children includes *"Honour thy father and thy mother"* (Exodus 20:12), *"Obey your parents in the Lord"* (Ephesians 6:1), and *"Listen . . . to a father's instruction; pay attention and gain understanding"* (Proverbs 4:1, NIV).

The family, like a body, needs all the parts working together to survive and grow. Divorce changes everything, separating the parts, dismantling God's plan.

That's why moms, dads, and kids in divorced homes need to depend on Jesus so much. He has offered to act as father to the fatherless, mother to the comfortless, and big brother or sister to children who feel lost and alone. When all else fails, God is still there, doing His best to form a family out of what's left.

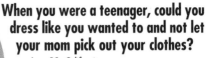

When you were a teenager, could you dress like you wanted to and not let your mom pick out your clothes?
—*Ana, 11, California*

I lived my teenage years during the sixties, when everyone who wanted to be cool looked like he or she had just climbed out of a dumpster. "We're unique, different, nonconformists!" was the battle cry. So everyone ended up looking like one another.

Fortunately for my mother, I was more of a clean-shirt, bell-bottom-jeans kind of guy. I left the beads, matted hair, and tie-dyed shirts to the sandal-and-leather set.

I understand what you're saying, Ana. You want to choose what to wear because clothes are an expression of who you are, right? Just as teens in my generation, you want the freedom to decorate your body with what you like. And someday, when you have the privilege of buying all your own clothes, you can.

For now, keep in mind that your mom has some very legitimate concerns that you should consider. Money may be an issue—a big issue. Modesty plays a role, too, as does making sure that what you select will last longer than the fashion whim that created it. You only think of how you'll look. Mom must consider value, length of wear, price, Christian principles, and addressing your more than likely ever-changing demands.

Why not be a part of the solution? Ask your mom to give you some choices in what she believes you should wear. Give her lots of choices, too, in what turns you on. Then you'll end up with a closet full of clothes you can both live with. Have fun!

DECEMBER 15

If you die and Jesus resurrects you, will you become the same person again?
—*Pacell, 11, California*

Yes . . . and no. It's a fact few people fully understand. But we Christians must learn the answer, for it can save us years of uncertainty. Let's take a closer look at this matter.

It's earth's last day. Jesus returns. Listen to what Paul says happens next: *"I tell you a mystery. . . . We will all be changed—in a flash, in the twinkling of an eye, at the last trumpet. For the trumpet will sound, the dead will be raised imperishable, and we will be changed. . . . When the perishable has been clothed with the imperishable, and the mortal with immortality, then the saying that is written will come true: 'Death has been swallowed up in victory'"* (1 Corinthians 15:51-54, NIV).

What is this great change that we're going to experience? That's right, we'll lose forever the threat of dying.

But doesn't God turn bad people into good people? Won't the sins we love to commit be taken away? That's not what it says. Consider this thought-provoking passage: *"He that is unjust, let him be unjust still: and he which is filthy, let him be filthy still: and he that is righteous, let him be righteous still: and he that is holy, let him be holy still. And, behold, I come quickly; and my reward is with me, to give every man according as his work shall be"* (Revelation 22:11).

Yes, when Jesus comes, we'll continue to be who we are, whether alive or resurrected. But something important will be removed from our lives. We'll find out what it is tomorrow.

DECEMBER
16

360

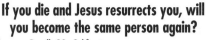

If you die and Jesus resurrects you, will you become the same person again?
—*Pacell, 11, California*

Yesterday we discovered that when Jesus comes, He'll remove the threat of death from us forever. We'll be changed from a "perishable" person to an "imperishable" heavenly citizen.

But God is going to remove something else from our lives—*temptation*. No longer will Satan have access to our thoughts. No longer will we need to constantly struggle to live a sin-free life. Day after day, year after year, millennium after millennium, we'll enjoy the freedom of perfection.

Our friend Ellen White reminds us, "We cannot say, 'I am sinless,' till this vile body is changed and fashioned like unto His glorious body" *(Selected Messages,* book 3, p. 355).

This change happens the moment we see Jesus coming in the clouds. Sin and its influence are swept from our lives by the mighty hand of God. In the twinkling of an eye, we stand as immortal beings and totally, forever, free from sin.

This transformation happens *only* to those who've been preparing for this glorious event by living their lives in constant, relentless battle with Satan. When temptation and sin are removed, they easily become citizens of heaven, for they've already prepared their characters, changing their desires and their wants to what God requires. They've long ago determined in their hearts that nothing will keep them from their future home.

We'll be the same person, Pacell. Now's the time for us to start preparing that person for heaven.

DECEMBER 17

Will the people who were with God, then separated, go to heaven?

—Daisy, 10, California

That's up to them, Daisy. But they can't *stay* separated from God and expect to be saved. After all, heaven is God's home. People who don't love or trust Him would hardly want to live for eternity in His presence.

There's only one road to heaven and it's found in this beautiful Bible text: *"Jesus saith unto him, I am the way, the truth, and the life: no man cometh unto the Father, but by me" (John 14:6).*

So what must a person do who has separated himself or herself from Jesus? God the Father says, *"If a wicked man turns away from the wickedness he has committed and does what is just and right, he will save his life" (Ezekiel 18:27, NIV).*

Did you notice who saves whom here? The wicked person, by turning from sin and coming back to Jesus, rescues his own life from eternal death through heaven's power!

Daisy, it's not fun to watch people reject Jesus, is it? Our hearts burn with concern and sadness. We think and think and think about how we can help them return to the safety and warmth of God's arms. But sometimes, all we can do is love them, and pray every night that they'll end the separation, and save themselves by God's redeeming might.

"He that keepeth the law, happy is he" (Proverbs 29:18). Let's determine to spread our happiness to those who've turned their backs on Jesus, reminding them of what they've left behind.

How was money made? Did God send it, or did Satan?

—Victoria, 11, California

Sometimes I wonder, Victoria. Often money tends to do more harm than good to those who have it.

The Bible even seems to support the thought that money wasn't exactly God's idea. *"For the love of money is the root of all evil: which while some coveted after, they have erred from the faith, and pierced themselves through with many sorrows" (1 Timothy 6:10).*

God's plan was for every man and woman to have all they need through simple, enjoyable labor. Short on food? Grow it. Don't have a house? Build one. Want to visit an uncle who lives by the river? Pack a lunch, grab a walking stick, and go. No malls, no bosses, no banks or mortgages, just faithful stewardship of everything God had provided.

But sin changed all that. Suddenly men and women wanted more than they needed. Jealousy, greed, love of wealth, and a pocketful of credit cards turned humanity into slaves to the mighty dollar.

Although the *love* of money might be the root of all evil, money itself doesn't have to become evil to us. I've seen it being put to wonderful uses such as paying for a child's Christian education, buying healthful food at the market, relieving the suffering of thousands in drought-stricken lands, or bringing a smile to a face on Christmas morning. Money, honestly earned and carefully spent, can glorify God and hasten His coming. Use it wisely, Victoria.

DECEMBER
19

I want to know more about the future.

—Jeremy, 13, Oklahoma

You and everyone else in this world, Jeremy. Walk down the street of any city, town, or village and you'll meet people whose faces are tight with worry. "What's going to happen to me?" they want to know. "Will the airplane I'm flying in tomorrow crash?" "Should I invest my money in this company or that business?" "When I die, will I go to heaven or to hell?"

You'd think most of us would want to know about the future so we can plan for it. But that's not the case. Everyone knows smoking shortens life and causes great suffering. Yet recent reports indicate that every day 3,000 teens take up smoking for the first time. They know the future, yet it doesn't affect their plans one bit.

Some say, "If I knew what was going to happen, I wouldn't be so frightened." In the Bible, God clearly outlines what the future holds, yet people fear even what they know. Some go so far as to be afraid of God Himself!

Jesus once said, *"Do not worry about your life, what you will eat or drink; or about your body,"* and *"tomorrow will worry about itself. Each day has enough trouble of its own" (Matthew 6:25, 34, NIV).*

When you look to the future, you should see Christ waiting for you with open arms. With that image planted firmly in your mind, turn your attention to today, and begin doing whatever it takes to win the victory over sin until Jesus comes.

Since Noah and his family were the only people on earth after the Flood, does that mean that from then on people were all family?
—*Michael, 10, California*

When the little door of the ark creaked open after the boat had come to rest *"upon the mountains of Ararat" (Genesis 8:4)*, the seagoing family looked out across a barren, lifeless land. *"So Noah came out, together with his sons [Shem, Ham, Japheth] and his wife and his sons' wives" (verse 18, NIV).* That makes eight travelers. Genesis 9 reports, *"From them came the people who were scattered over the earth" (verse 19, NIV).*

Today, we wouldn't think of marrying our cousins, as nice as they may be. It's just not done in this country. In other parts of the world, such marriages are still common.

Why was it accepted back then and not now? Medical research has shown that such unions tend to lower the mental powers of the offspring. There are other scientific reasons I won't get into, because I'm not a doctor. But those harmful effects must not have been a factor in Noah's day. After all, people were in much better health than we are. Captain Noah himself lived to be 950 years old. His sons and daughters-in-law probably lived for centuries too. A couple can have a bunch of kids during an 800-year marriage!

So, Michael, the next time a friend says something unkind about a person of another race or color, remind him or her of Noah, Shem, Ham, and Japheth. Tell this friend he or she shouldn't say such nasty things about a member of his or her own family.

DECEMBER
21

My dad doesn't go to church, but he loves God. I feel like he doesn't care. How can I convince him to go to church?
—*Girl, 14, Montana*

If your father isn't a Seventh-day Adventist, he needs to be taught about God's love, and how the Sabbath is a special day set aside for his benefit.

However, because you're attending an Adventist church school and you say your dad loves God, I have a feeling your father is an Adventist at heart but has lost interest in what the church has to offer.

There's a move on today throughout Adventism to make our churches "relevant." That means pastors and administrators are trying to find ways for our churches to meet the needs of their members. These days people don't go to church simply because they think they should. They attend because they believe they're receiving something of value. This value may be *social*—they enjoy being with other Christian friends; *mental*—their minds are challenged with new and interesting thoughts; or *spiritual*—they're learning how God can help them survive.

Your father may find the church you attend lacking in the area he enjoys or needs most. While you may love your Sabbath school class and the other fun activities, he finds little to get him out of bed on Sabbath morning.

The first step in getting your dad back to church is for you to realize he has needs that aren't being met. Ask him what they are. Tomorrow we'll dig for solutions to your concern.

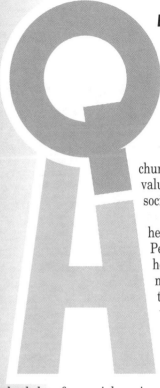

My dad doesn't go to church, but he loves God. I feel like he doesn't care. How can I convince him to go to church?

—*Girl, 14, Montana*

Yesterday we learned that people go to church because they find something of value there—something that meets their social, mental, or spiritual needs.

First, ask your dad what activities he'd really like to see at your church. Perhaps he's interested in health issues, how to be a good Christian businessman, finding effective ways to fight temptation and sin. Take these suggestions to your pastor.

Next, try to get yourself involved in the service in some way (giving the opening prayer, taking up the offering, singing with your Sabbath school class for special music, reading a text up front). Most dads love seeing their kids perform.

If all else fails, ask your dad to help you check out other Adventist churches in the area. Maybe one a few miles down the road is offering just what he's looking for.

And of course, pray, pray, pray. Ask God to open your eyes to your father's needs. Maybe someone hurt his feelings. Maybe he's carrying a load of guilt. Be patient as you let him see how much you enjoy attending church. Give God time to work.

One last thought. If Dad won't go to church, bring church to Dad. Repeat the high points of the sermon. Tell who was there and what you learned. In time, he may want to experience it for himself. What a happy day that will be for both of you, and for God.

DECEMBER
23

During the next few days, I'd like to dig into another important question many of my junior friends have asked. They write, "If I've done stuff I know Jesus doesn't like, how can I get back on track to heaven?"

As usual, the Bible doesn't disappoint. Strangely, the answers all begin with the letter C.

Let's say you cheated on a math exam. I know you wouldn't do such a dishonest thing, but we'll pretend, OK? You sneak a peek at someone else's paper and copy down a bunch of answers.

After turning in your test, how do you feel? Kind of weird inside, huh? Your lunch doesn't taste as good as it did yesterday. You can't get excited about the ball game during recess. For some reason, you snap at a friend and refuse to look your teacher in the eye. What's going on?

Sounds like you need the first C that the Bible says will get you back on track to heaven. It's found in Matthew 11:28. Listen: *"Come to me, all you who are weary and burdened, and I will give you rest" (NIV)*.

When our hearts are heavy with guilt, when our sins have separated us from our loving Saviour, it's time to *come* to Him.

How? It might be a moment of quiet reflection. It could be a silent prayer. Or you may decide you've been out on your own long enough. However you choose, it's not difficult. He's waiting, arms open wide, longing to welcome you into His fold of love.

"Come to me," Jesus says. It's the first step back.

"Coming" to Jesus is the first step back for those who've allowed sin to separate them from His protective love. What happens next also begins with the letter C. Can you spot it?

"What then shall we say? Is God unjust? Not at all! For he says to Moses, 'I will have mercy on whom I have mercy, and I will have compassion on whom I have compassion'" (Romans 9:14, 15, NIV).

Do you know what *compassion* is? "Oh, sure," I hear you say. "It's feeling sorry for someone." True, but that's only part of the picture.

One day a certain Samaritan happened upon the scene of a terrible crime. Thieves had ambushed a man traveling from Jerusalem to Jericho, leaving him for dead. The Bible records that the *"Samaritan, as he journeyed, came where he was: and when he saw him, he had compassion on him, and went to him, and bound up his wounds, pouring in oil and wine, and set him on his own beast, and brought him to an inn, and took care of him" (Luke 10:33, 34).*

Notice that this kind man did a whole lot more than feel sorry for the wounded traveler. He stopped and did something—in fact, a bunch of things. Why? Because having compassion involves *action!* It's more than words. Compassion moves people to do something about the situation.

When God has compassion on us, He's preparing to take action. What that action is depends on what we do after we come to Him. We'll discover the next step tomorrow.

DECEMBER

25

369

First we *come* to Jesus with our sins. He has compassion on us and prepares to do something. But before He can, we must take another C step. King David knew what it was. Try to catch it.

"Then I acknowledged my sin to you and did not cover up my iniquity. I said, 'I will confess my transgressions to the Lord'" (Psalm 32:5, NIV).

Did you find the C word? As a matter of fact, there were two. David didn't *cover* up his iniquity. And he did something more. He *confessed* his transgression.

When I was a lad living in the Philippines, my dad brought home an interesting souvenir someone had given him. It was a terrific, handmade bow and arrow. While my parents and brothers were off doing something next door, I decided to play with this mysterious weapon, even though I'd been told not to. Pretending I was a jungle warrior out hunting supper, I sneaked up on an unsuspecting couch and drew back the string, arrow feathers poised at my cheek. Then something happened that wasn't supposed to happen. The string slipped out of my grasp, sending the sharp pointed arrow arching across the living room. The good news was I missed the couch. The bad news was I killed the window screen, leaving a gaping hole in it large enough to allow the largest bugs in the Far East free access to our home.

No, I didn't try to cover up my sin. Yes, I confessed and took my punishment like any good jungle warrior. I learned confession feels better than guilt. When we confess our sins to God, He reaches for the soap. The soap? See you tomorrow!

Yesterday I said that when we confess our sins to God, He reaches for the soap. "What are you talking about?" you ask.

Listen for the C word in this hope-filled text: *"If we confess our sins, he is faithful and just to forgive us our sins, and to cleanse us from all unrighteousness"* (1 John 1:9).

Ever looked into a washing machine while it's hard at work taking out the ketchup stains on your favorite shirt, or the mud on your jeans from the game-winning slide? Things are really churning down there, aren't they? There are bubbles and waves and splashes.

When God cleanses us from our sins, something happens there, too. We get scrubbed. How? Maybe we need to ask forgiveness of the person we wronged. Perhaps we have to go to a teacher or parent and face whatever punishment we've got coming. Getting sin out of our lives isn't always easy, but it's always worth it.

Once the cleansing process is complete, we feel great! We can hold our heads up again knowing we're back on track for heaven. Our guilt is gone.

God says, *"Though your sins be as scarlet, they shall be as white as snow; though they be red like crimson, they shall be as wool"* (Isaiah 1:18).

First we *come*. God has *compassion*. We *confess*. God *cleanses*. But we're not finished yet. There are a few more C's waiting along our journey. However, the hard part is past.

DECEMBER 27

When I was a little boy, I got kind of sick. I had to stay home from school for six weeks! I couldn't go to Pathfinders. I couldn't play baseball with my buddies. I couldn't even ride my bike.

You see, there was something wrong with my knees. They hurt. The doctor said if I didn't conquer my disease I wouldn't live beyond the age of 30, because the disease would damage my heart.

One day while I was recovering, my Pathfinder Club had a camping trip. The doctor said I could go if I took it easy and didn't strain myself. Telling a 12-year-old not to strain himself is like asking a hurricane not to blow. Before the short hike from the parking area to the campsite, I loaded my backpack as full as those of the other guys, and we set off. My knees hurt, and I began to get tired. Soon I was struggling to keep up.

Suddenly the weight on my shoulders seemed to lessen. I turned and found one of the camp leaders taking some things out of my backpack as I walked along. Quietly, without attracting attention, she was placing them into her pack. When she finished the job, she moved away, keeping my pride and heart intact.

Now, whenever I read our C text for today, I think of that kind woman. First Peter 5:7 says, *"Cast all your anxiety on him because he cares for you" (NIV).* Did you hear the C word?

God wants to help us carry our load. He knows we're sick with sin. He knows our spiritual legs can get kinda wobbly. That's why He's happy to lift our burdens and place them on His strong shoulders. Do you have some burdens to *cast* today?

In several jungles of the world, people have discovered the perfect monkey trap. They tie a narrow-necked jar to a stake in the ground. In this jar they place a banana. Then they wait.

Soon, along comes their prey, looking around for something to eat. It sees the jar, smells the banana, reaches in, and discovers a problem. It can't get its hand back out while holding on to the fruit. The neck of the jar is too small.

Even while the jungle people are closing in for the kill, the monkey refuses to let go of the banana.

I wonder if Paul was thinking about this amazing method for capturing primates when he said *"Hate what is evil; cling to what is good" (Romans 12:9, NIV).*

Sometimes we may find ourselves clinging to stuff that could do us a great deal of harm. Bad habits, sinful secrets, evil thoughts, these can hold us as tightly as the monkey's fist around the banana.

You see, when the storms of life come, as they always do, if you're holding on to favorite sins, God can't help you. But when you *cling* to what is good, like pure thoughts, health-building habits, and faith in Jesus, you'll survive the storms and be able to assist others in the process.

Take a moment and think about your life. Is it time to let go of some things before the devil closes in for the kill? Reach for Jesus' hand. Take hold of the only object that will keep you solidly on the road to heaven.

We've found a lot of C's on our road to heaven. Can you remember them? *Come, compassion, confess, cleanse, cast,* **and** *cling.* **There are two more you should know about.**

The first is found in Psalm 51:10. Watch out. It comes quickly. *"Create in me a pure heart, O God, and renew a steadfast spirit within me" (NIV).*

Whew. That one tried to slip by, but you caught it. We must allow God to *create* a pure heart in us.

I once watched a fascinating documentary on television. It was all about heart transplants. Talk about amazing! Here's this sick person who's been waiting a long time. Suddenly the phone rings. A healthy heart has been located. Everyone starts running around like crazy. Doctors scrub in, nurses prepare the operating room, and the patient is quickly prepared and wheeled down to surgery. Family and friends hold each other and pray.

Then the head surgeon strolls into the waiting room and announces that everything's fine. The patient will recover fully and live a long life.

One fact struck me hard while watching this modern miracle of medicine. In order for that patient to get a new heart, someone, somewhere, had to have died.

When we ask God to create in us a pure heart, He performs a transplant of sorts. Our old, sinful organ is replaced with a new healthy one. Who died for us? Jesus.

Our last C text is found in the book of Joshua. Listen to what he said to the children of Israel as they stood with their toes on the border of the Promised Land:

"And if it seem evil unto you to serve the Lord, choose you this day whom ye will serve; whether the gods which your fathers served that were on the other side of the flood, or the gods of the Amorites, in whose land ye dwell: but as for me and my house, we will serve the Lord" (Joshua 24:15).

Human beings face endless *choices*. You've had to deal with dozens even today. Think back. Didn't you have to choose what to wear, what to eat, how nice to be to your friends, whether or not to commit a sin? Yes, you even made choices concerning your journey to heaven.

I'm making choices too. I'm deciding which words to use, what thoughts you might understand, the best way to get the message of God's love from my heart to yours. Making choices is what life is all about.

Juniors, we've come a long way on our C journey. Like in all expeditions through the Bible, we've been led to the feet of Jesus, where we must now make the most important decision of our lives. Do we *choose* Him? Do we *choose* to keep our hand firmly in His? Do we *choose* to allow Him to be our leader, our comforter, our friend?

Why don't we, like Joshua, announce to all, "As for me and my house, we will serve the Lord"? Today's the day. Now's the time. Make your choice.

✝ SCRIPTURE INDEX:

6:8, 9 . . . . Sept. 2	13:34-36 . . . . . May 20	14:16 . . . . Apr. 14
Sept. 3	16:16 . . . . July 4	Dec. 18
Sept. 4		14:18 . . . . Mar. 24
6:10 . . . . Sept. 5	**LUKE**	Apr. 14
Sept. 6	1:1-4 . . . . Feb. 19	June 6
6:11 . . . . Sept. 7	1:26, 27, 31, 32, 34, 38	14:21 . . . . Nov. 7
6:12 . . . . Sept. 8	Sept. 13	19:25-27 . . . . . Jan. 22
6:13 . . . . Sept. 9	2:1 . . . . June 12	
Sept. 10	2:10 . . . . May 19	**ACTS**
Sept. 11	4:16 . . . . Feb. 15	2:17 . . . . July 26
6:25, 34 . . . . . . Dec. 20	4:18 . . . . Aug. 29	2:38 . . . . Oct. 11
8:2, 3 . . . . Nov. 24	6:36 . . . . Jan. 1	5:19 . . . . May 19
8:20 . . . . Feb. 5	6:36, 37 . . . . . . Sept. 8	10:38 . . . . June 26
10:30, 31 . . . . June 28	10:33, 34 . . . . . Dec. 25	Aug. 29
11:28 . . . . Oct. 7	21:9-11, 26-28. Apr. 26	13:22 . . . . Aug. 19
Dec. 24	23:34 . . . . Dec. 8	
18:12 . . . . Aug. 10	23:42, 43 . . . . . Apr. 8	**ROMANS**
18:15-17 . . . . . Aug. 15	23:46 . . . . July 5	1:16 . . . . Mar. 3
Aug. 16	23:50-54 . . . . . June 14	1:22, 25 . . . . . . July 21
18:20 . . . . Oct. 8	24:1-3, 6 . . . . . June 14	2:13 . . . . Mar. 25
19:3-6, 9 . . . . . Mar. 20	24:36 . . . . Sept. 25	3:23 . . . . Sept. 18
June 17		6:4 . . . . May 31
22:21 . . . . Sept. 25	**JOHN**	6:14 . . . . July 20
23:37 . . . . Aug. 2	3:16 . . . . Mar. 4	6:23 . . . . Sept. 18
24:36 . . . . May 20	Apr. 25	Nov. 10
25:6 . . . . May 20	5:28, 29 . . . . . . Apr. 3	7:15 . . . . Mar. 28
25:31-39 . . . . . July 14	6:40 . . . . Feb. 1	7:19, 24, 25 . . . July 15
25:35, 36, 40 . . Apr. 24	Sept. 6	7:21-24 . . . . . . July 19
Nov. 25	8:7 . . . . Jan. 13	8:10 . . . . Jan. 5
25:40 . . . . Jan. 17	8:11 . . . . Jan. 13	8:28 . . . . Sept. 22
26:11 . . . . Jan. 16	8:58 . . . . Mar. 23	8:37 . . . . June 3
28:2 . . . . May 19	10:16 . . . . Oct. 28	9:14, 15 . . . . . . Dec. 25
	12:32 . . . . Feb. 4	9:27 . . . . Oct. 9
MARK	13:12-15 . . . . . Feb. 20	12:1 . . . . July 30
2:27 . . . . Feb. 15	Nov. 20	12:2 . . . . Jan. 27
Nov. 4	13:17 . . . . May 8	12:9 . . . . Dec. 29
5:38, 39 . . . . . . Jan. 11	13:34 . . . . Mar. 6	12:10 . . . . Oct. 14
9:23 . . . . May 11	Sept. 25	12:21 . . . . Mar. 16
12:24, 25 . . . . . Mar. 5	Nov. 25	Mar. 21
13:21, 22 . . . . . Oct. 18	14:9 . . . . Dec. 5	
13:32 . . . . May 2		